WASSERSTROM

P9-DTB-682

DISCARD
Mt. Angel Abbey Library

Jews, Greeks and Barbarians

DISCARD
Mt. Angel Abbey Library

MARTIN HENGEL

Jews, Greeks and Barbarians

Aspects of the Hellenization of Judaism
in the pre-Christian Period

DISCARD
Mt. Angel Abbey Library

FORTRESS PRESS   PHILADELPHIA

Mt. Angel Abbey Library
St. Benedict, Oregon 97373

DS
121.65
H 4513
1980
c. 2

Translated by John Bowden from the German *Juden, Griechen und Barbaren, Aspekte der Hellenisierung des Judentums in vorchristlicher Zeit,* no. 76 in the series Stuttgarter Bibelstudien, published by Verlag Katholisches Bibelwerk, Stuttgart 1976.

Translation copyright © 1980 by John Bowden

All rights reserved. No part of this publication may be reproduced, stored in a retrieval system, or transmitted, in any form or by any means, electronic, mechanical, photocopying, recording or otherwise, without the prior permission of the publisher.

First British Edition by SCM Press Ltd. 1980
First American Edition by Fortress Press 1980

Library of Congress Cataloging in Publication Data

Hengel, Martin.
  Jews, Greeks, and barbarians.

  Translation of Juden, Griechen und Barbaren.
  Bibliography: p.
  1. Jews—History—586 B. C.–70 A. D. 2. Jews—Civilization—Greek influences. 3. Hellenism. I. Title.
DS121.65.H4513   930ʹ.04924   80-8051
ISBN 0-8006-0647-7

8273F80   Printed in the United States of America   1–647

CONTENTS

To Elias Bickerman,
in gratitude and admiration

PREFACE

This study is a substantially enlarged version of two articles which will appear in English in the *Cambridge History of Judaism*. It deals with the encounter between Judaism and Hellenistic culture in the early period before the beginning of Roman domination in the Eastern Mediterranean. This is on the whole an obscure period in the history of Judaism because of the state of available sources, and is usually neglected by both biblical scholars and church historians. However, it was the time when the foundations were laid which proved decisive for the way in which the Jewish people understood themselves in the 'New Testament period', not only in the Diaspora of the Greek-speaking world, but also in their home country of Palestine. The following pages thus in fact present several chapters of a 'preparation for the gospel', and seek to build a bridge between the end of the Old Testament and the New Testament period. At times I have referred back to my much more detailed study, *Judaism and Hellenism. Studies in their Encounter in Palestine during the Early Hellenistic Period*, ET London and Philadelphia 1974, though at a number of points the present work goes further than its predecessor. Ongoing new archaeological discoveries and the constant progress of scholarship are providing an abundance of material. This book takes a quite independent course above all in Part II, 'Aspects of the "Hellenization" of Judaism', and in Part III, which discusses the crucial point of developments in the Diaspora. Thus it is less a summary than an expansion of my earlier and more voluminous work.

Part I deals with the history of Palestine and the Jews in the brief 150 years between Alexander's expedition in 334 BC and the death of the Seleucid Antiochus III in 187 BC, which is relatively neglected in German scholarship. This is the time of the first fertile and ongoing encounter of ancient Judaism with Hellenistic culture, both in the home country and in the Diaspora, in the latter especially in Ptolemaic Egypt. The period with which we are concerned ends at the point when the Jewish sources begin to be more extensive again, with the account of the preliminaries to the Maccabean revolt in II Maccabees 3. Part II is concerned with the term 'Hellenization', which is often vague and tends to be used wrongly; it investigates the political, social and cultural elements of Hellenization. The section not only makes use of Jewish material, but also investigates the relationship between the 'Hellenes' and the oriental 'barbarians', and the possibilities which non-Greeks had of becoming 'assimilated' to the new civilization.

Part III deals with the development of the Jewish Diaspora in the Greek-speaking world of Egypt, Greece, Asia Minor and Syria, and its relationship to its Hellenistic environment; finally, there is a short summary of the situation in Palestine itself. The whole book does not set out to do more than provide an introduction, and prompt further study. There is therefore a detailed bibliography at the end for further reading.

I am grateful to Herr Klaus W. Müller for his help in getting hold of the relevant literature, and to Herren Helmut Kienle and Fritz Herrenbrück for checking the manuscript. In addition, Herr Kienle took over the task of preparing the genealogies of Hellenistic kings.

Tübingen, July 1975

I

The Political and Social History
of Palestine from Alexander to
Antiochus III (333-187 BC)

Alexander's Expedition and Palestine (333-331 BC)

We are largely in the dark about the political and social history of Palestine in the early Hellenistic period between Alexander's expedition and the death of Antiochus III, a few years after his defeat by Rome, which ushered in the downfall of the Hellenistic monarchies. Only small fragments of the ancient sources have been preserved, and where they mention the area with which we shall be concerned they do so only sporadically, in connection with larger political and military developments. It is necessary, therefore, to begin with an account of the wider context. We get some idea of social conditions only through a combination of chance archaeological and papyrological discoveries, which at some points, as with the Zeno papyri, cast a little light on the darkness. Information about the Jews is still more sparse: in our main source, Josephus, legends and historical accounts are closely interwoven.[1] So for some periods I can only draw a sketchy and partly even hypothetical picture, which will constantly be in need of revision as a result of new discoveries. Nevertheless, there can be no doubt that it was during this period, about which we know so little, that Palestine and ancient Judaism first became intensively preoccupied with the predominant Hellenistic culture which was to play a decisive role in their future development. That is why this period is so important.

The last decades of the Persian empire had already brought war and unrest to Palestine and the Jews. Egypt's fight for independence and even more the revolt of king Tennes of Sidon (from 401 in the former case, and between 354 and 346 in the latter) against Persian rule also affected Palestine, as a large area of the coastal plain was in the possession of Sidon; Judaea had probably also suffered heavily from Persian counter-measures.[2] A few years later, Artaxerxes III Ochus succeeded in reconquering Egypt, which two generations earlier had managed to shake off the Persian yoke with Greek help. He used Palestine as a base. The Western areas of the Persian empire, and especially Phoenicia, had long been oriented on Greece and the Aegean in economic, cultural and military terms. In the wars mentioned above, Greek mercenaries played a decisive role on both sides. Hardly any well-to-do home in Palestine will have been without Greek pottery, terra cotta and other luxury items, and Greek coinage, along with its local imitations, had long been an important means of payment.[3] That means that when the Greeks took power in the persons of the men from Macedon, they will certainly not have been unknown. Nevertheless, the victorious progress of the young Macedonian king had a cataclysmic effect on the Semitic population of Syria and Palestine. Up till now they had come to know the Greeks only as guests; now they discovered that the kindred Macedonians were harsh masters. The victory of Issus in November 333 BC demonstrated the military superiority of the twenty-three-year-old Alexander and his small army over the massed hosts of the Great King; even the Greek mercenaries of Darius could no longer save the aging empire. After the victory, Parmenio pressed on to Damascus, conquered the hinterland of Syria and plundered the immeasurably rich Persian supply column, with its war treasury.[4] Advancing along the coast, the king found that the Phoenician cities of Arados, Marathos, Byblos and Sidon readily surrendered to him; the last-mentioned could remember all too clearly the cruel revenge which the Persians had on it. Tyre was the only place which believed that it could maintain neutrality and freedom, relying on its island setting. It refused entrance to the king, who wanted to sacrifice in the sanctuary of the city god Heracles Melkart, his mythical ancestor.[5] However, 'what the king found most intolerable was that someone should seek to negotiate with him on an equal footing'.[6] As the Persian–Phoenician fleet in the Aegean was a constant threat, he needed to be sure that he had cover in this direction. The proud, sea-borne citadel was regarded as impregnable; it had once resisted Sennacherib for five years and Nebuchadnezzar for thirteen and emerged successful. Yet the young genius captured it in seven months, between January and August 332, with the help of the famous causeway and a fleet considerably supplemented by the Phoenician cities. His achievement is unique in the history of ancient siege warfare.[7] Astounded, the orientals discovered not only the superiority of Greek military technology and strategy, but also the harshness of their foreign conquerors. 30,000 survivors, mostly women and children, were put on the slave markets, while Alexander had 2,000 able-bodied men crucified along the coast. Over against that, Sidonian ships, fighting on the side of the besiegers, are said to have rescued 15,000 people. Here the solidarity of the Phoenician people was stronger than the victor's wrath.[8] The city was rased to the ground and rebuilt as a Macedonian fortress; its new inhabitants were country-dwellers and colonists. As it continued to be a city state, however, prosperity returned in an astonishingly short space of time.[9]

Without meeting further resistance, the king sped southwards from Tyre down the coastal route of Phoenicia and Palestine. He was, however, delayed in Gaza, the most important centre for Arabian trade and the only coastal city which was not under Phoenician control.[10] Here the Persian commander, Batis, refused to surrender and with his Persian and Arabian garrison offered desperate resistance for two whole months. Alexander himself was wounded as a result of one of their forays. However, here too the siege engines which had already brought down the walls of Tyre inevitably proved their strength. With their help the city was finally stormed at the fourth attempt, the male population was exterminated and, as in Tyre, the women and children were sold as slaves.[11] The brave Batis, wounded, fell into the hands of the victor, who dragged him round the city behind a chariot, as Achilles once did to the dead Hector.[12] The subsequent fate of the city also resembled that of Tyre. It was resettled with population from the neighbouring countryside and turned into a Macedonian fortress.[13] The stubborn resistance put up by Tyre and Gaza against Alexander resembles the resistance offered by Sidon to Artaxerxes III; it shows the vigorous sense of political independence to be found in these cities, which was just as great as that in any Greek *polis*.[14] At a later stage, this sense made it easier for them to be assimilated outwardly to political Hellenization while retaining their Semitic characteristics.

The ancient historians who wrote about Alexander were scarcely interested in the fate of the hinterland of Syria and Palestine; their accounts concentrated on the king's great feats at arms. After his account of the conquest of Tyre and Gaza, Arrian sums up the conquest of these areas in one sentence: 'the remainder of Palestine, called Syria, had already come under his control.' That means that the majority of Palestinian peoples and cities had already surrendered to him by the time of the siege of Tyre, and supported his laborious efforts in implementing the siege. Only one instance is described in more detail. At the beginning of the siege of Tyre, Alexander himself undertook an expedition against 'the Arabs living in the anti-Lebanon', who had killed thirty Macedonians while they were felling wood. 'He overcame some of the inhabitants by force and others by subjection. He was able to return within ten days.'[15] On this venture he almost lost his life through carelessness, but saved himself and his companions by his presence of mind.

Curtius Rufus has a somewhat obscure comment on the rapid advance made by Parmenio in the direction of Damascus and his appointment as governor of Coele Syria: 'The Syrians, not yet humbled by defeat, rejected the new rule, but were soon subjected and now obeyed orders readily.' There is some doubt as to whether this is a reference to a subjection of the hinterland of Syria and Palestine by Parmenio, or whether it alludes to the campaigns of Alexander himself. However, Arrian's parallel report is confirmed by a comment which follows a little later: when he reached Tyre, Alexander 'already had possession of the whole of Syria and also Phoenicia, apart from Tyre'.[16] A note in Pliny the Elder,[17] which connects Alexander with the balsam plantations in Jericho, is ambiguous and as historically dubious as the late-Roman, Byzantine reports of cities which Alexander is supposed to have founded in Transjordania.[18] A large number of ancient cities made attempts to associate themselves with the most famous ruler of the ancient world in order to boost their own reputations. No limits were set to the making of local legends, even here in Syria and Palestine.

This critical judgment also applies to Josephus' account of Alexander's visit to Jerusalem and the disputes with the Samaritans that are associated with it. There are parallels in the rabbinic literature and in the Samaritan tradition (where the account is slanted the other way).[19] A. Büchler already recognized that Josephus' account is not all of a piece, but was made up of Jewish and Samaritan reports.[20] Least historical value of all is to be attached to the legend of Alexander's visit to the holy city and his sacrifice in the Temple after the conquest of Gaza. On that occasion the king is said to have paid homage to the Jewish high priest, who had earlier appeared to him in a dream in Dio of Macedon and called him to the conquest of Asia. We must give unconditional assent to Tcherikover's judgment: 'It is a historical myth designed to bring the king into direct contact with the Jews, and to speak of both in laudatory terms.' He supposes that it is based on 'a Palestinian folk-story' which came to be recorded in the Talmudic tradition: the literary version which Josephus used was produced in Alexandria in the first century AD.[21] A version of the Greek Alexander romance written by Pseudo-Callisthenes has also adopted features of the Jewish Alexander legend from Alexandrian circles.[22] We are most likely to find historical traces in Josephus' account of the building of the temple on Mount Gerizim by the Samaritans. According to this, while the Persians were still in control, Manasseh, brother of Jaddus the Jewish high priest, had fled from Jerusalem to Samaria because he was forbidden to marry Nikaso – note the Greek name[23] – the daughter of Sanballat, governor of Samaria; his father-in-law had promised 'to build a temple on mount Gerizim like the one in Jerusalem'.[24]

When Alexander began to lay siege to Tyre, he asked the Jewish high priest for support and for the tribute which had previously been paid to Darius. The high priest refused his request, pointing out that he had sworn an oath of allegiance to Darius. Sanballat, on the other hand, rushed to the help of Alexander with 8,000 Samaritans, recognized him as ruler and asked for permission to build the temple. He died several months later.[25] Scholars previously thought that Sanballat the governor of Samaria was not a historical figure, but had come into being as a result of confusion with Nehemiah's opponent of the same name;[26] however, the discovery of Samaritan papyri in a cave in Wādi Dāliya north of Jericho, with numerous documents going down to the year 335 BC, makes it probable that a third Sanballat really did live in Samaria at the time of Alexander's expedition.[27] It is not unlikely that this Sanballat – like other tribes and cities in Syria and Palestine – accepted Alexander as ruler and provided him with manpower for the siege of Tyre. In military activities Alexander may have relied principally on his well-tried Macedonian soldiers, but he cannot have avoided using foreign auxiliaries, for example for siege works and guard duty. A remark of Curtius Rufus to the effect that 'soldiers enlisted from conquered tribes were less trustworthy than the nationals' is cited against this view, but in fact it confirms the use of barbarian mercenaries.[28] As a result, we must not mistrust the report that Alexander later took Samaritan auxiliaries with him to Egypt[29] or the note in Pseudo-Hecataeus and Josephus about Jewish mercenaries who served Alexander in Babylon and Egypt.[30] On the other hand, we should not follow Josephus' account of the resistance of the high priest; he will have yielded to the new authority without any dramatic events. It remains an open question whether this recognition of Alexander was made even before the siege of Tyre – as was the case with the Samaritans – or at Kephar Saba, later to become Antipatris, during the march through the coastal plain – according to the Talmudic tradition – or elsewhere.[31] On this change of rule the Jews will certainly have asked for and been granted the right 'to live in accordance with their ancestral laws', as had happened before Alexander with the Persian and later the Hellenistic kings. Alexander also granted this right to their 'own laws' to the Ionian cities, the Lydians, the Indians and the Arabians.[32]

Finally, there is also a historical nucleus in Josephus' reference to a conflict between Alexander and the Samaritans, which is depicted in an even more pointed way in the Talmudic tradition.[33] According to Curtius Rufus, at the beginning of 331, while Alexander was occupied in Egypt, the Samaritans rebelled against the Macedonians and burnt alive the new satrap, Andromachus of Coele Syria, Parmenio's successor. Alexander rushed back to Samaria and executed the leaders of the revolt, who were handed over to him; he appointed Meno as successor to Andromachus.[34] This report is supplemented by the Chronicles of Eusebius, which record that Alexander destroyed Samaria and settled it with Macedonian colonists, in other words, turned the city into a Macedonian military colony. According to a second note from the same source, the resettlement happened only in the time of Perdiccas.[35] These fragmentary reports have now been confirmed by the discovery of documents in the Wādi Dāliya, which has already been mentioned. Some eminent Samaritans evidently escaped there. Their hiding place was betrayed and the cave, in which the excavators found the bones of 205 people, was smoked out by the Macedonian pursuit.[36] It is quite possible that the Jewish Temple community in Jerusalem took advantage of this catastrophe to their compatriots in the north to extend their territory somewhat.[37] Perhaps the later apocalypse in Isaiah 24–27 with its countless references to the destruction of the 'city of chaos' is a reflection of the catastrophe which befell Samaria.[38] The threatening poem in Zechariah 9.1–8 shows that the descent of Alexander from the north, with his military successes against Tyre and other cities, inspired passages of late prophecy elsewhere.[39] A series of coin hoards and destroyed sites along the coastline of Palestine from the time round about 332 shows that not only Tyre and Gaza were destroyed. Smaller places also fell victim to the Macedonian invasion.[40] Apart from resettling the destroyed cities of Tyre and Gaza, Alexander himself hardly 'founded' any cities in the area with which we are concerned. Quite apart from the tragedy in Samaria, which was rapidly dealt with, he could not spend any more time in Palestine on his return from Egypt in early 331. After celebrating in Tyre in May with magnificent games, he set out for Mesopotamia, where on 1 October 331 victory at Gaugamela in his decisive battle with Darius III opened up an entirely new future for Asia and Europe.

The Macedonian foundation of the cities of Samaria and Gerasa, ascribed partly to Alexander and partly to Perdiccas, was perhaps planned by Alexander but in all probability was only implemented after the king's death by Perdiccas, the imperial regent (323–20). Other cities on the far side of the Jordan like Dio, Pella and imperial Capitolias later claimed Alexander as founder.[41] The resettlement of Shechem (Sikima) and the building of the temple on Mount Gerizim are probably connected with the catastrophe of Samaria and its refounding as a Macedonian military colony. We cannot exclude the possibility that the building of this temple was prompted by the secession of a group of priests from Jerusalem under the leadership of a brother of the high priest, and had been planned even before Alexander's expedition; the plan may have been put into effect at a later stage. The Samaritan source underlying Josephus' account pursues the tendentious aim of justifying the erection of this schismatic sanctuary by connecting it with the person of Alexander.[42] According to the excavations at Shechem, the place had been uninhabited between 480 and 330 BC; then followed an intensive period of building and a new period of prosperity towards 300 BC. G. E. Wright connects this discovery with the fate of Samaria: after the introduction of a Macedonian military settlement, the Samaritans needed a new centre and built it at ancient Shechem, at the foot of the sacred mount Gerizim.[43] Here earlier remains which might perhaps come from the Samaritan sanctuary have been discovered among the foundations of the temple of Jupiter dating from Hadrian's time.[44] The demarcation between the new Macedonian Hellenistic city and the Samaritans with their new centre of Shechem remains obscure. It is possible that after the detachment of certain Jewish areas, the rest of Samaria became the territory of the new *polis* and the Samaritan population was reduced to the status of *perioikoi* who – unlike, say, the Jews and Idumaeans – did not receive the rights of an independent *ethnos*. This would explain why Strabo speaks only of the four *ethnē* of the Jews, the Idumaeans, the Gazaeans and the Azoteans; why even in crisis situations the Samaritans did not term themselves an *ethnos*, but 'Sidonians in Shechem'; and why Sirach, taking up Deuteronomy 32.21, could mock them as being 'not a people'. Josephus is the first to call the Samaritans an *ethnos*;[45] that is, they will only have been given this status after Pompey.

We know almost nothing about the administration introduced by Alexander into Syria and Coele Syria. All we have is the name of the satraps, which change often. Damascus became the capital of the province which was identical with the old Persian satrapy of 'Abar-Nahara. It is striking that even a Persian, Bessos, appears as satrap from 329 to 325.[46] All this indicates that the king hardly interfered at all in the internal structure of the country, with its countless cities and peoples. Both the Phoenician city-kings and the Jewish high priest continued in office as before.[47] In only one respect did Alexander bring about a fundamental change. He restricted the colourful multiplicity of local mintings in Syria and Phoenicia and took the first steps towards a relatively unified coinage. As these new coins minted by Alexander were paid out promptly to the occupying forces and were not accumulated in treasuries, like the Persian darics, they soon also began to circulate among the population and furthered economic development.[48] Secondly, the king was also concerned to arrive at a better assessment and control of economic resources. He already regarded the territory he had conquered as his personal possession, as 'land won through the spear'.[49] In Syria and Palestine he will have turned the screw of taxes and tolls to improve upon the yield in the Persian period, just as he did in Egypt with the help of the organizing genius of Cleomenes of Naucratis. One reason for the regular and rapid change of satraps in Syria may have been that the king was not satisfied with its financial performance. Thus Meno and his successor Arimnas were deposed in rapid succession, the latter because he had not taken sufficient care in equipping the army for the expedition beyond the Euphrates in the summer of 331.[50] Thus in connection with monetary and financial policy Alexander adopted principles which were also put forward in the Pseudo-Aristotelian *Oeconomica* and which later laid the basis for the economic power of the Hellenistic monarchies, especially the Ptolemaic empire. Of course he could do no more than make a beginning; it was impossible for him really to consolidate the empire. A full year after his return from India, on 10 June 323, Alexander surprisingly died in Babylon at the age of thirty-three.

His influence is unmistakable. Like the later Talmudic and Christian legends, the Hellenistic Jewish legends about Alexander in Alexandria made him a worshipper of the God of Israel and thus a monotheist.[51] First of all, however, critical judgments could not be ignored. This is particularly true of the Jewish tradition. The apocalyptic, say, of the Book of Daniel or the apocalypse of the symbolic beasts in Ethiopian Enoch saw Alexander's expedition as the last turning point in world history: 'Then a mighty king (*melek gibbōr*) shall arise, who shall rule with great dominion and do according to his will.'[52] True, his kingdom will soon be broken and divided, and what will come after that will not be according to 'the dominion with which he ruled'.[53] At the same time, however, the 'fourth kingdom' of the Macedonians and Greeks which he introduced represents the ultimate height of violence and godlessness: 'Then appeared a fourth beast, terrible and dreadful and exceeding strong; and it had great iron teeth (and claws of bronze); it devoured and broke in pieces, and stamped the residue with its feet.'[54]

I Maccabees also begins its account with a negative description of the world conqueror: 'He fought many battles, conquered strongholds, and put to death the kings of the earth. He advanced to the ends of the earth, and plundered many nations. When the earth became quiet before him, he became arrogant, and his heart was lifted up ...'[55] The last, telling sentence has close connections with the taunt-song to the prince of Tyre in Ezekiel 28.2:

> Because your heart is proud,
> and you have said, 'I am a god ...'

Thus Jewish criticism of Alexander and his successors is prompted not least by a condemnation of their claim to merit divine worship. The Jews could never accept this demand.[56] Here we come up against a critical point which was decisive in shaping the predominantly negative attitude of ancient Judaism towards the Hellenistic Roman world. By contrast, the picture of the past became more positive: the greater the rejection of the Hellenistic domination which had now begun, the brighter the picture of the Persian empire which had been destroyed by Alexander.

Palestine during the Struggle between the Diadochoi (323-301 BC)

In the quarrels over Alexander's heritage which followed his death, Palestine soon again became the focal point of political and military events. The military assembly in Babylon which had to decide the destiny of the empire agreed on a compromise. The world empire would remain a unity under the nominal rule of Philip Arrhidaeus, Alexander's feeble-minded brother. Perdiccas became 'chiliarch' of the Asian part and thus at the same time represented the unity of the empire. New appointments were made to the most important satrapies. Ptolemy, son of Lagus, secured Egypt for himself; it was rich and difficult of access. Together with Lysimachus of Thrace he was successful in championing the formation of particular states. Laomedon, who was bilingual (that will have been in Aramaic and Greek), was given the satrapy of Syria.[1]

In November 322, Ptolemy, then forty-four, arrived in Egypt and skilfully took over Cyrenaica. A little later, despite the resistance of supporters of Perdiccas, he got hold of Alexander's body and brought the precious relic under military escort to Memphis, right through the satrapy controlled by Laomedon. Laomedon did not dare to raise a hand against him. Diodore describes how the gilded ornamental carriage was stared at in amazement by people who flocked to see it in every city on its way from Babylon to Egypt.[2] In May/June 320 Perdiccas was murdered at Memphis in a mutiny by his officers, including Seleucus. In an attempt to break the growing might of Ptolemy, he had left Damascus to invade Egypt. Power was redistributed at a meeting at Triparadeisus in Syria, on the upper part of the Orontes. Ptolemy's territory was confirmed, but not extended as he had wanted.[3] Like the ancient Pharaohs before him he saw – in Diodore's words – that 'Phoenicia and so-called Coele Syria[4] were a favourable area from which an attack could be launched on Egypt, and he regarded it as a matter of supreme importance to bring this area under his rule.' Control of this glacis seemed to him to be necessary to protect his empire in Egypt; furthermore, if he was to achieve the military supremacy in the Eastern Mediterranean that he sought, he had to take over the harbours and fleets of Phoenicia. He sent an army and a fleet under the command of his friend Nicanor. 'In a short and successful campaign', Laomedon was captured and the most important 'Phoenician cities' – which also included the coastal areas of Palestine – were secured by garrisons.[5] Two years later (318 BC), Eumenes of Cardia, Alexander's former secretary, the only Greek among the Macedonian generals and the most faithful supporter of the royal family, tried to take Phoenicia and Coele Syria; however, he was forced eastwards by Antigonus Monophthalmus, the '*stratēgos* of Asia'.[6] The capture and execution of Eumenes by Antigonus in 317/6 destroyed all hopes for Alexander's dynasty; instead, the idea of the 'unity of the empire' passed over to Antigonus, who was now the most powerful man in Asia. To escape the threat of his wrath, the young satrap Seleucus of Babylon fled to Ptolemy in Egypt. Antigonus himself invaded Syria and rejected a delegation from an alliance of his rivals which called for the recognition of the rights of Ptolemy to the disputed province. All-out war became inevitable. A host of workers was forced to fell trees for Antigonus in the Lebanon and in the Taurus mountains; four shipyards were used to accelerate the production of a fleet. Ptolemy's garrisons were driven from the harbours of Phoenicia, Joppa and Gaza were taken by storm, and the garrison of Tyre eventually surrendered after a fifteen-month siege.[7]

Summoned back to Asia Minor, Antigonus handed over command in Palestine to his twenty-year-old son Demetrius, later to gain a reputation for his success at sieges. On the advice of Seleucus, who had escaped to his protection, Ptolemy advanced into the territory he had lost. Early in 312 there was a battle south of Gaza in which the two experienced soldiers, former officers of Alexander, inflicted a devastating defeat on the young Demetrius.[8] In this way, for the second time within a few years Ptolemy became master of Palestine, and the Phoenician cities which he coveted once again came into his hands. After the capture of Tyre he allowed his friend and ally Seleucus to take an army to Babylon and try to win back the satrapy which he had lost. The return of

Seleucus to Babylon in the early spring of 312 (1 October in the Julian calendar) marks the beginning of the Seleucid era, a period much imitated, and significant in the East right down to modern times.[9] Of course, Ptolemy did not remain master of the territory he had reconquered for long. Six months after the victory his General Killes, with a force of seven thousand men, was surprised by Demetrius in a swampy area in central Syria and taken captive.[10] When Demetrius' father Antigonus himself marched into Syria, the wary Ptolemy avoided a new encounter and after the destruction of the fortresses of Ake (Acco), Joppa, Samaria and Gaza, withdrew to the safety of Egypt.[11] In the years that followed, father and son worked hard to develop the strategically important southern province which they had regained, and which at the same time formed a base for an attack on Ptolemy in Egypt. In connection with this they made a not altogether successful attempt to conquer the Nabataeans of Arabia, who in this way first make their appearance in history as a political power. They played a key role in caravan trade with Gerrha on the Persian Gulf and southern Arabia, which supplied the Hellenistic world with highly prized scents, spices and other luxury goods. A surprise attack launched by Demetrius on the rocky fortress of the Nabataeans, the later Petra, proved a dismal failure.[12] Jerome of Cardia, 'the standard historian of the first fifty years after the death of Alexander', an officer of Eumenes and later of Antigonus, had taken part in this unsuccessful enterprise. He gives us a vivid picture not only of these battles, but also of the Dead Sea. His attempt to get bitumen there failed because of Arab attacks.[13] More important than these clashes with the Nabataeans, who were well able to keep their independence, were the cities which Antigonus founded in Palestine. In the decade between the reconquest of Palestine and the battle of Ipsus the country had its first relatively peaceful period for development since the death of Alexander. The first beginnings of a new administration became evident, and Macedonian veterans were given settlements. The first real *polis* which Antigonus founded was Antigoneia in northern Syria, which was intended to be the capital of his empire. Those Palestinian cities which bear typically Macedonian, northern Greek names, probably owe their foundation to his initiative. By contrast, the later Ptolemaic and Seleucid foundations almost always bear dynastic names. These would include Apollonia, Arethusa and Anthedon in the coastal plain, and Pella, Dio, Hippos and Gadara in Transjordania. Pella – named after Alexander's birthplace – and Apollonia (present-day Arṣūf) may represent the Hellenization of former Semitic places.[14] Whereas the settlements in the coastal plain, already densely populated with Phoenician cities, were meant to strengthen the Macedonian military presence, the military settlements in sparsely-populated Transjordania were to protect the caravan routes and the agricultural land against the Arabs.[15] As with Alexander, monetary policy and financial administration became very important. The continual struggle between the rivals over Alexander's heritage swallowed up enormous sums which had to be extracted from subject territories if the armies were to be paid. Presumably Antigonus continued the division of Syria and Palestine into toparchies, which had already been attempted by Alexander. From now until the time of Herod the toparchy formed the basic administrative and fiscal unit;[16] the next largest was the hyparchy, which corresponded to the 'nomos' in Egypt. It is the successor of the small satrapy of the Persian empire. The Graecized names of these administrative units, which end in -itis, like Ammanitis, Esbonitis, Gaulanitis, Galaaditis, etc., probably come from the time of Antigonus or Ptolemy I. In Egypt, the names of the 'nomoi' were Graecized in a similar way. Other hyparchies were given the ending -aea, like Judaea, Samaraea (and also Samareitis), Idumaea and Galilaea.[17]

After the destruction of Ptolemy's fleet by Demetrius before Salamis in Cyprus in the early part of 306, father and son once again attempted to launch an attack on Egypt using Palestine as a base. However, the fleet which sailed from the harbour of Gaza was forced back by a sudden storm from the north and decimated; finally, the whole enterprise came to grief because of the unfavourable weather and the impossibility of reducing Ptolemy's fortresses at Pelusium.[18] After his victory at Salamis, Antigonus adopted the title 'king' for himself and his son; Ptolemy followed suit after his successful repulse of the attack on Egypt in 305. The other Diadochoi did the same; thus in constitutional terms, too, Alexander's kingdom was divided into five parts. The final issue between Antigonus and his rivals was not, of course, settled at the Egyptian frontier, but at Ipsus in Phrygia, in the summer of 301 BC. Antigonus 'the one-eyed', now eighty years old, lost the battle and his life to the combined armies of Seleucus and Lysimachus. His most dogged opponent, Ptolemy Soter, as he now liked to be called, did not take part. He left the risk to the allies and instead seized Palestine for himself. Hearing a rumour that his friends had been defeated, he abandoned the province again rapidly, despite his involvement with the siege of Sidon, and left garrisons behind. Going against earlier agreements, the victors assigned Coele Syria in its entirety to Seleucus. However, by rapidly reoccupying the area, Ptolemy beat him to it. The new master of Asia did not want to wage war against the former friend to whom he owed so much, but he did not want to renounce his claims altogether. This incipient strife over Phoenicia and Palestine was from now on to be a decisive influence on the politics of the two empires for the next 150 years.[19]

It is striking that in the histories of the Diadochoi, as in the histories of Alexander, the Greek chroniclers make hardly any reference to the Jews. Even Josephus is offended that Jerome of Cardia does not mention them 'anywhere in his history, though he lived quite near their land'. 'Blind passion obscured his sense of the truth.'[20] In reality, we may conclude from this that the political and economic significance of the little temple state of Judaea in the hill-country between the Dead Sea and the coastal plain was too slight to attract the attention of historians. 'Why should a Greek author, at a time when the whole fabulous Orient was open to his inquiry, concentrate on a Lilliputian place in the arid mountains?'[21] The only exception is that of writers who were interested in strange and indeed abnormal religious groups and customs, like Theophrastus[22] and Megasthenes[23] or Hecataeus of Abdera, who gives an account of the exodus of Moses and the founding of Jerusalem in his Egyptian history.[24] In the *Contra Apionem*, Josephus gives further extracts from a writing 'on the Jews' which is ascribed to him, but this may come from a Jewish forger of the middle of the second century BC.[25] However, this does not exclude the possibility that this writer used some good historical sources. The report says that after Ptolemy's victory at Gaza, many inhabitants of Syria followed him to Egypt because of the 'friendliness and graciousness' of the ruler. These will have included the Jewish high priest Hezekiah, at sixty-six a man of exceptional gifts, not least in economic matters. He is said to have invited many of his friends to emigrate to Egypt because of the favourable political status of the Jews there.[26] It is by no means improbable that this report is to be taken quite seriously in historical terms, even if as a whole it contains clear allusions to the settling of the high priest Onias IV in Leontopolis around 160 BC. As at a later date, we may suppose that Ptolemy's Jewish supporters left Jerusalem in the face of the advancing enemy and followed him to Egypt (see pp. 40f. below). A popular move is to connect this Hezekiah with a Hezekiah who appears on the earliest Jewish coins with the inscription *yḥzkyh hpḥh*, Hezekiah the governor. It is well within the realms of possibility that the last governor in Judaea in the final stages of Persian rule came from the high priestly family and went to Egypt in 312 as a follower of Ptolemy. Another possibility is that the title *peḥah* continued to be used even after Alexander for the supreme official in the small satrapy. There could be a pointer here to conflict which we shall meet again towards the end of the third century. However, we cannot do better than guess at this.[27]

The hypothesis of a continuity in administration between Persian rule and the beginnings of the Ptolemaic era and the possibility of partisan struggles in the province of Yehud is strengthened by a new find of coins. While these coins follow the earlier minting of Yehud coins in silver – presumably during the Persian period – in form and symbolism, they also show striking innovations. A number of the copies of Yehud coins known so far depict various human heads, one of which is perhaps meant to represent a Persian ruler; the other side of the coin, however, has the traditional Athenian owl, a falcon and a god on a winged wheel (Yahweh?). By contrast, the newly-discovered coins very probably have the head of Ptolemy I with the diadem(?) on one side and the royal eagle with Zeus' lightning flash on the other. The inscription is no longer *yhd* (Yehud, the Aramaic name for the province), but *yhdh* (Yehudah, the Hebrew name for the province), in Old Hebrew letters. Does this remarkable change point to a strengthening of the Hebrew nationalistic self-awareness in connection with Ptolemy I's seizure of power in 302/1 BC, which presumably had its violent side?[28] The prohibition against images was evidently not observed as strictly then as it was in the post-Maccabaean and early Roman period.

A further report has come down to us through the geographer and historian Agatharchides of Cnidus (second century BC).[29] According to this, Ptolemy Lagus overcame the difficulties of capturing Jerusalem by attacking on a sabbath, when the inhabitants did not take up arms because of their 'superstition'; they found him a 'cruel master'. This harshness of Ptolemy I towards the Jews is confirmed by Pseudo-Aristeas. After capturing Jerusalem, the founder of the dynasty is said to have shipped 100,000 Jews to Egypt. He selected 30,000 of them as soldiers, and made the rest of them, old men, women and children, slaves. The numbers are certainly exaggerated, but the event itself is historical. His son Ptolemy II Philadelphus later ordered that the enslaved Jews should be set free.[30] Tcherikover[31] will be right in saying that we can hardly connect this attack on Jerusalem with the siege of Gaza in 312 BC when Ptolemy immediately returned to Phoenicia. It is more likely to have taken place when the country was last attacked in 302/1 BC. At that time the Jewish leaders in Jerusalem seem to have taken sides with their former masters, the Antigonids. In the following period, Jewish slaves and mercenaries formed the basis of the Jewish Diaspora in wide areas of the Hellenistic world, though it should be pointed out that there was already a considerable Jewish minority in Egypt from the time of Persian domination on.[32]

Like the rest of Coele Syria, which was very much a bone of contention during the struggle of the Diadochoi, Judaea had to suffer the disturbances of war, and it is understandable that this time of distress made its mark on the Jewish tradition. I Maccabees still says of Alexander's successors: 'They caused many evils on the earth.' Zechariah 14.1ff. may possibly reflect the capture of Jerusalem by Ptolemy I: 'The city shall be taken and the houses plundered and the women ravished; half the city shall go into exile, but the rest of the people shall not be cut off from the city.' In Joel 4.4ff., in a text which perhaps comes from the Persian period, the Phoenicians and the inhabitants of the coastal plain are accused of selling Jewish slaves to the Greeks and in turn are threatened that the people of Judah will sell their children to the South Arabians.[33] The constant demonstration of Greek military power revived interest in the ancient Israelite tradition of the 'holy war'. This is the case in the books of Chronicles,[34] where the repeated stress on the army of Judah equipped 'with lance and shield' recalls the Greek phalanx, known in Palestine since Persian times. The proud description of king Uzziah's fortification and military organization, and above all his effective siege engines, may also follow a Graeco-Macedonian model. The prophet's command to the people of Judah not to fight alongside mercenaries from the northern kingdom, and the plundering foray made by those who are rejected, both point to tensions with the Samaritans and at the same time illustrate the havoc caused by the mercenaries of the Hellenistic period. Finally, hate of the military supremacy of the foreign conquerors can be seen in Zechariah 9.13f.:

> For I have bent Judah as my bow;
> I have made Ephraim its arrow.
> I will brandish your sons, O Zion,
> over your sons, O Yawan (=Ionia, i.e. Greece),
> and wield you like a warrior's sword.

Israel itself becomes God's weapon against the Macedonians and the Greeks. Here we have the beginnings of an attitude which comes to full fruition in the war scroll of Qumran. Of course the way in which the holy war takes on 'the dimensions of a world war'[35] in Chronicles and in the prophetic and apocalyptic tradition of the time stands in marked contradiction to the political insignificance of the tiny Jewish state. Here religious claim and political reality are in irreconcilable opposition. This contrast will dominate the Jewish history of the next 450 years.

Palestine under the Ptolemies down to the Accession of the Seleucid Antiochus III (301-223 BC)

The final occupation of Palestine by Ptolemy I after Ipsus (301) led to a century of Ptolemaic domination. This shaped and changed Palestine in a new way. Apart from the Fourth Syrian War (219–17), for most of the country this was a time of peace, and Palestinian Judaism in particular was not to experience its like again in the 350 years which followed. This may be the source of Polybius' note about the sympathies of the inhabitants of Coele Syria for the Lagids.[1] Unfortunately, our sources are more than scanty, and the few that we do have we have only by chance. The result is that we can only construct a very fragmentary picture of this important period. Here the situation in Palestine or Coele Syria can be seen only in the wider context of the history of the Hellenistic monarchies.

To begin with, Ptolemy was not yet undisputed master of the whole province of 'Syria and Phoenicia', as the official Ptolemaic designation ran.[2] Demetrius Poliorcetes, the 'sea king', continued to dominate the Phoenician cities of Tyre and Sidon even after the defeat of Ipsus and the death of his father. He even launched another attack on Palestine in 296, during which, according to the Chronicle of Eusebius, Samaria is said to have been destroyed. Step by step, however, Ptolemy took over the maritime empire of the Antigonids. Within ten years, at the latest, he also had control of the Phoenician coastal cities.[3] The frontier with the Seleucid empire still remained relatively stable, though Seleucus did not surrender his claim.[4] This frontier ran from the tiny stream of Eleutheros, present-day Nahr al-Kabīr, through the Biqaʻ north of Baalbek to Damascus, which was in dispute.[5] Thus the territory under Ptolemaic control comprised Coele Syria,[6] i.e. Palestine and the Biqa', and the Phoenician cities – apart from Aradus, which played an independent role.[7] Along with Cyprus, the southern coast of Asia Minor and the forests of the Lebanon, this formed the basis of Ptolemaic sea power.

E. Will describes the relationship between the two great empires in the period between the murder of Seleucus I and the accession of Antiochus III as 'l'impossible stabilité'.[8] Because of the internal weakness of the Seleucid empire, to begin with, the Ptolemies, who had control of the Eastern Mediterranean, were at an advantage. Ptolemy II Philadelphus ([284] 282–246), vigorous and highly gifted, took Egypt to the pinnacle of its power. The first clash, the so-called Syrian war of succession (280/279), began with a mutiny of Seleucid troops in Seleucus, in northern Syria, above all at the military base of Apameia. This was presumably sparked off by the agitation of Ptolemy II. However, Ptolemy's frontier was not moved northwards as a result; instead, Egypt was able to extend its possessions along the coast of Asia Minor.[9] Two years later, Ptolemy II subdued the Nabataeans in a successful expedition and in so doing took over control of the spice trade with Gerrha and southern Arabia, which from now on was principally directed through the Ptolemaic fortress of Gaza. As a result trade links between Petra and northern Syria were cut. The southern and eastern frontiers of Palestine were also given increased military protection in order to hold the Arabian tribes further in check. Traces of these Ptolemaic 'military frontiers' have come to light again in very recent times.[10] The so-called First (in reality the Second) Syrian War was sparked off by an attack launched on Egypt from Cyrenaica by Magas, an ally of Antiochus I. This proved unsuccessful. We can make only a hypothetical reconstruction of subsequent events. In order to anticipate a Seleucid advance on Coele Syria, Ptolemy II invaded Syria in the neighbourhood of Hamath,[11] while Antiochus seized Damascus by a ruse of war. However, his attack as a whole seems to have proved a failure, and victory was celebrated with pomp in Alexandria in 271/70. The *pompē* of Ptolemy II was at the same time a special recognition of the cult of Dionysus, from whom the ruler traced his descent on his mother's side. As 'conqueror of the world', Dionysus was at the same time the guarantor of the royal victory. According to the Zeno papyri, in 259 BC Damascus was again firmly under the control of the Ptolemies; however, the city had probably lost a good deal of its significance as a result of the diversion of the trade from Arabia.[12] The so-called Second Syrian War (260–253) was waged almost exclusively in Asia Minor and the Aegean, and hardly affected Palestine at all. The supposition that Antiochus II succeeded in shifting the frontier south to a line between Berytus and Sidon is very questionable.[13]

We get more detailed information about Palestine at this time from the Zeno archive. Of the roughly 2,000 documents which it contains, about forty relate to Syria and Phoenicia.[14] The turmoils of war have left hardly any trace; what we find, rather, is intensive political and economic activity.[15] From January 259 BC to February 258, Zeno travelled all over the country on behalf of Apollonius, the finance minister. The first and greatest journey took him and a marvellous entourage of senior officials and officers from the Tower of Strato on the coast, through Jerusalem and Jericho into Transjordania, to the fortress of the Jewish magnate Tobias in Ammanitis, and then northwards into the Hauran and to the sources of the Jordan. From there he returned via Galilee, where Apollonius had an enormous vineyard in Bet 'Anat (Baitanata), to Ake-Ptolemais on the coast.[16] There followed trips to the Phoenician cities, to Gaza and to Marisa and Adora, the chief centres of Idumaea. In addition to this, other agents for Apollonius or Zeno were regularly active in various parts of the country. This extended activity on the part of Zeno as a plenipotentiary of Apollonius, who was himself the king's right-hand man, shows the lively interest of people in Alexandria in the province on the north-eastern frontier. The aim was evidently to arrange its political administration and economic development as expeditiously and effectively as had been the case in Egypt. The underlying idea here was one that was fundamental to the Hellenistic monarchies: the whole territory was the king's property, over which he had sovereign control in the same way as a Macedonian landlord had control over his estate. In Egypt this principle was developed to the ultimate degree. Thus when it was part of the Ptolemaic empire, not only did it have a strict monopoly of coinage with an independent monetary standard which differed from the usual Attic one; there was also a monopoly in the production and supply of the most important economic raw materials, especially grain, oil, linen, etc. Agricultural production from the royal land was strictly planned in advance; a complicated system of leasehold and state supervision covered virtually every branch of production and trade, so that considerable financial resources constantly found their way into the royal treasure. Foreign trade was subject to particularly strict control, and high duty was imposed. This intensive exploitation of the riches of Egypt in the third century formed the basis for the political and military supremacy of the Ptolemaeans in the Eastern Mediterranean. Alexandria became the greatest economic centre of the Hellenistic world, and in the Greece of the third century Egyptian gold played the same kind of role against Macedonian predominance as had Persian gold in an earlier age.[17] Thus, in the words of W. W. Tarn, the Egypt of the Ptolemies was 'a money-making machine'.[18] Athenaeus (V, 203b) ends his account of the unique *pompē* of Ptolemy II with the question, 'What kingdom was so rich in gold?' Two royal laws enacted barely a year before Zeno's journey, relating to a fiscal census of cattle and to slaves born in 'Syria and Phoenicia', show that attempts were now made to introduce Egyptian 'state capitalism' into this province as well.[19] They were to be implemented, even in the smallest hamlet, by local tax officials and mayors, and false information was punishable with severe penalties.[20] Zeno's journey may have been connected with the supervision of this law. Contacts with Transjordania and Gaza also indicate some interest in the spice trade, which was a further source of wealth. The intensification of economic productivity can also be seen in the marked increase of discoveries in Palestine of coins from the time of Ptolemy II, for the first time also including copper, the money of the small man. Only now did coinage replace the traditional barter. We may conclude from this that the king and his minister succeeded in making a marked improvement not only in the productivity of Egypt, but also in that of the province of Syria and Phoenicia. We hear of exports of slaves, corn, oil and wine – of course under strict supervision; the world-famous balsam plantations in Jericho and 'En Gedi (Engaddi) were used more intensively as a 'royal estate' than they were in the Persian period. From Egypt came imports of papyrus, linen, glass and luxury goods. As in Egypt, technological improvements were carried out in Palestine and the cultivation of new plants and species was introduced. Thus, for example, in Apollonius' vineyard in Bet 'Anat in Galilee, 80,000 high quality vines were introduced from the island of Cos, the produce of which was identical with popular imported wine from the Aegean. Further improvements were effected by artificial irrigation, water-wheels, the plough, the wine-press and other similar implements.[21] The ostraca from Khirbet et Kom demonstrate that Hellenistic influence primarily made itself felt in Palestine in the economic sphere. These ostraca probably date from the sixth year of Ptolemy II, 277 BC, that is, eighteen years before Zeno's journey. They come from the archive of an Idumaean money-lender Ḳos-yada' bin Hanna'. Four of them are in Edomite, one is in Greek and one is bilingual. Here in essentials we already have that culturally mixed milieu which we shall come across again later in Marisa, the capital of Idumaea (where in addition there is also Phoenician influence).[22]

The development of administration was inextricably bound up with economic exploitation. The capital of the province was presumably Ake-Ptolemais, which had been given its new name shortly before Zeno's journey in 261 BC.[23] The royal decree mentioned above names a 'financial administrator' for 'Syria and Phoenicia'; H. Bengtson will be right in arguing that he will have had a *stratēgos* beside him as chief-in-command, for political and military administration. The division of the country into hyparchies and toparchies, already dating back to the time of either Alexander or Antigonus, was taken further with the aim of making each individual village, as in Egypt, the smallest administrative unit and exploiting it to the greatest possible degree. Like the *nomoi* in Egypt, the hyparchies were also under a political and military *stratēgos* and an *oikonomos* for financial administration. In Marisa, the capital of the 'hyparchy' of Idumaea, Zeno's letter makes mention of five different officials from Ptolemy's administration. Thus Hellenistic bureaucratic administration also found a footing in the province, and Greek merchants and officials made their way into every last Palestinian farmstead.[24] It is striking that there is not a word about any Seleucid city or about the Seleucid empire anywhere in the Zeno correspondence. For this agent of the finance minister, the neighbouring country was to some degree non-existent, a way of treating it which is reminiscent of forms of modern censorship.[25] Military defence against the Seleucids in the north and the Arabs in the east and south was provided by an intensive chain of fortifications, of which a large number of archaeological traces still remain. These are particularly impressive in Samaria. New military settlements and cities were also founded. They include Philoteria on Lake Genessaret, the former Bet

Yerah, which was named after a sister of Philadelphus. In Scythopolis, the old Beth Shean, it seems that mercenaries were settled
from the kingdom on the Bosphorus. The city developed into a
centre for the cult of Dionysus; his nurse – presumably a Hellenized Semitic goddess – was accorded particular reverence here. The
founding of the city was ascribed to the god himself.[26] It is possible
that Damascus was refounded as Arsinoe, and there was perhaps a
second settlement under this name in the Biqa'.[27] Pella became
known as Berenice, the old fortress of Rabbat–'Ammon became
Philadelpheia, and Baalbek became Heliopolis. A whole series of
smaller places on the coast of Phoenicia, like Leontopolis, Ornithon-
polis, Sykaminonpolis, Boukolonpolis, Krokodelionpolis and Porphyreonpolis will also have been given their names, formed on an
analogy with Graeco-Egyptian place names, during the Ptolemaic
period.[28] II Maccabees 6.8 speaks in general terms of the 'Hellenistic cities' (*Hellēnidas poleis*) neighbouring on Judaea. For the
most part their 'Hellenization' will go back to the relatively peaceful period of Ptolemaic rule. A purely Hellenistic settlement with
great economic activity and considerable riches, so far unnamed,
was excavated in Tel 'Anafa in the Hūla basin. True, the results of
the excavations so far relate above all to the Seleucid era of the
second century BC, but still earlier strata from the Ptolemaic period
have been discovered below this.[29] Even the Phoenician cities on
the coast with their rich traditions partly adopted Hellenistic forms
of constitution. Thus after the death of its last king, Ptolemy's
admiral Philocles, Sidon gave itself a democratic constitution. By
contrast its rival Tyre chose an aristocratic constitution with suf-
fetes. We may suppose that there were similar changes in civic
constitutions of a 'Hellenistic' kind in other coastal cities down as
far as Gaza.[30] From the end of the third century on, men from
Tyre and Sidon appear as competitors at games in Greece – which
were only open to 'Hellenes'.[31] We find the remains of the typical
early Hellenistic, rectangular, Hippodamian city plan in a number
of towns: Damascus, Gerasa, Samaria, Philoteria and Marisa, as
also in the Seleucid Dura-Europos on the Euphrates. The numerous sagas of the founding of Palestinian and Syro-Phoenician
cities, much indebted to Greek myth, which then found expression
during the Roman period in city coinage and finally in the *Ethnica*
of Stephen of Byzantium, may partly go back to this period.[32]

From a political point of view, of course, it was not so easy to

unify the province, despite all the attempts of the Ptolemies. It was
far too varied. There were relatively independent cities on the
coast, and 'peoples' organized as *ethnē* in the interior;[33] in addition,
above all there were the military colonies established on royal land,
which had only limited 'civic rights'. The strict distinction between
native-born and Greek and Macedonian which was deliberately
maintained in Egypt does not seem to have been forced through so
vigorously in 'Syria and Palestine'. The taking of native-born concubines was probably relatively frequent,[34] and in the fortress of
the Jewish magnate Tobias in Transjordania we find Macedonian
and Jewish soldiers together in harmony. Tobias himself employed
a Greek secretary, and his correspondence with Apollonius and the
king shows him to have been a very self-conscious master. According to Josephus he was the brother-in-law of the high priest Onias
II; leaving aside the high priest Hezekiah in Pseudo-Hecataeus, he
was the first Jew to gain a position of influence during the Hellenistic period.[35] Because the situation was so different from Egypt,
the Ptolemaic administration had to make use of the indigenous
aristocracy on an equal footing. At the same time, the Zeno papyri
clearly show the difficulties which the new masters had with the
indigenous population and its marked self-awareness. An elder in
a Jewish village, called Jeddus, forcibly ejected from the village
both Zeno's agent and the representative of the Ptolemaic administration, who were trying to collect a debt. Two Idumaean sheikhs
sold two slaves to Zeno. When the slaves ran away, they refused
to hand them back and asked for a further payment.[36] The men
working in the vineyard in Apollonius' great estate at Bet 'Anat
protested vigorously against excessive taxes and appealed to the
minister.[37] On the other hand, in the interests of stable conditions
for agricultural work and the collection of taxes, the royal administration had to protect the semi-tributary peasants (*sōmata laika
eleuthera*) against Greek adventurers and freebooters. It therefore
prohibited the arbitrary enslavement of the country population.
Thus there were many aspects to the social situation in Palestine
under the rule of the first Ptolemies. Whereas the indigenous
aristocracy tended to improve their position under the new masters,
because they were involved in the economic boom and were ready
in at least some respects to adapt their life-style and language to
that of the Hellenistic upper classes, there was much greater
exploitation of the lower strata of the population, as a result of the

more intensive forms of state and private revenue collection. However, as the king wanted to maintain the productivity of the land, he had to respect certain basic rights of the population and take counter-measures against any direct oppression. The possibility of presenting petitions and complaints within the hierarchical structure of the royal bureaucracy, which in this respect followed an ancient royal Egyptian tradition, also afforded some degree of relief.[38]

The Phoenicians represented an important intermediary link in the communication of Hellenistic culture in Palestine. For a long time there had been economic and cultural interaction between the Greeks and the Phoenicians, whom they regarded as being a cut above other barbarians. In the Persian period the Phoenicians controlled the whole of the coastal plain, and their influence still seems to have been strong under the Ptolemies. This is clear from the Sidonian colony in the Idumaean capital Marisa. It was formed towards the middle of the third century and proved to be the setting for a mixed Hellenistic, Phoenician and Idumaean culture. The colony of the 'Sidonians' in Marisa was governed by an *archōn*; Greek was the principal language, and the tomb paintings with scenes of Dionysian dancing and representations of animals and hunting scenes show Alexandrian influence. Presumably there were similar Sidonian colonies in Shechem and Rabbath-'Ammon Philadelphia.[39]

That the real skill of Ptolemy II lay in the sphere of economics and administration and not least in the art of diplomacy, rather than in the waging of war, is clear not only from the conditions in Egypt and Palestine depicted in the Zeno papyri, but also from the development of relationships with the Seleucid empire after the Second Syrian War. As a result of the successes of the Macedonian king Antigonus Gonatas, the supremacy of the Ptolemies in the Aegean had been shattered. Nevertheless, in 253, Philadelphus succeeded in signing a peace treaty with his former opponent Antiochus II and allied himself with him in marriage. The Seleucid left his wife Laodice and her sons and declared himself ready to marry Berenice, Ptolemy's daughter. Apollonius, the minister, accompanied the princess from Pelusium along the coast of Palestine and Phoenicia to the frontier.[40] However, this 'diplomatic *tour de force*'[41] ended seven years later, after the death of Philadelphus in a tragedy (246). At the end of his life, Antiochus II again recognized the legitimacy of his first marriage to Laodice, and nominated her son Seleucus II as a successor. Berenice opposed this solution in the interests of her young son, and the intervention of her brother Ptolemy III Euergetes led to the Third Syrian War (246–241). However, immediately before the arrival of Euergetes in Antioch, Berenice and her son fell victim to a murder plot, and the astonishing initial successes of Ptolemy III, who not only gained control of Northern Syria and Cilicia, but is also said to have advanced as far as Babylon, were followed by severe setbacks. A rebellion forced him to return to Egypt.[42] The counter-attack led by Seleucus II Callinicus led to the capture of Ptolemy's fortresses of Damascus and Orthosia on the coast; the Egyptians seem vainly to have laid siege to them in 242/41.[43] However, the Seleucid attempt to seize the whole of Coele Syria failed completely, and the struggle with his brother Antiochus Hierax finally led the king to sign a peace treaty. This gave Ptolemy III substantial gains in territory in southern Asia Minor, including the enclave of Seleuceia in Pieria, the port of Antioch.[44] As Josephus records in *Contra Apionem*, Ptolemy III Euergetes may have visited Jerusalem on a journey through the province in connection with the conclusion of the war, and may there have offered a sacrifice to mark his victory.[45] Even the Book of Daniel follows the fate of Berenice and the successes of Ptolemy III with great interest, in the *vaticinium ex eventu* in Daniel 11; this is an indication of the degree to which people in Jewish apocalyptic circles were personally concerned about the argument between Ptolemies and Seleucids over the fate of Syria.[46] The apocalyptic author possibly incorporated a chronicle of the empires of the Diadochoi into his *vaticinium*.

The dismissal of the *dioikētēs* Apollonius and the attempt to simplify the administration by the introduction of local *stratēgoi*, coupled with the abolition of the distinction between military and economic executives, evidently led to a set-back in economic productivity. The king had to resort to a debasement of coinage which continued under Ptolemy IV and gradually led to inflation of copper currency.[47] The first part of the history of the Tobiads, which has been preserved for us by Josephus, presumably belongs to the time of Euergetes; Josephus puts it in the wrong period.[48] For all its romance-like elaborations, the narrative illuminates the changed situation in Palestine under Ptolemy III. According to the story, the high priest Onias II, the brother-in-law of the feudal lord Tobias, known to us from the Zeno papyri, refused to pay the annual instalment of tribute to the king. This was probably not because of an old man's stubbornness, as the Tobiad romance relates; people would have become weary of the regimentation of the Ptolemaic administration, and perhaps expected that Seleucus II Callinicus would take over the reins of power. The king promptly threatened to confiscate Jewish land and to settle military colonists on it. The threat was averted as a result of the intervention of Joseph, a nephew of the high priest and son of the feudal lord Tobias; in recompense, Josephus received the office of *prostasia*, i.e., he became political representative of the Jewish *ethnos* to the Ptolemaic administration. He now had in Judaea a similar position to that formerly held by the *pehah* under the Persians. By offering to double the tax yield, in Alexandria he succeeded in taking over responsibility for collecting taxes from the whole of 'Syria and Phoenicia'. When individual Hellenized cities, like Ashkelon and Scythopolis, rebelled against the increase in taxation, he succeeded in overcoming their resistance; he held office for twenty-two years, presumably down to the outbreak of the Third Syrian War, i.e. from about 240 to 218 BC.[49] In this capacity he became the first great Jewish banker, maintaining a permanent agency in Alexandria and depositing large sums there. These developments fit in well with the administrative reforms of the king who, after the dismissal of the financial genius Apollonius, attempted to simplify the complicated bureaucratic administration and increase the revenue from tax. However, as discoveries of coins in Palestine indicate, the additional exploitation reduced the amount of currency in circulation, and under his regime the economic power of the Ptolemies gradually began to decline (see n. 47 above). The rise of the Tobiad Joseph did, however, have advantages as far as the Jews were concerned: Jerusalem, which hitherto had been relatively unimportant, now became a significant economic and political centre. Polybius still sees Jerusalem primarily as a holy place: he speaks of the Jews who 'live around the temple called Hierosolyma'.[50] Whereas the feudal lord Tobias lived in Transjordania, Joseph and the later Tobiads worked in the city; that means that the nobility, too, increasingly began to live in the capital, thus opening it up more and more to Hellenistic influence. Like his father Tobias before him, Joseph seems to have sat relatively loosely to the precepts of the Torah. After describing his life, the Tobiad romance praises him in the following terms. 'A noble and generous man, who led the Jewish people out of poverty and misery into a splendid way of life.'[51] Here we have clear signs of a viewpoint which at a later date the Jewish Hellenists in the time of Antiochus IV wanted to adopt as their programme. It is expressed in I Maccabees 1.11: only close economic, political and cultural contact with their non-Jewish, Hellenized – or, as we would now put it, 'progressive' – environment will improve the lot of the Jews in Palestine; cutting themselves off from it had been a constant source of misfortune.

The book of Koheleth (Ecclesiastes) is another work which sheds light on the situation of the Jews in Palestine under Ptolemaic rule. While it would be wrong to find in it direct influence from Greek philosophical schools, we can certainly detect the atmosphere of the early Hellenistic period and familiarity with Greek proverbial wisdom and poetry.[52] Reference to political and social conditions are of interest to us here:

> If you see in a province the poor oppressed and justice and right violently taken away, do not be amazed at the matter; for the high official is watched by a higher, and there are yet higher ones over them (5.7).

We may see this as an allusion to the bureaucratic administration of the Ptolemies which we find, say, in the Zeno papyri. We may see a reference in 10.20 to the practice of denunciation, which was widespread in the Hellenistic monarchies;[53] the wise man, who himself stands 'under the shadow of money', sees through the cupidity of the new Hellenistic-oriental manager and criticizes it:

> He who loves money will not be satisfied with money;
> nor he who loves wealth, with gain: this also is vanity.
> When goods increase, they increase who eat them (5.10f.).

An addition to 5.7 probably alludes to the interest of the Ptolemies in increasing the agricultural yield: 'But in all, a king is an advantage to a land with cultivated fields.'[54] The work of the Chronicler, which also comes from the early Hellenistic period, describes the interest of king Uzziah in agriculture in similar terms. Not only did he build fortresses and equip them with engines of war (see pp. 19f. above); he 'had large herds in the . . . plain, and he had farmers and vinedressers in the hills and in the fertile lands, for he loved the soil.'[55]

We can understand how the old prophetic criticism of riches, luxury and the violence of those in power took on a new topicality, and how the anti-Hellenistic opposition could interpret the social term 'poor' in the sense of 'pious'. The piety of the poor, a theme developed above all in apocalyptic circles, thus implied a clear protest against the change of social structures by the alien Hellenistic government and its aristocratic accomplices.[56]

4

Palestine down to its Conquest by Antiochus III (223-200 BC)

During the first eighty years of the third century the Seleucids, who had a far larger kingdom with inexhaustible resources, failed to take control of the disputed territory of Coele Syria. A number of things stood in their way: dynastic struggles which kept flaring up again, the invasion of Asia Minor by the Gauls, the rivalry of the ambitious kingdom of Pergamum and the premature, violent death of their most capable ruler.[1] Ptolemaic diplomacy, combined with a militant defensive strategy, had been stronger than all the Seleucid attacks. However, in 223, when Antiochus III became king shortly after his twentieth birthday,[2] following the murder of his brother Seleucus III Soter, old plans for the conquest of the territory were revived. Although Molon, satrap of Media, had defected, in summer 221 the young king launched a first attack – on the advice of his 'vizier' Hermias – and crossed the northern frontier of Ptolemaic territory in Syria.[3] It seemed an opportune moment, as Ptolemy III had died at the end of 222 BC and his son Ptolemy IV Philopator, then only seventeen and tutored by Eratosthenes, showed more interest in abstract thinking and the arts than in the harsh reality of politics and administration. Polybius describes him as the spoilt *rex otiosus* who, shielded from the sycophants at court, did what pleased him without bothering about the national interest.[4]

Antiochus occupied the plain of Massyas, present-day Biqa', but his attack was halted at the line of defence set up by the Ptolemaic general Theodotus in its narrow southern end, between the fortresses of Gerrha and Brochoi.[5] After a number of unsuccessful assaults, Antiochus was forced to retreat. In the following year he crushed the revolt of the satrapies in the East and made preparations for a new attack. Despite the defection of his kinsman

Achaeus, who made himself king of Asia Minor, Antiochus concentrated all his attention on the conquest of Coele Syria. Philopator was given bad advice by his ministers Sosibius and Agathocles. Not only had he failed to prepare for a new attack from the north; in addition he fell foul of the capable general Theodotus, governor of the province and victor at the time of the first attack. Antiochus began the Fourth Syrian War – which was in fact the sixth military encounter – in the spring of 219 by capturing the Ptolemaic enclave of Seleuceia in Pieria, at the very gates of Antioch.[6] There he received a letter from Ptolemy's general Theodotus, who had rebelled against Philopator in Ake-Ptolemais, inviting him to attack Coele Syria. For the first time, thanks to Polybius, we have a detailed account of a Seleucid campaign in Phoenicia and Palestine. Antiochus again invaded the Biqa', by-passed the fortresses of Brochoi and Gerrha, and seized the pass near Berytus. Thereupon Ptolemy's army, which had been laying siege to Ptolemais, capital of a rebel province, abandoned the attempt and withdrew. The acquisition of Tyre and Ptolemais brought the king massive provisions, and forty ships.[7] He gave up his plan to launch a direct attack on Pelusium, which had proved fatal to so many attacks on Egypt, as soon as he heard of the massive defence measures of the Egyptians. Instead of this he proceeded to occupy the smaller cities of Phoenicia and Palestine. They readily surrendered; only the larger fortresses, as for example Dora, on the coast, were bold enough to offer any resistance. Treachery broke open the splendid Ptolemaic system of defence in depth. Taken aback by the defection of Theodotus and the rapid successes of Antiochus, Philopator and his counsellor Sosibius felt too weak to invade Palestine immediately. Instead, they tried to gain time to make proper preparations, and entered into negotiations with the Seleucids. Antiochus, preoccupied with the siege of Dora, agreed to a cease-fire for four months during the winter. He left behind garrisons in the territory which he had captured under the command of the renegade Theodotus, and with the greater part of his army moved to Seleuceia in the hope (which was reinforced by Philopator) that no attempts would be made to recapture lost ground and that in effect the province was already his.[8] Of course the negotiations in Memphis, skilfully manipulated by the Egyptians, came to nothing – the Egyptians even managed to conceal their preparations for war from the eyes of the Seleucid delegation – and in the spring of 218

Antiochus set out to conquer the rest of Palestine. However, in the meantime, Ptolemy's general Nicolaus – like Theodotus, an Aetolian – had advanced into Phoenicia and occupied both the 'pass of the planes' and Porphyreonpolis, between Berytus and Sidon.[9] In a combined action by land and sea, Antiochus forced him to retreat to Sidon. The victor refrained from laying siege to the city, and instead invaded Galilee, occupying Philoteria, where the Jordan flows out of Lake Genessaret, and Scythopolis, in an important strategic position. He also captured the mountain fortress of Atabyrion, i.e. Tabor, by a stratagem. A whole series of Ptolemy's officers came over to his side, some with their troops, a clear indication of the decline of Ptolemaic rule over Palestine. Antiochus largely owed his successes to these renegades.[10] He crossed the Jordan, took Pella in the Jordan valley, and Camus and Ephron (Gephrus) in the hill-country of Gilead. The aim of this thrust into Transjordania was to join forces with the Arab tribes, who promptly and with one accord took his side. We may assume that this reference is above all to the Nabataeans, who had not forgotten the way in which Philadelphus had humiliated them and the Ptolemies had restricted their power.[11] Strengthened by their support, and abundantly provided for, Antiochus siezed the fortress of Abila to which Nicias, the friend and kinsman of a local ruler, Menneos, had vainly attempted to give aid. Evidently the Ptolemies had to some degree entrusted the defence of the eastern frontier, against the Arabs and other enemies (as in the cleruchy of the Jewish feudal lord Tobias), to local forces.[12] Following that, after a short siege he occupied the particularly powerful fortress of Gadara. There he heard news that a powerful force was assembling in Rabbath-'Ammon which was plundering the territory of the Arabs who had gone over to Antiochus; this presumably consisted of units from the Ptolemaic 'military frontier' in Ammanitis, the military colony of the Tobiads.[13] He shelved his other plans and attacked the almost inaccessible fortress. All attempts came to nothing until a prisoner disclosed the secret source of its water supply and lack of water forced the garrison to capitulate. Following this, Antiochus sent two of Ptolemy's former officers who had come over to him, with a force of five thousand men, 'into the territory near Samaria'; we may take this to include Judaea and Jerusalem, even though they are not mentioned by name.[14] There is perhaps an intrinsic connection between the conquest of the territory of the Tobiads in Ammanitis and the advance into Samaria-Judaea. It is remarkable that at this point – in contrast to his account of the Fifth Syrian War – the historian passes over the *ethnos* of the Jews in silence. Evidently they had no independent military significance in Palestine for a reporter whose attention was drawn primarily to the great Ptolemaic fortresses. Towards the end of 218 Antiochus went to his winter quarters in Ptolemais.

By the early part of the next year, Philopator had completed his preparations and marched east from Pelusium. Antiochus moved south along the coast. On 22 June 217 BC, the two armies met at Raphia on the southern frontier of Palestine. A mad attempt by the renegade Theodotus to assassinate Ptolemy IV misfired; the king was saved by a young Jewish apostate, Dositheos the son of Drimylos.[15] The kaleidoscopic Seleucid army included ten thousand Arabs under the command of a certain Zabdibelus, and select Syrian troops;[16] Antiochus' riders and his Indian elephants were superior to the African ones on the Egyptian side. However, the decisive factor was the firmness of the Ptolemaic phalanx, trained by Greek mercenaries and Egyptians well versed in Macedonian ways. While the young Antiochus III was pursuing the fleeing cavalry of his opponents, an annihilating defeat was inflicted on his own army.[17] Over the following years this decisive contribution by native Egyptian troops bolstered up the confidence of the fellahin, and led to constant unrest in Egypt. Antiochus fled with the rest of his army to Gaza and negotiated a brief cease-fire in order to bury the dead. His losses amounted to 10,000 infantry and 300 cavalry, whereas Ptolemy's casualties were only 1,500 and 700 respectively. The Seleucid was forced to retreat from the conquered province as rapidly as possible,[18] while the Phoenician cities vied with one another in paying homage to their legitimate ruler. Polybius explicitly stresses that the sympathies of the Palestinians had always been with the royal house in Alexandria.[19]

As soon as he reached Antioch, Antiochus began peace negotiations without delay, as he was afraid of being squeezed between Achaeus in Asia Minor and Ptolemy in the south. After some delay, the Egyptian king, delighted at his unexpected success and without any political or military ambition, gladly acceded to the request. He had not impeded his opponent's retreat and – after the decree of Raphia – only advanced into Seleucid territory, for three weeks, when the negotiations seemed to be dragging on too long.[20] He had no plans for conquest and did not even ask for the restoration of Seleuceia in Pieria, which had been lost some time before. All that happened was that the old frontier was largely restored. Possibly the unrest among the Egyptian detachments encouraged him to work towards peace.[21] Instead of further military successes, he and his consort, Arsinoe, his sister, allowed themselves to be feted by the cities of the province which he had won back. He visited its sanctuaries, to demonstrate his reverence for the gods of the land and to receive the manifold demonstrations of homage from its inhabitants.[22] Honorific inscriptions from Marisa, Joppa and the neighbourhood of Tyre[23] bear witness to this royal visit to the province, which is said to have lasted for four months after the decree òf Raphia.[24] Despite all the romance-like elaboration, there may well be a historical nucleus to the legendary account in III Maccabees of Philopator's unfortunate visit to the Temple in Jerusalem.[25] The book of Daniel, which describes the Fourth Syrian War in some detail, also talks in the end of the 'arrogance' of Philopator, who overthrew ten thousand but whose power had no endurance.[26] As a result of his laziness and indolence, Ptolemy IV all too quickly gave away the fruits of his victory; 'he could have robbed Antiochus of his kingdom had he supported his good fortune with action'.[27]

As a result, developments in the two kingdoms over the following years went in opposite directions. Whereas Antiochus III first overthrew the usurper Achaeus in Asia Minor (216–213) and after that undertook his famous *anabasis* into the eastern provinces which led to the restoration of the kingdom of his great-grandfather Seleucus I (212–205), Ptolemaic Egypt was troubled with increasing internal unrest. Above all in Upper Egypt, the native inhabitants, goaded on by their priests, rebelled against the rising taxation by means of which the king sought to make good his financial losses caused by the war. In 207 BC Thebais left the confederate kingdom and for twenty years was an independent kingdom with native Nubian monarchs.[28] Here we can see a basic crisis in the relationship between the Hellenistic monarchy and the indigenous population which was to become even more serious in the second century. The mood of the Egyptian *laoi* is illuminated by apocalyptic-sounding texts such as the Demotic chronicle and the Potter's Oracle, which dreamed of the end of foreign rule in Egypt.[29] The king was compelled to make an attempt to counter this development by yielding to some extent to the wishes of the indigenous population. Greater importance was now attached to early Egyptian religion and its traditions. We may expect that this crisis also left its mark on conditions in Palestine, though our sources only drop hints in this direction. For example, the Tobiad romance in Josephus reports that Joseph, the man with ultimate responsibility for collecting taxes, whose relationship with the royal house seemed to have become rather cooler, sent his youngest son Hyrcanus to Alexandria to celebrate the birth of the heir to the throne – perhaps the later Ptolemy V Epiphanes, 210 BC – where he won favour from the king and his friends as a result of generous gifts. Having returned to Jerusalem, however, Hyrcanus fell foul of his father and above all his brothers, with the result that he had to retreat to the old Tobiad property on the other side of the Jordan, where he 'waged war on the Arabs' and 'exacted tribute from the barbarians'.[30] This probably means that he was given supreme command over the Ptolemaic cleruchy in Ammanitis, while his position in Jerusalem had become untenable. This points to a change in the political situation in Jerusalem. The vigorous new high priest Simon II, 'the Just', son of Onias II who had once been suppressed by Joseph, had gained new influence – perhaps in connection with the split in the Tobiad family, in which he followed the majority of the aristocracy by siding with Hyrcanus' brothers. The Tobiad romance reports that the whole people was divided into two parties as a result of this dispute in the leading family, the Tobiads.[31]

However, it is very probable that there was a political and religious background to the division, and that it was not just a family quarrel involving the most powerful family in the land. Down to the time of his suicide under Antiochus IV Epiphanes, Hyrcanus, who had acquired a considerable sphere of power in Transjordania, remained a supporter of the Ptolemies, whereas the 'Tobiads' in Jerusalem, along with the high priest Simon, now supported the Seleucid party. When Antiochus III finally conquered Palestine, this pro-Seleucid group was evidently in the majority in Jerusalem, while the interests of the people were again wholly represented by the high priest Simon, who was very conscious of his own status and of the tradition. His contemporary Ben Sira cannot praise him highly enough:

> He considered how to save his people from ruin, and fortified the city to withstand a siege.[32]

It is probable that in the province of Syria and Phoenicia, too, there had been a shift of mood in favour of the Seleucids as a result of the obvious political collapse of Ptolemaic rule in Egypt, coupled with increasing financial difficulties, which could be seen not least in the inflation of copper currency.[33] Among the Jews in particular, this change may also have been helped on by a somewhat anti-semitic policy of Philopater in Egypt, which is described by III Maccabees (legendary though it is). According to this account the king, whose interest in the cult of Dionysus is also attested elsewhere, attempted to convert the Jews by force to the worship of Dionysus.[34]

Antiochus III reaped the fruits of this development in the so-called Fifth Syrian War of 202–200 BC. His successful expedition into the eastern provinces as far as Bactria and 'India', a kind of imitation of Alexander, had also increased his prestige in the West; he took the title 'the great king' (*basileus megas*) to distinguish himself from the kings of Armenia, Parthia and Bactria who had now become his vassals.[35] The letter of Antiochus to Zeuxis, the *stratēgos* of Asia Minor, handed down by Josephus, in which he orders the settlement of two thousand Jewish cleruchs from Babylonia, together with their families, in Phrygia and Lydia, probably also comes from the time of the '*anabasis*'.[36] This means that not only the Ptolemies, but also the Seleucids, relied on Jewish mercenaries. A note inserted into II Maccabees speaks of 8,000 Jewish soldiers who proved decisive in a fight against the Galatians – presumably under Antiochus I.[37] As a result of his expedition to India, Antiochus had not only extended his sphere of influence quite considerably; at the same time he had carried through an administrative reform which replaced the great satrapies, which had grown too powerful, with smaller administrative units. At the same time, the advancement of the ruler cult served to strengthen the unity of the kingdom.[38] His son Antiochus IV Epiphanes later sought to continue this policy – on essentially less favourable presuppositions.

At the end of 205 BC, Philopator had died in Egypt – in mysterious circumstances. The court kept his death secret for a long time. The throne was then occupied by Ptolemy V Epiphanes, a five-year-old child. Antiochus took advantage of the weakness of his opponent first of all to seize the Ptolemaic possessions in southern Asia Minor and then to attack Coele Syria, after making a secret agreement with Philip V of Macedon (202 BC).[39] We are considerably less well informed about the Fifth Syrian War than we are about the Fourth, as the relevant passages in Polybius have almost all been lost. We know only the most important events.[40] The province was evidently much easier prey than eighteen years before. Only Gaza, which had special links with Egypt because it was the terminus of trade with Arabia, offered lengthy resistance before it was taken.[41] When the king had withdrawn to winter quarters, the Ptolemaic general Scopas took the opportunity of advancing into Palestine with his army and recapturing the southern part of the country (winter 201/200). The Jews in Jerusalem, who had largely become Seleucid supporters – presumably following the lead of the high priest Simon and the Tobiads – were the chief to feel the weight of Ptolemy's vengeance. Josephus quotes Polybius, who in this connection for the first time gives a lengthy account of the Jews, though all that we now have is the brief quotation in Josephus: in the winter Scopas 'conquered the people (*ethnos*) of the Jews'.[42] Evidently the Jewish *ethnos* in Palestine, under the leadership of the high priest Simon the Just, now played a larger role than in earlier campaigns. By contrast, the seer in the book of Daniel describes this revolt against the Ptolemies in negative terms: 'In those times many shall rise against the king of the south; and the men of violence among your own people shall lift themselves up in order to fulfil the vision; but they shall fall.'[43] Jerome (following Porphyry) already saw that this is a description of the fight between the supporters of the Ptolemies and the pro-Seleucid party.[44] Thus the century-long struggle of the great powers over Coele Syria led to a division in the religious community in Palestine, a division which appeared again at the time of Antiochus IV Epiphanes, provoked the period of religious oppression and led to the Maccabean rebellion. However, a little later Scopas suffered a devastating defeat at the hands of Antiochus III at Paneion, by the sources of the Jordan.[45] He escaped to Sidon with ten thousand men, the ruins of his force. After three unsuccessful attempts at a relief, he was forced to capitulate in 199 BC in exchange for safe conduct.[46] After his victory at Paneion, Antiochus occupied Palestine for the second time. Polybius mentions Batanaea in Transjordania, Samaria, Abila and Hadara – three fortresses which had already played a role in 218 – and finally also the city of Jerusalem and its Temple. According to Josephus and Porphyry-Jerome, the Jews gave powerful support to the king by overpowering the Ptolemaic garrison in the citadel of the city, and also provided copious provisions for the Seleucid army, including its elephants.[47] We also hear from Jerome that Egyptian troops evacuated to Egypt the Jews who had supported Ptolemy.[48] Thus the 'hundred-year war' over Phoenicia and Palestine was finally decided in favour of the Seleucids. To begin with, it seemed as though the indigenous population, including the Jews, were well pleased with the new solution, despite their considerable sufferings in the battles which had been waged over them – Jerusalem itself had been partially destroyed.[49]

Palestine under Seleucid Rule down to the Death of Antiochus (III 200-187 BC)

Antiochus sought to gain or to retain the sympathies of his new subjects in Coele Syria by means of a skilful policy. We have three pieces of evidence for this statement, two of which have been preserved by Josephus, while the third was discovered a number of years ago in Ḥefzibah, west of Scythopolis. They are: 1) a letter from the king to Ptolemy, *stratēgos* of Coele Syria, in favour of the Jews and their Temple;[1] 2) extracts from a royal edict[2] concerned to preserve the ritual purity of Jerusalem and the Temple; and 3) a correspondence consisting of six letters from the period between 201 and 195 BC which was given the form of an inscription and which relates to the possessions of Ptolemy son of Thraseas, the *stratēgos*, in the plain of Megiddo.[3] The communication of the king to the same *stratēgos*, concerning the Jews, takes the form of an edict in which Antiochus expresses his thanks for the powerful support given by the Jews in the battles fought on their territory. In reality, these 'demonstrations of royal favour' did not rest on a spontaneous act of the king; they were the fruits of negotiations in which the priest Johanan had played a decisive part in the role of chief delegate. His son Eupolemus was later to be the leader of a Jewish delegation to Rome in the time of Judas Maccabaeus.[4] The content of the royal decree is no more than it was customary for the king to concede to other war-torn cities, say in Asia Minor, from the Persian period onwards. However, the recipient here is the *ethnos* of the Jews rather than the city of Jerusalem. Jerusalem is mentioned only as a 'city of the Jews'; in other words, it had no 'civic rights' corresponding to those of a Greek *polis*.[5] The king promised to support the rebuilding of the Temple and the daily sacrifice by the provision of goods in kind. Certain people were exempt from personal taxation (poll-tax, tax on produce and salt tax): the leaders of the *ethnos*, the *gerousia* as the supreme political authority (it must have come into being in the Ptolemaic period);[6] the priests, the Temple scribes (i.e. the forerunners of the later scribes) and the Temple singers (but not all Levites). Those who returned to the city, which had been largely destroyed, were to have three years exemption from tax,[7] and the tribute to be paid by the Jewish *ethnos* was to be reduced by a third as compensation for war damage. The annual contribution under the Ptolemies probably amounted to three hundred talents, but this was again raised considerably by the successors of Antiochus III.[8] All those who had been wrongfully enslaved under war conditions were to be given their freedom. Finally, all members of the *ethnos* – including those living in the Diaspora – were given the right to 'live in accordance with the laws of their fathers', as had already happened under the Persians and Alexander. In this way the traditional Law of Moses was given its legitimation as the 'royal law' for the Jews.[9] About twenty-five years later there were Jewish 'Hellenists' from Jerusalem who were given permission by the new king Antiochus IV Epiphanes to disregard the 'royal favour' and to give Jerusalem a new constitution, namely that of a Greek city called Antiocheia.[10] We have a new parallel to this edict of Antiochus III in the *philanthrōpiai* which he showed to the city of Teos in Ionia. Here he granted complete exemption from tax to citizens on account of the war damage they had endured and previous exploitations by the Attalids, along with the right of asylum; in other words, the concessions to this Greek *polis* went far beyond those made to the Jewish *ethnos*.[11]

The second edict prohibited foreigners entering the sanctuary – a privilege which the Romans also recognized at a later date[12] – together with the introduction of the meat and skins and also the breeding of unclean animals. Only sacrificial animals could be kept in the city. Infringements were to be punished with heavy fines. These regulations, presumably prompted by the high priest Simon and the orthodox members of the priesthood, inevitably limited the significance of Jerusalem as a trading centre. With such inconvenient rules, non-Jewish trading caravans will have avoided the city as far as possible. Right down to the time of the Jewish war against Rome in AD 66–70[13] we keep finding this tendency to use ritual prohibitions to restrict economic contacts with the Gentile world, which were thought to be dangerous. Conflicts which were to flare up soon afterwards should be seen against the background of this edict concerning the 'sanctification' of the Temple and the city, which was promulgated to serve the interests of the orthodox.[14] Such an edict, with its restrictions on trade, represented a challenge to the 'progressive' group for whom segregation from their Hellenistic-Semitic environment had long been a painful matter.

The inscription in Ḥefzibah near Scythopolis relates to the protection of the village population in the far-flung possessions of Ptolemy son of Thraseas from outrages by the Seleucid occupying forces. In 219 BC, at the beginning of the Fourth Syrian War, this Ptolemy had still been an army commander in the Ptolemaic service, but he later went over to the Seleucid side and under Antiochus III became *stratēgos* of the new province of Coele Syria and chief priest of the ruler cult.[15] The king's letter about the 'demonstrations of favour' to the Jews had been addressed to him. It remains uncertain whether his property in the plain of Megiddo already belonged to him when he was serving Ptolemy, or whether it was given him out of the 'royal land' as a reward for his defection; the inscription speaks both of private property and of (royal) investment (*eis to patrikon*). In the earliest letter, written in 201 when the war was still on, Ptolemy is given permission for his villages to enter into reciprocal exchanges and trade – presumably without being taxed. In a further, later correspondence the soldiers are forbidden to take up quarters in these villages, to make requisitions, or to drive the inhabitants from their homes. A tenfold fine is threatened for any damage done.[16]

That Antiochus took pains to tread carefully during the transfer of power is also clear from the fact that he left Ptolemy's supporter Hyrcanus the Tobiad, unmolested in his territory in Ammanitis – his power was only broken by Antiochus IV Epiphanes.[17] In contrast to Ptolemaic Egypt, the administration of the Seleucid empire was 'federal' rather than central, and even after the administrative reforms carried out by Antiochus III, individual cities, peoples and dynasts were allowed a considerable degree of independence.[18] Thus to begin with the Seleucid rule in Palestine will have come as an improvement in the situation for the population of the province, especially as it had been combined with a reduction in taxation. The activity of the new rulers in the new province is also illustrated by the founding or renaming of a number of cities; as a rule, however, they are usually to be attributed to the sons of

Antiochus III, Seleucus IV and Antiochus IV Epiphanes. Tcherikover conjectures that Antiochus III founded only an Antiocheia and a Seleuceia on Lake Hulah in honour of his decisive victory over Scopas in 200 BC.[19]

In the meantime, of course, a new power had appeared on the scene. In the year in which Antiochus III finally conquered Palestine, Rome declared war on Philip V of Macedon. The Roman delegation which presented the ultimatum to the Macedonian king, requiring him to give up all his conquests in Asia Minor and the Aegean, also went on to visit Antiochus – possibly while he was still in Palestine – and to secure his neutrality in the coming conflict. It did not accept Egypt's offer of an alliance. In its dealings with the Hellenistic monarchies, then, Rome relied on the well-tried policy of 'divide and conquer'. Antiochus was to be prevented from coming to the aid of Philip V of Macedon, his ally against Egypt and Rome's chief enemy; the Ptolemies were the chief ones to suffer. The Seleucid conquest of Coele Syria hardly affected the Romans. However, Antiochus probably promised that he himself would not attack Egypt.[20] This gave Rome a free hand against Macedon, which suffered an annihilating defeat at the hands of Titus Flaminius in 197, at Cynoscephalae in Thessaly. The final decline of the Hellenistic monarchies had begun. Antiochus must have been aware of the threat in the West, even if he underestimated the new opponent. He rejected a Roman delegation which in 196 BC asked him to grant freedom to the Greek cities in Asia Minor and at the same time offered mediation in the conflict between the Seleucids and the Ptolemies, and himself took the initiative in coming to terms with his old enemy. In 197 BC, Ptolemy V Epiphanes, barely fourteen years old, was declared of age and crowned. The Seleucid peace negotiations began with him and came to a final conclusion in 194/93 with the marriage of the young ruler to Antiochus' daughter Cleopatra, the first Ptolemaic queen of this name. It is possible that the king provisionally ceded some of the produce of Coele Syria to Ptolemy as a 'dowry', to alleviate his loss of the province. At a later date the guardians of his son, Ptolemy VI Philometor, attempted to claim this from Antiochus IV Epiphanes as a right. However, the Seleucids emphatically retained political jurisdiction and military power.[21] With peace buttressed by this linking of dynasties, Antiochus felt that he had secured his rear and could devote attention to his enterprises in Western Asia Minor and in Greece; thus war with Rome had become inevitable. He ended 190 in Magnesia in Lydia with a catastrophe both for him and for the Seleucid monarchy. Antiochus' multi-national army – which included Medes, Elamites, Syrians and Arab camel troops[22] – suffered an annihilating defeat from an army of Romans and their allies only half the size, under the command of the Scipio brothers. The defeat was pressed home by the peace conditions laid upon the king at Apameia in 188 BC. Seleucid possessions in Asia Minor as far as the Taurus had to be forfeited; they were transferred to the kingdom of Pergamum. The elephants used in war had to be handed over and the fleet reduced to ten ships. This made any active policy in the west impossible. Furthermore, Antiochus had to pay the victor 12,000 talents within twelve years as war damage,[23] a considerable amount which proved a heavy burden on the finances of the kingdom, especially as the king took great pains to keep to the conditions of the treaty. The loss of the silver mines in Asia Minor caused difficulties in the future for his monetary policy. Consequently the lessening of taxation in Palestine which had initially been introduced by Antiochus will not have lasted for long.[24] The inroads continually made by Seleucid rulers into the rich sanctuaries in their kingdom must be seen in this light. Local inhabitants killed Antiochus III 'comme un vulgaire bandit', only a year after the peace treaty, when he was attempting to plunder the treasures of a temple in Elymais (187 BC).[25] Under his son Seleucus IV, the 'vizier' Heliodorus seized the Temple treasure in Jerusalem, and Polybius says of Antiochus IV Epiphanes: 'He plundered numerous sanctuaries'. In particular, he completely stripped the rich Temple in Jerusalem. What the Hellenistic rulers took for granted as their right must have seemed sacrilege and wickedness to their subjects, and will have strengthened opposition against them.[26] A further consequence was that Ptolemy V Epiphanes had renewed hopes of winning back Palestine and Phoenicia, and the conflict which had apparently been settled broke out again. Ptolemy's supporters were given considerable encouragement – in Judaea also.[27] Thus the catastrophe of Magnesia proved to be the start of new and bitter conflicts for Palestine, as a frontier province of the Seleucid kingdom. For ages the prestige of the Hellenistic monarchies had been bound up entirely with the success of their kings in war. Defeat at the hands of republican Rome had shaken the Seleucid kingdom, giving encouragement to the national independence movements in the eastern provinces and in Phoenicia and Coele Syria. It is one of the contradictions of history that at the very point when the decline of the Hellenistic kingdoms became obvious, radical reformers in Jerusalem set about changing the holy city into a Seleucid *polis* with a Greek constitution.

We again find the apocalyptic historian of the book of Daniel a careful observer of the catastrophic fate of Antiochus III:[28] 'Afterward he (the king of the north) shall turn his face to the coastlands, and shall take many of them. But a commander (*qaṣin* here for consul) shall put an end to his insolence; with a curse[29] he shall pay him out for it. Then he shall turn his face back towards the fortresses of his own land; but he shall stumble and fall, and shall not be found.'

The new situation in Judaea at the beginning of Seleucid rule is illustrated by a series of allusions in Ben Sira, who himself may have been one of the 'Temple scribes' mentioned in the edict of Antiochus III. His work combines the high estimation of modest possessions and hard work held by ancient wisdom, with terse, prophetic-sounding polemic against the extravagance of riches and the exploitation of the worker; he also warns against foreign traders.[30] The heroes of his great national and religious past, down to Simon the Just, are celebrated in the 'praise of the fathers'; but at the same time the sons are warned to keep together.[31] There is also an unmistakable warning given to those who despise the Law, to apostates and doubters.[32] Behind this stands the threatening influence of Hellenistic civilization on the aristocracy. In contrast to this, Ben Sira identifies the divine wisdom which permeates the whole world with the Torah of Moses.[33] His political attitude is illuminated by his prayer for the eschatological liberation from heathen and Seleucid rule. It is also typical of the feelings of the Jewish worshipping community throughout the early Hellenistic period, who no longer wanted to be a pawn in the game constantly played by the godless world-powers:

> Have mercy upon us, O Lord, the God of all, and look upon us,
> and cause the fear of thee to fall upon all the nations.
> Lift up thy hand against foreign nations
> and let them see thy might.

A cryptic allusion is made to the Gentile ruler and his cult:

> Crush the head of the prince of Moab,
> who says, 'There is no (God) but me.'

The concluding formula, following Deutero-Isaiah, shows that universal breadth which becomes typical of Jewish apocalyptic in Hellenistic times:

> And all who are on the earth will know
> that thou art the Lord, the God of the ages.[34]

II

Aspects of the 'Hellenization' of Judaism

The Problem of 'Hellenization' in the Early Hellenistic Period

Two difficulties stand in the way of a description of the 'Hellenization' of Judaism or, in other words, the interplay between Judaism and Hellenistic culture in the pre-Maccabean period, i.e. in the brief 160 years between 333 and 175 BC. First, we only have very fragmentary and sporadic information about the Jews in Palestine and in the Diaspora during this period. The non-Jewish literary sources are almost completely silent, and where they do provide any information, very little of it is concerned with the adoption of Hellenistic culture by the Jews. By and large, too, the epigraphic, papyrological and archaeological evidence is scanty and often difficult to interpret. We can only guess at the dating of Jewish writings from the period and they can usually be used only as 'indirect evidence' of the penetration (or rejection) of Hellenism, since either – at least on the surface – there is no mention at all of links with the Hellenistic world or, if the writing is polemical or apologetic, the accounts are tendentious. Almost all the Jewish literature from this period that has come down to us is essentially religious and nationalistic propaganda.[1] Given this source material, then, we shall never arrive at a complete picture; at best, it is only possible to attempt to describe individual situations and lines of development as information happens to have come down to us from the sources.

Secondly, while we can gain a fairly clear understanding of 'Judaism', i.e. the members of the Jewish *ethnos* in their home country of Palestine and in the Diaspora, their religion, literature and way of life, the much-used terms 'Hellenism' or 'Hellenization' are blurred and disputed. Historians and theologians use them frequently, but it does not follow that we can be certain about what they mean. It is therefore worth while looking at the terms rather more closely. In this context, 'Hellenism' does not mean just a historical period,[2] say between Alexander's expedition (334 BC) and the battle of Actium (31 BC); it is to be understood as the designation of an apparently clearly defined culture which because of its aggressive character also sought to take over ancient Judaism. This description of Hellenism as a 'world culture', which 'permeated' those parts of the East which had been conquered by Alexander, goes back to the first great historian of the period, Gustav Droysen, who was influenced by Hegel's philosophy of history. To him the Greek world seemed to be the antithesis to the ancient East, and 'Hellenism' was the synthesis which found its consummation in Christianity.[3] There is some foundation for this understanding in antiquity itself, specifically in Plutarch's work *De fortuna aut virtute Alexandri Magni*. Here Alexander appears not only as conqueror of the world, but also as an educator with philosophical training and a 'reconciler of the world',[4] who 'civilized barbarian kings', 'founded Greek cities among the wild peoples', and 'taught laws and peace to lawless and uneducated tribes'.[5]

Plutarch paints this idealistic picture under the influence of the Stoic idea of the citizen of the world and against the background of a Roman empire at peace, which had become relatively humane,[6] and had not yet been shaken by the crises of the third century AD. Originally the conception of the political unity of the world, along the lines of an 'imperial idea', which he took for granted, was completely alien to the thought of the Greeks, which was oriented on the specific *polis*. By contrast, we find it in the Persian empire[7] – which the Greeks regarded as barbaric – and later in Jewish apocalyptic.[8] In fact Alexander began his expedition as a war of vengeance. Even today scholars still dispute when and in what way he was first struck by the idea of world rule, and indeed whether he aimed at it at all.[9] This means that the notion of a self-contained 'Hellen(ist)ic culture', concerned with expansion, backed by the philosophical and political idea of a humanitarian amalgamation of peoples, can hardly be projected back on the early Hellenistic period of Alexander's expedition, the struggles of the Diadochoi and the monarchies of the third century. The victorious Macedonians had themselves been accepted only in the upper strata of Greek culture; to Greeks proper and to orientals they therefore seemed to be destroyers rather than 'bringers of culture'. Both

Demosthenes, who hated the Macedonians, and Isocrates, who marvelled at Philip II, still describe them as 'barbarians'.[10] If we discount Alexander, who was an exceptional figure, they certainly did not have a missionary zeal for civilization. Even the young king presumably did not do more than aim at a 'fusing' of the new Macedonian ruling class with the old Persian aristocracy, in the practical concern to stabilize the enormous territory over which he ruled.[11] In other words, his motivation lay in the pragmatic sphere of power politics rather than in the humanitarian realm. Significantly, the Macedonian military assembly held after the death of the king immediately gave these plans up. It is of course astonishing how quickly the Macedonians, who until shortly beforehand had been regarded as 'barbarians', now took over the 'élitist' conceptions of the Greeks and did so without reservation.

Thus in the first place the interest of the Diadochoi and the later Hellenistic kings lay not so much in extending Greek culture towards their oriental subjects as in securing and extending their own personal power. This, however, was done less by mixing with the orientals than by keeping apart from them, and was helped on by the intensive usage of Macedonians and Greeks in military matters and in the royal administration. The king's power was rooted in the Macedonian phalanx, Greek mercenaries, officials and technicians. It called for collaborators able to think rationally, with a talent for organization and as few moral scruples as possible. This is why the kings founded numerous cities and military settlements in the 'colonial territories' which they had conquered in order to safeguard their power. The cultural 'unity' of the new 'Hellenistic' world, which had grown so much greater, did not lie within their field of vision; on the contrary, they often pursued a narrow-minded mercantile policy of mutual segregation (and detachment), and wrought destruction on one another in constant suicidal wars from the death of Alexander until the final victory of Rome. In the West, the power of Rome inherited their legacy, bringing peace with a great deal of force; in the East it fell to nationalistic, oriental rulers, and particularly to the Parthian kingdom. A more thorough 'Hellenization', which also included the lower classes, only became a complete reality in Syria and Palestine under the protection of Rome, which here could come forward as the 'saviour' of the Greek cultural heritage. It was Rome which first helped 'Hellenism' to its real victory in the East – as far as the Euphrates frontier. In historical terms, the 'age of Hellenism' does not come to an end with the battle of Actium in AD 31; that is at the point when it really begins to have a profound effect. It is quite remarkable that the innovation of using the verb *aphellēnizein* in the transitive sense is to be found for the very first time in the writing of a Jew, Philo of Alexandria. In his encomium on the emperor Augustus, he enumerates the benefits brought by Roman rule, referring to the ending of the civil wars and the menace of the pirates, the pacification of 'wild and bestial peoples' and finally to the 'Hellenization' of barbarians. 'He enlarged Greece with many other Greek lands and Hellenized the most important parts of the barbarian world, a guardian of the peace, who gave each man his due . . .' (*Legatio ad Gaium* 147).[12] This transitive use of *hellēnizein* only appears again very much later in Libanius; the subject-matter, on the other hand, mentioned in connection with Alexander, appears again in the work of Plutarch which I have already mentioned.[13] In other words, the cultural programme of the 'Hellenization of barbarians' only became a general theme in the time of the Romans.

Thus the theme of a 'mutual interpenetration' of Judaism and Hellenism is a very complicated and even contradictory phenomenon, to be found at many levels, and a first task must be to look more closely at the elusive and controversial terms 'Hellenism' and 'Hellenization' in relation to particular historical phenomena.

7

Hellenes, Barbarians and Jews: the Fight for Political and Social Status

Our starting point is the traditional Greek distinction between Greeks and barbarians, which became particularly pointed above all as a result of the victorious outcome of the Persian wars.[1] Both words are blanket terms. The barbarians were those who spoke a 'foreign' language. This negative, derogatory designation 'in a striking way lumped together peoples outside the Greek world, whether they were highly cultured, semi-cultured or had no culture at all'.[2] The 'Hellenes', too, were not a 'people' in the strict sense, but a community of peoples and cities. This becomes clear from their original designation, *Panhellēnes*. The theory of a blood relationship through a common descent from one ancestor, *Hellēn*, the son of Deucalion, was secondary. This is comparable with the positive Jewish selection of Shem as son of Noah after the great flood.[3] The community of the 'Hellenes' manifested itself in a way of life with a particular stamp, a culture governed by a view of the freedom of man and the political institutions that went with it, like shared games and sanctuaries drawing worshippers from wide areas. A shared aristocratic model of the heroes of Homer's epics was stronger than the bond of a common language, which only arose over a long period of time out of a variety of dialects. The experiences of the fight for freedom against the Persians strengthened the sense of togetherness and superiority, and resulted in the image of the barbarian becoming a negative caricature. They were regarded as uneducated and even bestial, hostile to strangers, despotic or enslaved, superstitious, cruel, cowardly and faithless.[4] This negative catalogue can easily be extended. At a later date Cicero describes Syrians and Jews as peoples 'who are born to slavery'; Livy dismisses the army of Antiochus III as 'Syrians . . . who because of their servile race (*servilia ingenia*) are a people of slaves rather than soldiers'; Titus affirms that the Jews 'learnt to be slaves', and Tacitus even calls them *despectissima pars servientium*. These are only specific instances of the prejudiced view, widespread in the classical period, that the barbarians are slaves by nature and the Greeks (and later the Romans) by the same token masters. The notion of a 'master race' is as old an invention as the idea of the equality of all men. Even now we take over more of the commonplaces of the ancient world than we imagine. In the speech which he attributes to Apollonius of Tyana, who himself came from Lycaonia in Asia Minor, Philostratus shows that even in the Roman period, at the beginning of the third century AD, the genuine 'Hellene' looked down on the 'barbarians' of Asia Minor with real contempt. The 'barbarians' of Asia Minor, from Pontus, Lydia and Phrygia, sell their children as slaves, so that they come up in droves on the Italian slave market, 'for like other barbarian peoples they had been constantly subjected to alien masters and even now do not see anything shameful in slavery'. By contrast, 'even now the Greeks love their freedom', and no Greek would sell a Greek slave outside his homeland.[5] Aristotle, who took up this view that barbarians were slaves in his doctrine of the state, is said to have advised the young Alexander to treat the Greeks as a leader would his men, and the barbarians as a master would his slaves.[6] As he thought that slaves only had the function of 'implements', the underlying view here is that 'barbarian' subjects, too, are essentially only the tools of the victor, in other words, objects for exploitation.[7] Lysander sold the inhabitants of Cedreiae in Caria as slaves, as they were only *mixobarbaroi*, whereas he gave their freedom to the inhabitants (Greeks) of Lampsacus in Ionia, which was conquered a short time later.[8] Similarly, even the intermingling of Greeks and barbarians was taboo. According to Plato's *Menexenos*, the Athenian boast was that unlike other Greek cities, they did not have Phoenician or Egyptian ancestors: 'The mind of this city is so noble and free and so powerful and healthy and by nature hating the barbarians because we are pure Hellenes and are not commingled with barbarians. No Pelops or Cadmus or Aegyptus or Danaus or others who are barbarians by nature and Hellenes only by law dwell with us, but we live here as pure Hellenes who are not mixed with barbarians (*ou mixobarbaroi*). Therefore the city has acquired a real hate of alien nature.'[9] This prejudice remained even in the Hellenistic period. Livy, or Polybius as his Greek source, puts quite similar statements on the lips of the delegation sent by Philip of Macedon to the pan-Aetolian congress in 200 BC: 'There is, and always will be, eternal war between the barbarians and all the Greeks. They are enemies because of their unchanging nature.'[10] We often find arguments of this kind in Polybius. They are put forward by representatives of Greek states and are directed against a new threat to Greece, which now of course no longer comes from the East, as in the time of the Persian danger, but from the Romans in the West. Thus in 207 BC a delegation from Rhodes accused the worst troublemakers in Greece, the Aetolians, of siding with the Romans against all the Greeks: 'When you have captured a city, you do not allow the freemen to be harmed or their houses to be burnt down. You would regard such behaviour as cruel and barbaric. But now you have made an alliance with the Romans, as a result of which you expose all other Greeks to the worst possible acts of violence and wickedness.' Here Polybius aptly reflects the mood in his homeland at the end of the third century and the beginning of the second. Here the old contrast still retained its force. Even Philo, the cosmopolitan who thinks in nationalistic Jewish terms, can still find fault with the 'lack of any closer contact' between Greeks and barbarians (*to amikton kai akoinōnēton*), as this is one of the chief reasons for the lamentable difference between the various laws of the nations. By contrast the Jews, as citizens of the world, possess the true Law which is in accord with nature.[11]

Given this situation, we can understand how individual 'barbarian' cities and peoples were very concerned either to reconstruct some original relationship with the Greeks or at least to regard themselves as an early 'Hellenic' colony. Thus the Phoenicians argued that Cadmus, the founder of Thebes, was one of their number; Hellenized Jews claimed that the Spartans, like themselves, were descendants of Abraham (see pp. 116f. below); the Romans saw themselves as descendants of fugitives from Troy; the inhabitants of Tarsus, an old Semitic city, claimed that they were true Hellenes, whose ancestors came from Argos, and that their city was founded by Heracles, or at least Triptolemos, in person (Dio Chrysostom XXXIII 1,47; cf. Strabo XIV 5,12/673). To have some direct connection with the heroic, classical dawn of Greek history was thought to be noble and honourable. The counter-argument, that compared with Egyptian, Babylonian or even Jewish history, Greek history was a relatively recent affair, carried little weight to begin with, and only became more important when coupled with the claim that the eastern, barbarian religions had a greater claim to truth.

Alexander's expedition seemed to confirm the absolute military and political superiority of the 'Hellenes' – who also included among their number the Macedonian aristocracy and above all the royal house of the Argeads.[12] Especially in the newly founded *poleis* and military settlements of the conquered territories, people tried to maintain the distinction between 'Hellenes' and 'barbarians'. This came about through a stress on Graeco-Macedonian descent, restriction in the granting of civic rights in the newly-founded cities and the conservative education of the gymnasia, which provided the foundation for the typically Greek, aristocratic life-style. For example, in Alexandria in the late Ptolemaic and Roman period down to the edict of Claudius, the acquisition of civil rights was bound up with graduation from the gymnasium. By making it difficult for the Jews to join the gymnasium in Alexandria, Claudius also made it virtually impossible for them to acquire Roman citizenship, for which Egyptians were eligible only if they were citizens of Alexandria. Thus the old dispute about equal civil rites, dating from the Ptolemaic period, continued in Roman times; in the end, discrimination against the Jews led to the bloody rebellion under Trajan in AD 115–117.[13] While there may have been mixed marriages between Graeco-Macedonian settlers and local inhabitants in new 'colonial territories' – say at the foundation of new cities –, for the most part successful attempts were made to keep citizenship intact and free from contamination by 'barbarians'.[14] In the speech of the delegation from Rhodes to the Senate in 190 BC it is stressed that the new cities in Asia are just as Greek as their mother cities on the mainland: 'the change of location did not involve any change in descent or customs.'[15] Even under Parthian rule and at the time of the Empire, the citizens of Dura-Europos, founded by Seleucus I, felt that they were authentic 'Macedonians'. Mixed marriages occurred, but they were the exception rather than the rule.[16] The numerous marriages confined to the ancient families helped to keep the Graeco-Macedonian heritage intact. Even Tacitus praises the citizens of Seleuceia in Babylonia, still under Parthian rule, that 'they were not corrupted by barbarian ways, but kept to (the life-style) of their founder Seleucus (I)'. He must have found this verdict in his Greek sources, since in classical Greece it was a stereotyped theme that the greatest misfortune for a Greek *polis* was 'to become barbarian'.[17] Thus, for example, Isocrates describes how Salamis in Cyprus was 'barbarized' and 'subjected to the Great King' through Phoenician rulers, until Euagoras brought a new time of political and economic prosperity to the city and the island.[18] According to Josephus, even in the first century AD the inhabitants of Seleuceia in Babylonia, which has already been mentioned, were made up of three groups: the Greeks, the 'Syrians' and the Jews. The Greek citizens vigorously defended their position of power in the city over against the other two groups.[19] Strabo reports that the population of Pentapolis in Cyrene was divided into four groups:[20] Greek citizens, Libyan peasants, *metoikoi* and Jews, whereas Josephus and Polybius[21] each report that the population of Alexandria fell into three groups. When conflicts broke out between the various groups, being in the minority the Jews always came off worst. We can see from these examples how attempts were made – with greater or lesser success – to perpetuate the old prejudice against the barbarians in some places down to the Roman period, though at the same time it must be stressed that these limitations were ethnic as well as legal and social. Thus the idealistic picture of a mixed population coming closer together in an atmosphere of humanism after the time of Alexander hardly bears much critical examination. Eduard Meyer was making a rare exception, at least in the early Hellenistic period, into a rule contradicting political and social reality when in his classic article 'The Rise and Fall of Hellenism in Asia' he wrote: 'So the Hellenism of the peoples continued, and they came increasingly close together. We find a shift in the use of the term Hellene, already expressed by Isocrates and taken for granted by Eratosthenes. From now on the Hellenes are the educated class, no matter where they may come from. Being able to speak Greek is a basic qualification: the unlettered masses are the barbarians.'[22]

In the 'early Hellenistic' period of the third century BC there was a virtually unsurmountable wall between the Graeco-Macedonian ruling class and the subject peoples. For example, in the third century, native-born Egyptians required a special permit to live in Alexandria. Among other things, details about place of birth required in official documents were meant to prevent Egyptians from claiming the rights of Greek citizens. Only in the second century was there increased immigration of Egyptians from the Chora, which produced the unruly mass portrayed by Polybius, probably made up predominantly of Graecized Egyptians with no political rights.[23] The Jews saw themselves as a 'third force' between the Greek citizens and the native population; in Syria and Egypt, even in Roman times, they tended not to be given full civic rights for political and religious reasons, although for a long period they had adopted Greek as their language and the upper classes had even had a Greek education. The biassed and misleading accounts given by Josephus of the Jewish *isopoliteia* in Alexandria and Antioch, and the struggles of the Jews in Alexandria and Caesarea to obtain civil rights, which were refused by Claudius and Nero,[24] show how difficult it was to overcome these barriers. Nor is the situation limited to Egyptians and Jews. We also hear of similar situations from other parts of Greek 'colonial territory', for example from Massilia on the southern coast of Gaul, from Asia Minor, and from the Greek cities on the northern coast of the Black Sea.[25] The 'Hellenes' of the Greek cities in 'colonial territories' old and new worked hard, and in some cases successfully, right down to Roman times, to prevent 'non-Greeks' gaining citizenship. Polybius complains that towards the end of the second century BC the citizens of Alexandria were unfit to be involved in a well ordered civic administration because of their 'mixed descent'. This may be because Ptolemy VIII Euergetes II decimated the citizenry in about 127 BC and made up the numbers with aliens. However, it is uncertain whether these were Greeks from the mother country or Graeco-Egyptians. It should be noted that in the same breath Polybius singles out the Alexandrians from the two other groups of Egyptians and mercenaries in a positive way, 'as they have not forgotten the original way of life which is common to all Greeks'.[26] Livy, probably following Poseidonius, says that the Macedonians dispersed in the 'colonies' of the East degenerated into Syrians, Parthians and Egyptians, but ascribes this less to the mixing of races than to the change of climate and situation: 'Everything turns out more appropriately (*generosius*) at the place of his origin; when transplanted to alien soil it changes its nature in accordance with the material which it draws from there.'[27]

Thus when analysing the concept of 'Hellenization', we have to distinguish between very different components. These would include: first, close professional contacts; secondly, the physical mixing of populations caused by mixed marriages; thirdly, the adoption of Greek language and culture by orientals; and fourthly, the complete assimilation of 'orientalized' Greeks and 'Hellenized' orientals. It was not always possible to avoid mixed marriages, for example because of the lack of women in new military settlements and newly founded cities. On the other hand, complete assimilation was the rare exception, at least in the early period, during the third century. We come across 'assimilation' most frequently with orientals, but even here it did not as a rule affect the mass population. We find real interpenetration only in the Roman period.

There was considerable resistance even over the question of mixed marriages. The marriages arranged by Alexander between his Macedonian *hetairoi* and Persian princesses were later all annulled at the request of the military assembly – with the exception of that of Seleucus, who remained faithful to his Persian consort Apame and thus became the founder of a Macedonian-Persian dynasty. Alexander ordered the ten thousand veterans brought back to Macedon from Krateros to leave behind 'their children by barbarian wives'; the king himself wanted to have them brought up the Macedonian way.[28] According to a historical romance written by Hermesianax (third century BC), the city-king of Salamis on Cyprus, Nikokreon, refused to give his daughter as wife to the rich Arkeophon 'because of the base origins of Arkeophon, since his ancestors were Phoenicians'.[29] When the Seleucid Demetrius II Nikator was taken prisoner by Mithridates, king of the Parthians, he was held captive 'in a golden cage' and forced to take to wife Rhodogune, daughter of the Parthian king; in fury at this, his lawful wife Cleopatra Thea, the daughter of Ptolemy VI, allied herself with his brother Antiochus VII Sidetes. After the death of Antiochus in the Parthian war, she refused to be reconciled with Demetrius, who had been set free and now sported a Parthian-style beard; she was not content until he was dead. The pride of the trueborn Macedonian queen could not forgive him his alliance with the barbarian princess.[30]

In the middle of the third century, in Ptolemaic Palestine, we hear that the occupying forces took local women as concubines. However, these were not accorded the same status as legal wives, and a royal decree was necessary to prevent them from being regarded as slaves.[31] There is isolated evidence of mixed marriages between Greeks and Egyptian women in the Egyptian Chora, say in the Fayum,[32] but mixed marriages with Jews are very rare (see p. 91f. below). Even in these exceptional instances, however, attempts were made to secure the status of 'Greeks' for the children. It is very rare to find Greeks becoming Egyptians in every respect: that always involved a sharp drop in social status. At most it happened to the 'Hellenomemphites', who had already immigrated before the time of the Ptolemies, and is later connected with the impoverishment of the Chora in the second and first centuries BC.[33]

We find a move in the opposite direction much more frequently. Gifted members of the local population turned Greek in order to climb the social ladder; they learnt Greek and sometimes also adopted Greek names. It is often difficult to tell whether those who had Greek names were Egyptians, Jews (see pp. 85f., 93f., below) or genuine Greeks. Countless Greek documents from the time of the Ptolemies show that only the language of the 'rulers' was officially recognized; this meant that only bilingual Egyptians could gain positions in the lower and middle grades of the royal administration. In order to exploit the agricultural economy to the full, the state relied on bilingual officials at the lower levels of bureaucratic administration. The fact that a list of qualities required of a Ptolemaic official states that he must not only be *philobasileus* but also *philhellēn*, must indicate that the person concerned is a non-Greek, Jewish or native official.[34] The Ptolemies and the Greek upper class did not regard the Egyptians as their opponents, nor was a preference for Greeks and Macedonians fixed in law or a matter of principle; however, this did not prevent natives of lower social status becoming the objects of exploitation. A. Świderek endorses the comment by W. W. Tarn that 'the Greek came to Egypt to grow rich', and points out that every document from the Zeno archives, dating from the middle of the third century, confirms this judgment.[35] From the beginning, the kings' policy towards the Egyptians was governed by considerations of economics and power politics. Because an efficient administration run by Greek officials had yet to be built up, Ptolemy I had initially included high Egyptian officials and counsellors in his administration,[36] but later he used only Greeks in prominent positions and was followed in this practice by his son – presumably for greater economic efficiency. A prototype here is the finance minister Apollonius from Caunus in Caria,[37] who brought further fellow-citizens, including Zeno, to work in Egypt. Thus the Egyptians were removed from higher office, though this did not prevent the kings from referring back to them where that seemed a useful thing to do. The best-known instance of this occurs with the Egyptian Phalangists, trained by Macedonians, with whose help Ptolemy IV Philopator won the battle of Raphia in 217 BC (see pp. 36f. above) Of course this promotion of native inhabitants, forced upon the Ptolemies by the needs of the moment, led to inner unrest. In any case, it was impossible to do without Egyptian collaboration at lower administrative levels, in the villages and the toparchies.

Thus the Hellenistic rulers did not intend a real 'Hellenization' of the indigenous *laoi*, that is, the able-bodied inhabitants of the country. The main task of the natives was to cultivate the land as agricultural workers within the strictly 'mercantile and capitalist' system practised by the state, and to hand over as much of its produce as possible. Compared with them, foreign military settlers, who mostly came from Greece or Macedon, were in a much better economic position. They had to pay over less, and for the most part did not cultivate the land assigned to them in person, but leased it out to the native inhabitants.[38] A number of factors prevented the native population from becoming a threat by breaking through the political and social limitations imposed on them: the centralized government of the king, which was administered from the Greek metropolis of Alexandria; the nationalistic solidarity of the Greeks living in the country; education in the gymnasia, from which the Egyptians tended to be excluded; and the cohesion of the civic bodies in the few *poleis* in the country. Even in Roman times – for fiscal reasons – this 'well-tried' policy was continued: in a new form, but with no less repression. As a rule the local population responded with resignation, and on some occasions with passive resistance, migration and open rebellion.[39] The third possibility was an attempt at assimilation and social improvement.

Some changes began to make themselves felt in the second century BC, both in Egypt, about which we are best informed, and in the Seleucid empire, where the contrasts were perhaps not so marked, but equally effective. As the influx of new Greek immigrants from the home country receded quite markedly, some of the 'Graecized' Egyptians and Semites became much more influential. The tendency towards 'Hellenization' and social 'acceptance' of the local upper class was much stronger in the Seleucid empire, with its very mixed population, than in Ptolemaic Egypt, as Egypt did not have a real native aristocracy (always excepting the priesthood). In Egypt the priests, as the backbone of national resistance, provided support for the native inhabitants in the anti-Greek disturbances which broke out from the end of the third century onwards, above all in Upper Egypt. Because of this, when immigration from Greece declined, the Ptolemies largely relied on foreign mercenaries, above all from their 'colonial territories'. Semitic mercenaries, and again Jewish mercenaries in particular, played an important role here.[40]

By contrast, after the harsh peace of Apamia in 188 BC, which drove them out of Asia Minor, the Seleucids tried to strengthen the Hellenistic element in their empire by allowing the aristocracy of local cities to adopt the constitution of a Hellenized *polis* if they so wished, in return for an appropriate contribution to the royal treasury. From the beginning, they had been much more active in encouraging the foundation of cities in their extensive empire than the Ptolemies, who only founded new 'cities' in their foreign provinces. To some extent the Graeco-Macedonian cities formed the framework of Seleucid power, and were intended to hold the multinational empire together. Polybius reports that Media was 'encircled with newly founded Greek cities, following Alexander's plan to protect it from the surrounding barbarians'. According to Pliny the Elder, the Macedonian, i.e. Seleucid, kings reorganized Mesopotamia into cities to enable them to make better use of the abundant fertility of its soil; before that, with the exception of Babylon and Nineveh, all the settlements were villages. For this reason, Eduard Meyer calls the first two Seleucids, Seleucus and his son Antiochus I, 'the greatest founders of cities, not only in this period, but at any time in world history'. At a later date, Antiochus IV Epiphanes was particularly concerned to revive this policy in a new form – perhaps influenced by the successful Roman pattern of colonization; he encouraged the transformation of the Semitic aristocracy of oriental cities into 'Hellenic citizens' of new *poleis*, though after a promising beginning, the policy proved to be a complete failure, at least as far as the Jews were concerned.[41] Even here, however, the initiative for such a transformation came from the Hellenized aristocracy of these cities and not from outside.

Thus especially from the second century onwards, in Egypt, Palestine and Syria, as earlier in Asia Minor and on the north coast of the Black Sea, there came into being a new class which might be called 'Graeco-Egyptians' or 'Graeco-Syrians'.[42] They were not of Greek or Macedonian descent, nor were they citizens of the old and proud colonial cities in their territories, but their language and culture clearly differentiated them from the local 'barbarian' population. That this new class could also be regarded as 'Hellenes' in view of their education and life-style – at least in a later period – is clear from the criticism Strabo (*c.* 63 BC – AD 21) makes of Ephoros (*c.* 405–330 BC), who distinguished three Greek peoples from the sixteen to be found in Asia Minor and called the rest barbarians (though he qualified this judgment by remarking that some of the barbarians were 'mixed'). Strabo retorts: 'We cannot call any of those . . . included among the "mixed races" . . . since even if they were mixed, the predominant element would make them either Greek or barbarian. We do not acknowledge a third, "mixed" people.'[43] It becomes quite clear here that the collective term 'Hellenes' did not always have unequivocal ethnic connotations. Aetolians, Acharnians, Epirotes and Macedonians only joined the community of 'Hellenes' at a later date, and the same may also be true of Graecized Asia Minor. In the Hellenistic period, after their victory over the Illyrian pirates in 229 BC the Romans were allowed to participate in the pan-Hellenic Isthmian games.[44] Because of their superior political and military power, people evidently wanted to stop treating them as mere 'barbarians'. That is why Polybius can no longer call the Romans barbarians – that is, if these are his own words and not those of a Greek delegation (see pp. 57f. above), though he is well aware of the old contrast between Greeks and barbarians and the prejudices associated with it. Of course he does not call the Romans 'Hellenes' either, but in stressing their good qualities, which culminate in the ideal form of a state with a 'mixed' constitution, he also includes their national character.[45] The Romans acquired a new, unique and special status midway between Greeks and barbarians. This leads Cicero to divide the world into three parts: *Italia, Graecia, omnis barbaria.* The Jew could go on to make the same kind of distinction: Jews, Greeks and barbarians.[46] In the East, the Phoenician cities, which had had all kinds of contacts with the Greeks for centuries and gave them their script, had taken part in the exclusively 'Hellenic' games from the beginning of the third century onwards.[47] For example, the 'city-king' of Sidon, Philocles, son of Rešefiaton Apollodorus, was a capable admiral under the first Ptolemies and after 286 BC secured naval supremacy for them in the eastern Mediterranean.[48] However, the Phoenicians, who at least to outward appearance had adopted Greek culture very quickly, had long had a special relationship with the Greeks. Finally, the passage from Strabo cited above confirms that 'Hellenization' was largely bound up with the lifestyle of the leading classes of a people. Thus Strabo himself can no longer recognize the traditional distinction. For him – in the time of Augustus – the designation 'Hellene' is bound up with the cultural status of the upper class.

8

'Hellenization' as a Literary, Philosophical, Linguistic and Religious Problem

We have seen that the problem of 'Hellenism' or 'Hellenization' in the early Hellenistic period has a very strong political and social element. Compared with that, to begin with its philosophical, literary and religious aspect was of secondary importance, though it gradually became much more prominent. We have a long chain of evidence – above all from philosophers – which departs from the negative pattern of 'Greek – barbarian' and stresses man's common 'humanity' or even the superiority of the barbarians. What we find here is usually the opinion of outsiders, whose views gain ground only gradually. Nor should we overestimate the influence of such evidence on the Hellenistic rulers and their Graeco-Macedonian subjects. As a rule, both of these were governed by considerations of power politics and economics. The question of 'humanity' only played its part to the degree that the royal *philanthrōpia* also had some real use.[1] Single-mindedly bent on increasing productivity, neither Apollonius nor his agent Zeno will have thought very much about purely humanitarian problems. Nevertheless, at this stage conceptions came into being which later became more widespread under Roman rule, when Stoic philosophy became common currency, and which could also be used by Jewish-Hellenistic and later Christian apologetic for their 'counter-attack'.

Even with the Sophist Antiphon, the idea appears that all men are 'by nature', i.e. biologically, equal. However, at that time political equality was not yet demanded.[2] Similar notions were taken over by the Cynics[3] and Stoics in the form of the idea of 'world citizenship', which to begin with was quite apolitical. It is perhaps no coincidence that the founder of the Stoa, Zeno of Citium, was himself of Phoenician descent and was ridiculed by opponents on that account. By contrast, his opponent Epicurus held the view that 'only the Greeks can philosophize'.[4] He might perhaps be described as a genuine 'Hellenic' philosopher, as opposed to the universalism of the Stoa. However, in accordance with the trend of the times the cosmopolitan spirit of the Stoa was in the last resort to prove the stronger. It met the needs of the Hellenistic monarchies, who in the long run had to integrate their multi-national subjects. Inspired by this spirit, Eratosthenes, tutor of Ptolemy IV Philopator and leader of the Museion, protested against the generally prevalent division of the human race into Greeks and barbarians and thus against Aristotle's advice to Alexander that the barbarians should be treated as slaves. He praised Alexander for his way of judging men by their qualities and not by their descent. He argued that, rather than being divided into Greeks and barbarians, people should be classified in accordance with their *aretē* or *kakia*.[5] It is doubtful whether the somewhat unfortunate domestic and foreign policies of his pupil were helped by considerations of this kind. Political circumstances compelled Philopator to make concessions to the native Egyptian populace, but this caused him even more difficulties. Within Stoicism, which above all from the second century BC onwards became the dominant philosophy of the late-Hellenistic and early Roman period, the old contrast between Greeks and barbarians was replaced by the idea of world citizenship, and the Stoics proclaimed the ideal of 'Hellenism' through education. This development was furthered by the fact that not only Zeno, the founder of Stoicism, but subsequently a large number of Stoic philosophers did not come from Greece, but from the colonial territories of the East or from 'barbarian' surroundings. Chrysippus and Aratus came from Soloi in Cilicia (though that was founded from Rhodes as early as the eighth century). However, Chrysippus' father was said to come from Semitic Tarsus, and the successor of this philosopher, so influential on literature, another Zeno, also came from there. Another pupil of Chrysippus, Diogenes, came from Seleuceia near Babylon, and a third Zeno, a pupil of the founder, came from Sidon. I ought also to mention Antipater and Archedemos from Tarsus, Boethus from Sidon and Herillus, a pupil of Zeno, from Carthage. Posidonius, the greatest representative of middle Stoicism, came from Apameia in Syria. We find a very good example of this new idea of world-citizenship, influenced by philosophy, in a number of epigrams by the founder of the Greek Anthology, Meleager from Gadara in Transjordania (*c.* 140–70 BC). Like his older compatriot Menippus, he had more than a touch of Cynicism in his approach:[6]

> Island Tyre was my nurse, and Gadara, which is Attic, but lies in Syria, gave birth to me. From Eucrates I sprang, Meleager, who first by the help of the Muses ran abreast of the Graces of Menippus. If I am a Syrian, what wonder? Stranger, we dwell in one country, the world; one Chaos gave birth to all mortals.

Here we find a mixture of national pride at his Syrian descent with a rejection of any attempt to scorn his non-Greek descent. Presumably he encountered resistance of this kind on Cos, where he acquired Greek citizenship in his old age. His argument, 'Stranger, we dwell in one country, the world' (*mian, xene, patrida kosmon naiomen*), speaks for itself. In another epigram he refers to his command of several languages: Aramaic, Phoenician and Greek:

> Heavenborn Tyre and Gadara's holy soil reared him to manhood, and beloved Cos of the Meropes tended his old age. If you are a Syrian, 'Salam!' If you are a Phoenician, 'Naidius!' If you are a Greek, 'Chaire!', and say the same yourself.

I must, of course, add that this is a late paradigm from the first century BC, i.e. from a time when a bitter blow had been dealt to Greek consciousness by the devastation of the Hellenistic monarchies and the rise of Rome in the West, along with the successes of 'barbarian' rulers in the east like Tigranes of Armenia, the Parthian kings, or Mithridates VI of Pontus. Towards 100 BC Gadara, the native city of Meleager, had been destroyed by the Jewish king Alexander Jannaeus. Such an attitude would hardly have been possible in the third century BC.

Even the reports and speculations of Greek scholars on the greater antiquity of Eastern cultures and the first inventors from among the 'barbarians', to whom the young Greek nation owed a great deal, could hardly have much impact on the élitist attitude of the Greeks, with the whole of the Eastern world at their feet. Moreover, they were too restricted to particular philosophical groups. Thus in the early Academy people treasured the ancient wisdom of the oriental 'barbarians', but at the same time, like Plato himself, were very well aware of Greek superiority.[7] The

Cynics tried to turn this into self-criticism by holding up to the Greeks the mirror of an alleged 'barbarian philosophy' with its extreme simplicity.[8] The oriental fantasies of a Ctesias[9] or the learned utopia of Hecataeus of Abdera, who believed that the earliest culture was handed down from Egypt, and was the first to give a detailed and relatively positive account of the Jews and became the model for Euhemerus,[10] provided entertainment for an avid and curious reading public rather than having any political effects. Hecataeus certainly did not influence the policy of the first Ptolemies towards their Egyptian subjects. On the other hand, this writing provided valuable arguments first for the Jewish and then for the Christian apologists, who could then attack the theory of the superiority of the Greeks.[11]

The early Hellenistic period, especially the third century BC, was also for the most part a time of the collapse of traditional religion and of enlightenment. Tyche, the goddess of fortune, emerged as the predominant deity, and it is not surprising that at a later date she took the place of the local Astarte on so many coins minted by Syrian cities. A Hellenistic hymn calls her 'all-powerful Tyche', who 'has the beginning and end of all things in her hands', and according to Pliny the Elder, this ambiguous deity, invented by men because of their mortality, 'is alone invoked and praised throughout the world, in all places, at all hours and through the voices of all men'. Closely connected with this celebration of Tyche is the most cultivated religion of this period, the 'pseudo-religion' of the ruler cult, that is, the divinization of the 'superman' endowed by Tyche with success. By transforming the ancient gods into the rulers of former times, Euhemerism furthered both the ruler cult and the Judaeo-Christian polemic against traditional polytheism.[12] To begin with, even the oriental religions had little attraction for the immigrant Greeks, who – if they had any religion at all – primarily worshipped their gods in traditional fashion. Only with the collapse of the Hellenistic monarchies did general religious interest increase, and here astrology came to occupy a central position. Of course there are a few striking exceptions. Thus there was an expansion of the cult of the Graeco-Egyptian Sarapis,[13] and in its train, of that of Isis, as early as the third and second centuries BC. The Ptolemies played a part in this. However, Sarapis was presented as a Greek god with Egyptian features, who found acceptance only among Greeks and Graeco-Egyptians, and not among the Egyptian *laoi*. Sarapis owed his success in the Hellenistic world to the fact that – like other oriental deities, the kindred Isis, the God of the Jews and later Mithras, the god of light – he was stronger than fickle Tyche or inexorable Heimarmene.

Another deity – in contrast to Sarapis thoroughly Greek in character – who was hardly affected by the Hellenistic enlightenment was Dionysus. Indeed, in the wake of Alexander he showed signs of conquering the non-Greek world. According to W. W. Tarn he was 'the most important Greek god outside Greece . . . in this period . . . whom the Dionysian artists bore throughout the world; with the help of art and literature, he succeeded in making a triumphal progress through Asia similar to that of Alexander . . . If any Greek god could have conquered the world, Dionysus would certainly have been capable of it.'[14] The Ptolemies and Attalids derived their dynasty from him; Ptolemy IV was a particularly enthusiastic follower of his mysteries, and a little later the scandal of the Bacchanalia reveals his influence in Rome. More than any other deity, he was identified with oriental gods: from the time of Herodotus with Egyptian Osiris, later with Sarapis, Phoenician Adonis, Sabazius from Asia Minor and Dusares from Arabia and Nabataea. Of all the ancient gods he was also most persistently associated with the Jewish God in Jerusalem. He owed his tremendous influence not least to his humanity – he is the son of Zeus by a mortal mother – and also to his strange, barbarian-sounding character, the liberating experience of ecstasy and his involvement in all spheres of existence, the exuberant joys of life as well as the kingdom of the dead. In his last work, the *Bacchae*, quoted more than any other in antiquity and known to everyone, Euripides portrays Dionysius as a barbarian stranger from Asia, accompanied by a host of strange female worshippers and clothed in human form, intent on conquering the cities of Greece. A true Greek, Pentheus of Thebes, boldly goes against this barbarian monster and pays for his 'fight against the god' with a gruesome death. The very un-Greek advice given by the seer Tiresias to Pentheus, 'We must serve (as slaves) Bacchus, the son of Zeus' (*tōi Bakkhiōi tōi Dios douleuteon*, 366), ushers in a new personal relationship with the deity which was essentially to be found among the oriental gods rather than in the Greek pantheon. This is the secret of the success of this most polymorphous of all Greek gods: he was less a deity from the official Greek world of the gods – that is why fewer inscriptions are dedicated to him than to the other gods – but was worshipped above all in private religious associations (*thiasoi*). The fact that the Septuagint already interpreted the much-hated Canaanite cults with terms derived from the mysteries of Dionysius shows that Greek-speaking Judaism saw his mysteries as dangerous competition (see below, p. 165 n. 28).

The full extent of the victorious power of Hellenistic civilization and its supremacy over the 'barbarians' only emerged when the political power of the Hellenistic monarchies had largely been shattered and the 'barbarian' victors themselves submitted to the rationality and effectiveness of 'Hellenistic' state administration and – to some degree – to the harmony and powers of expression of Greek language and poetry. In Rome, those who pressed for a synthesis of Roman tradition and Greek education were by no means the worst: they included the brothers Scipio, who defeated Antiochus III in 190 at Magnesia and thus ushered in the decline of the Seleucid monarchy, or L. Aemilius Paullus, who destroyed the Macedonian empire in 168, after the battle of Pydna. The son of Aemilius Paullus, Scipio the younger, then became a close friend of Polybius, who after Pydna had come to Rome as an Achaean hostage. In the East, from Arsaces III (191–176 BC onwards), the Parthian kings had adopted the epithet *philhellēn*, which regularly appears on their coins, in order to express their loyalty towards the Hellenistic cities on their territory. Originally this had been a title of honour for the Greek patriots;[15] now it became an honorific name for barbarian kings. That the Parthian kings were also by no means averse to 'Hellenistic education' is illustrated by the famous episode after the victory of the Parthians over Crassus in 53 BC. The last scene of Euripides' *Bacchae* was being performed at court at the very moment when the messengers of victory brought the head of the Roman commander to Artaxata, the Armenian capital, where the Parthian king Orodes was celebrating the wedding of his son with the sister of the Armenian king Artavasdes. Instead of carrying the mask of Pentheus, the Greek actor who was playing Agave held the head of the Roman general, with the words:

> From the mountains we bring
> a newly-cut shoot, a happy capture.

Plutarch's account suggests that the whole scene had been arranged to celebrate the triumph,[16] but it remains impressive enough. We find the designation *philhellēn* again with the Nabataean king Aretas III (say 85–62 BC), who had coins minted with this inscription in Damascus, after he had conquered it.[17] Indeed the term was even used by the Jewish high priest Aristobulus (104/3 BC), who according to Josephus was the first to adopt the title of king.[18] His brother Alexander Jannaeus then minted coins with a Greek inscription, brought mercenaries into the country from Asia Minor, and largely changed the Hasmonean high-priestly state into a 'Hellenistic monarchy'. On the other hand, this did not prevent him from capturing and to a large degree destroying all the Hellenistic cities in the country apart from Askhelon, forcibly converting some of the non-Jewish population to Judaism. Some light has been shed on the mixed Jewish-Hellenistic culture which came into being under him by the recent discovery in Jerusalem of the tomb of Jason, a Jewish pirate captain from the time of Alexander Jannaeus. The Pharisaic pietists responded to the Hellenizing tendencies of the high priest/king with a bitter rebellion which ended with a mass crucifixion of 800 Pharisees.[19] We then find the complete synthesis between 'Hellenism' and the East with king Antiochus I Epiphanes of Commagene (about 69–38 BC). In the famous inscription of Nemrud Dagh he stresses his descent from Greeks and Persians – he derived 'his family from Alexander and from Darius' – and 'proclaimed a Graeco-Persian syncretism'.[20] Naturally, *philhellēn* also appears among his countless honorific titles, though of course this now has to take second place behind the politically opportune *philorōmaios*. H. Dörrie has shown that Antiochus inherited this title and that it goes back to petty kings friendly to Rome, who according to Strabo made an alliance in 95 BC, under the leadership of Rhodes, against the pirates and Mithridates Eupator of Pontus, Rome's enemy. Mithridates was in fact just as well disposed towards Hellenistic culture as Antiochus, and had advocated the liberation of Greece from the Roman yoke. However, from the end of the second century BC onwards support for 'Hellenistic civilization' became more and more identical with loyalty to Rome, which was the sole means of protecting the petty Hellenistic states from barbarian alienation.[21]

This integrating, civilizing power of Hellenistic culture, which became effective at a time when the political and economic 'decline' of the Hellenistic monarchies was well under way, can also be seen in a series of analogous phenomena. True, from the time of the downfall of the Seleucid empire, i.e. from the time of Antiochus Epiphanes, the 'Hellenized' Phoenician cities from Arados to Ptolemais had successfully pressed for an increasing degree of freedom, but in doing so they quite deliberately maintained their 'Hellenistic' character, which became fused in a remarkable way with their own national Phoenician tradition. In the second and first centuries BC, Tyre and Sidon became significant literary and philosophical centres of Greek education. That nevertheless they deliberately kept their own Phoenician tradition is clear from the euhemeristic interpretation of early Phoenician religion given by Philo of Byblos (AD 64–141).[22] In Egypt, too, the various attempts at rebellion in upper Egypt, which were connected with anti-Hellenistic, nationalist reforms, did not have any lasting success, despite the comparative political weakness of the Ptolemaic empire in the second half of the second century and the first century BC. On the contrary, increasing advances were made by the unique type of Graeco-Egyptian 'mixed culture' which became characteristic of the late Ptolemaic and Roman period, while the difference between Alexandria and the Chora persisted. One example of this synthesis is the Egyptian priest Chairemon, a Stoic and president of the Museion, who in AD 49 was invited to become the tutor of the young Nero. He attempted to represent the Egyptian priesthood as the true Stoic philosophers, in the same way as Philo and Josephus gave an idealistic description of the Jewish Essenes as supremely wise men.[23] It should, of course, be noted that such neat syntheses were hardly possible in the early Hellenistic period, i.e. in the third century BC – the time of a Berossus or a Manetho – though analogous attempts appear from the second century on, not least in Jewish Hellenistic literature or in the attempt at reform in Jerusalem. The synthesis was effectively achieved only in the Roman period. The best Jewish example of this is Philo of Alexandria.

The concept of 'Hellenization' holds on many levels, and is sometimes self-contradictory. As far as the early Hellenistic period is concerned – and it is in that that we are particularly interested – we must begin from the fact that the initiative towards 'Hellenization' was a one-sided one. It came from the indigenous Semitic and Egyptian population, who sought in this way to improve their social and cultural status and to share in the prosperity and the success of the Greeks. Thus in the first place 'Hellenization', i.e.

the adoption of the Greek language, Greek education and the Greek life-style, was usually the individual contribution of particular orientals. The most obvious exception here are the Phoenicians, with whom adaptability was combined with national pride: they had long cultivated contact with the Greeks. By contrast, the Graeco-Macedonian ruling class – at least in the fourth and third centuries – had little interest in Hellenizing the 'barbarians'. They had a one-sided interest in preserving their power and their social status and exploiting their innate capacity for work to the greatest possible degree; this of course required co-operation, which meant a certain amount of contact. The possibilities of complete 'assimilation' and 'equal rights' could only rarely be achieved by the native population in one generation, and some obstacles – as for example acquiring civil rights in a city conscious of its tradition – remained unsurmountable for a long period. These sharp limitations in the third century were diminished in the second and first centuries. However, the contrasts remained – at least as social barriers – until Roman times and were identical there with the fundamental opposition between the citizens of cities and the local populace. The latter largely resisted 'Hellenization',[24] and proved to be the starting point for the Coptic and Syrian renaissance in a Christian context during the late Roman and Byzantine period. 'Hellenistic culture' always remained a city culture. Those orientals who attempted to break down the barriers between 'Greeks' and 'barbarians' and to adopt Hellenistic civilization – with its manifold possibilities – would have been members of the local 'aristocracy', the 'civil body', or perhaps natives who had come into close contact with the Greeks as mercenaries, subordinate officials, wage earners or slaves. It was, of course, extremely important for the 'Hellenized' aristocracy of an oriental city which legally had only the status of a *kōmē* to be given the status of a *polis* formed on the Greek model, as a result of royal recognition.[25] Of course, in Egypt this possibility was completely ruled out, as the Ptolemies deliberately recognized only old Naucratis, Alexandria and the new dynastic foundation of Ptolemais in Upper Egypt as *poleis*. However, the situation was substantially more favourable even in Ptolemaic 'colonial territory'. The first cities which attained this new status without being new foundations by the Macedonians were evidently the Phoenician coastal cities (see pp. 65f. above); this again confirms the special status of this seafaring people.

For individuals, the first and most important step towards Hellenization was an ability to cross the language barrier and to speak impeccable Greek. The Greeks seldom took the trouble to learn the language of their new surroundings. Before the battle of Raphia, Ptolemy IV exhorted the Egyptian phalangists by means of an interpreter. Of the Ptolemaic rulers, Cleopatra VII, the last queen of the dynasty, is said to have been the first to learn Egyptian. The fact that in the second century BC a Greek mother congratulates her son for learning Egyptian and therefore having found a post as teacher with an Egyptian doctor is just the exception which proves the rule.[26]

Greek language in the form of Attic *koinē* became all the more important because it was the bond which held together all the 'Greeks' throughout the world, beyond individual kingdoms, from Bactria to Massalia. The basic foundation of 'Hellenistic culture' was not the political power of the Greek states, split up and fighting against one another, but a common language. Thus it did not come to an end even after the victory of the 'barbarian' Romans and Parthians, but continued in the two empires and indeed reached its consummation under the protection of the *pax Romana*. There is a famous saying of Isocrates: 'He who shares in our *paideia* is a Greek in a higher sense than he who simply shares in our descent.'[27] This sees *paideia* primarily as a proper command of Attic Greek and thus defines the 'true Hellene as the one who speak Attic'.[28] We should not draw more profound conclusions from this remark. It quite certainly is not concerned with a universal Hellenic cultural mission or with the idea of amalgamating the nations through education. Isocrates himself, who incited Philip of Macedon to a pan-Hellenic war of vengeance against the Persians, was an outspoken despiser of the 'barbarians'. In accordance with the stress on this language, the verb *hellēnizein* does not mean the adoption of Greek culture but 'to speak (and write) Greek correctly'.[29] Strabo calls barbarians who begin to learn Greek and therefore cannot yet pronounce it properly, *hoi eisagomenoi eis ton hellēnismon*.[30] The degree to which this language barrier was at the same time a social barrier is clear from the desperate complaint of a collaborator – presumably Palestinian and Semitic – whom Zeno left behind in Joppa at the end of his journey through Palestine in 258 BC (see p. 23 above) without giving him the wages he had been promised. He ran away 'to Syria', i.e. to the interior, explainıng that it was 'so that I do not die of hunger'; When he was summoned back to Egypt, he was still refused a living wage: 'So I am in need in both summer and winter. (Jason) told me that I should accept sour wine as wages. Now they are treating me despicably because I am a barbarian. Please . . . give them instructions so that I receive my due and so that they pay me in full in future, lest I die of hunger, because I do not have a proper command of Greek' (*hoti ouk epistamai hellēnizein*).[31] The complaint of a prominent Egyptian priest of Ammon with regard to the misdeeds of a Greek military settler Androbius, who was billetted on him, is in similar vein: 'He despised me because I am an Egyptian.'[32] It is a sign of the way in which things had changed that about a century later, in the middle of the second century BC, Ptolemy the Graeco-Egyptian and *katochos* from the Sarapeion in Memphis complains that he has been attacked by Egyptians 'because I am a Hellene'.[33] Here we come up against an instance of the nationalistic Egyptian reaction against the unsuccessful Ptolemaic policy over native-born Egyptians which, above all in Upper Egypt, even took the form of armed rebellions (see below, p. 149 n. 29). The Maccabean revolt, too, must be seen in the perspective of a 'nationalistic' attempt at rebellion against the Hellenistic policy of alienation, though those who supported it were of course primarily aristocratic Jews who were ripe for assimilation.

Consequently, it is no coincidence that the rare noun *Hellēnismos*, with an extended meaning which embraces both the Greek lifestyle and Greek culture, appears for the first time in a Hellenistic Jewish work which thus seeks to describe this 'alienation' and glorifies the Maccabean revolt. The unknown epitomator of the work of Jason of Cyrene, or Jason himself, accuses another Jason, son of Simon the Just, high priest and leader of the Jewish reform party, in a sharp piece of polemic, of having brought about in Jerusalem, through his own initiative, 'a peak of attempts at Hellenization (*akmē tis hellēnismou*) and an invasion of a strange kind'.[34] By means of a piece of polemical transposition, the Jewish Hellenists and their Seleucid accomplices are described as 'barbarians', and those Jews who are faithful to the Law appear as 'patriotic citizens'.[35] The word *ioudaismos*, as referring to Jewish veneration of the Law and Jewish customs, makes its first appearance in II Maccabees and does so often, to some degree as a counterpart to *hellēnismos*.[36] By contrast, we find the verb *ioudaizein*,

along with *peritemnesthai*, 'be circumcised', in the Greek version of
the book of Esther as a translation of the hithpael participle
mityah^adim (root *yhd*): 'and many of the Gentiles had themselves
circumcised and adopted Jewish customs for fear of the Jews.'[37]
Josephus still uses the same terminology when he writes that
Metilius, the commandant of the Roman garrison, was the only
one to get away with his life because after surrendering the towers
of Herod's citadel in AD 66 he promised *mechri peritomēs ioudaizein*,
i.e. to become a Jew and accept circumcision. If command of
Greek was the distinguishing feature of *hellēnizein*, then the observance of the Law, and especially circumcision, was that of
ioudaizein. Thus the terminology of II Maccabees is very significant. The Jews seem to have felt the new Greek way of life to be
an 'aggressive' civilization which threatened to alienate them from
the distinctive tradition of their fathers. They opposed it with their
own tradition of the Law, which could be equally 'aggressive', i.e.
could have just as great a missionary effect. As sovereign lord of
history, the God of the Jews was at the same time the universal
lord of Tyche and Heimarmene, of chance and destiny; he forbade
any divinization of men, and was an inexorable judge of all human
hybris. As creator of the world he was at the same time the giver of
all the joys of life, the God of the feasts of Israel and also the victor
over death, the one who gives eternal life. He could be the fulfil-
ment of the religious longing of Greeks and Romans, while on the
other hand opposing all natural and ecstatic forms of religion.
Consequently Jewish ethical monotheism could present itself as
the true religion of philosophers. However, the special element of
this conflict is that the Jews attempted to counter the new civilization threatening them with their own forms of language, literature
and thought. In this controversy we cannot mistake the fact that
the Greek feeling of superiority with its contrast between 'Hellenes'
and 'barbarians' was matched on the Jewish side by a sense of
election, unique in antiquity, which was expressed in the contrast
between 'Israel' and the 'nations of the world'. One example may
illustrate this. Both Socrates and Thales, i.e. the earliest as well as
the most famous Greek philosophers, were credited with the following saying: 'I thank Tyche that I was born a human being and not
an animal, a man and not a woman, a Greek and not a barbarian.'[38]
A saying of R. Jehuda b. Elai, *c.* AD 150, is on similar lines: 'Three
thanksgivings must be said every day: Praised (be God) . . . that he

has not made me a woman. Praised be God that he has not made me ignorant. Praised be God that he has not made me a *goy* (Gentile): "For all *gōyim* are like nothing before him" (Isa. 40.17).'[39] Against this background of almost similar but highly controversial sayings we can understand the revolutionary character of Paul's remark: 'There is neither Jew nor Greek, there is neither slave nor free, there is neither male nor female; for you are all one in Christ Jesus' (Gal. 3.28). In this confrontation there was a whole series of analogous phenomena: mixed marriages were tabu not only among Greek citizens conscious of their status, but even more among the Jews; and faithful observance of ancestral laws, the mark of the true *polis*, was also the foundation of Jewish life. If, according to Eratosthenes and others, the mark of the 'Hellene' was a sense for 'law and community' (*to nomimon kai to politikon*),[40] this was also the strength of the Jewish people. It is no coincidence that from II Maccabees and the Letter of Aristeas onwards we often find the term *politeia* for the Torah and the verb *politeuesthai* for life in accordance with the Torah. The attempt at reform in Jerusalem brought about 'the destruction of the *politeia* inherited from the ancestral past',[41] the special value of which was that it was of divine origin. Like the antithetical use of *hellēnismos* and *ioudaismos*, this turn of phrase is also significant terminology from Hellenistic Judaism. It shows both the inner affinity of Judaism to the Greek world and also its opposition. Both together governed the political, spiritual and religious existence of the Jews in the mother country and even more in the Diaspora, where they lived in constant tension between assimilation and self-assertion. Apion, opponent of the Jews, asked: 'If they are citizens, why do they not worship the same gods as the people of Alexandria?'[42] His question could have been asked in any Greek *polis* in which a Jewish minority sought civil rights. This is the cause of the difficulties to which the Jews were exposed not only in Alexandria and Syria but also in individual cities of Asia Minor, even at the time of the later republic.[43] Josephus' answer, that 'our people is one and the same' and that it is mindful to live 'in the laws given from the beginning',[44] would have been respected by any Greek, but at the same time it inevitably clashed with the laws of a city which included the recognition of the official city cult. A Greek *polis*, conscious of its tradition, could hardly have been tolerant at this point.[45]

Even the additional argument of the Jews in the Ionian cities, that they were in the first place 'locally born' (*eggeneis*), and in the second place did not harm any fellow citizens through faithfulness to their laws,[46] did not provide a way out of the fundamentally religious division. The only protection which could be offered here were the edicts of the Hellenistic kings and the later Roman emperors, which were more than mere regional policy. Here was also one of the roots of ancient antisemitism.

Apollonius Molon from Rhodes, at the beginning of the first century BC, is a vivid example of this. In his blind hatred, he not only calls the Jews *atheoi* and *misanthropoi* – because of their way of life in the Greek cities – but claims that they are 'the most stupid of the barbarians' (*aphyestatous einai tōn barbarōn*), and have therefore failed to produce 'a single invention which is of any use for living',[47] a charge which the Jewish apologists countered by glorifying the patriarchs and Moses as 'first inventors'. In his *Apology*, Josephus responds by stressing 'that we have introduced to the rest of the world a very great number of very fine ideas'.[48] Cicero, a pupil of Apollonius Molon, continues this sort of defamation of Judaism as a *barbara superstitio* a little later,[49] and then it becomes a stereotyped theme which enters anti-Christian polemic. In other words, at this point the Roman reaction was hardly better than that of the Greeks. According to Acts 16.20f., the charge was made against Paul and Silas in the Roman colony of Philippi that 'These men are Jews and they are disturbing our city. They advocate customs which it is not lawful for us Romans to accept or practise.' Even in Rome itself, the growing Jewish minority met with mistrust and restrictive measures, and indeed from time to time with direct expulsion. There is a direct connection between Roman hatred of the Jews and later Christian persecutions. On social grounds, the Jews in the Diaspora could become assimilated to the alien civilization around them to such a degree that they themselves sought completely equal rights, yet at the same time – like the Christians later – they inevitably had to remain a 'theocratic' alien body,[50] a 'third people'[51] between Greeks and barbarians,[52] which for its own self-assertion appealed to a higher law than that of the particular state under which they happened to be living. This is probably the root of the inner strength which ancient Judaism developed in the Graeco-Roman world, and also of ancient anti-Judaism with all its fearful consequences.[53]

Conflict was also unavoidable even in the Jewish homeland in

Palestine itself. The new 'Hellenistic' state, with its intensive administration, single-mindedly intent on fiscal and military 'efficiency', was essentially different from its oriental predecessors. Because the new rule in Judaea gave the upper class a chance to become assimilated to the superior Hellenistic civilization and encouraged it to break down the barriers which had been erected from the time of the exile to that of Nehemiah and Ezra, a tension arose between those who remained faithful to the Law and the aristocracy, with a delight in reform, who wanted to participate without restrictions in the 'blessings' of the new civilization. This led to the open conflict of the Maccabaean revolt, which of course did not produce an ultimate solution to the problem, since even the new Hasmonean state, which wanted to base itself wholly on the Torah of Moses, could not avoid the autonomy of Hellenistic rationalism in its state administration. Even the attempt of the Hasmoneans 'to build a Hellenistic state on a Jewish national foundation' was doomed to failure. The revolt of the Pharisees against the new Hasmonean Sadducean state was no less bitter, cruel and wasteful than the Maccabean fight for liberation. In the end, with Roman help the Hellenistic monarchy proved victorious again in the form of the Herodian kingdom. 'A Hellenistic state could not be founded on the Jewish theocracy. A Jewish High Priest could not be a Hellenistic king, and the two conceptions had to be separated.'[54] On the other hand, at that time the only possible form of state was that of the Hellenistic monarchy or *polis*. It was necessary to have control of an army with modern equipment and an effective administrative and financial apparatus, and to participate in a competitive way in world trade. These problems were not understood by the Jewish religious zealots under Hasmonean and Roman rule. The Jewish 'theocracy' had to be a failure in the Roman and Hellenistic period at the point where it attempted to translate its theocratic ideal into the political reality of another kind of world. Refuge in an apocalyptic future was no solution to the problem, and the complete destruction of autonomous statehood, the metropolis of Jerusalem with its central sanctuary and the closed territory of Judaea, as a result of the unsuccessful rebellions of 66–74[55] and 132–135, was the fearful price which the Jewish people had to pay in its vain fight for the realization of utopian 'theocracy'. Only the liberal wing of Pharisaism under the leadership of the 'school of Hillel' showed a viable way forward, the way of obedience to the Law without self-destructive political ambition, in the clear recognition that as long as God allowed the rule of Hellenistic Roman power, the godless 'fourth empire', to endure, the *politeia* of Israel was not of *this* world.

III

The Encounter between Judaism
and Hellenism in the Diaspora
and in the Home Country

9

Jews in a Greek-Speaking Environment: Mercenaries, Slaves, Peasants, Craftsmen and Merchants

The milieu in which Jews came into the closest contact with Greeks, and were compelled to adapt to their environment as far as possible, was that of Hellenistic mercenary forces and military settlements. The Hellenistic kings not only maintained a standing army in garrisons, but also settled soldiers, by preference on 'estates' from the royal land. In Egypt, this was done not so much by means of self-contained settlements as by estates spread all over the country. In this way the soldiers became farmers or landlords who had their property cultivated on a leasehold basis. According to Pseudo-Hecataeus and Josephus, auxiliaries from Judaea and Samaria served even in Alexander's army, in Egypt and in Babylonia, and we have no reason to mistrust this information in principle.[1] The king was only continuing an old tradition which had already been widespread under the Saitic dynasty and the Persians in Egypt. It is possible that even Jewish military settlements in Egypt were taken over by the Macedonians. Thus the Aramaic Cowley Papyrus 81, *c.* 310 BC, mentions ten places between Migdal on the north-eastern frontier of Egypt and Syene in the south where Jews were settled. The papyrus illuminates the complex economic activities of a Jewish merchant 'Abihai, and we find in it not only numerous Jewish names but also Greek names, a sign of the contact between the two groups of people. Only in one case, however, does a Jew seem to have had a Greek name: Haggai (son of) *dyprs* (Diaphoros?).[2] After capturing Jerusalem (302 BC?), Ptolemy I Soter brought a large number of Jewish prisoners to Egypt. He is said to have taken 30,000 select men into his army and settled them as cleruchs.[3] At least a proportion of the Jewish immigrants mentioned by Pseudo-Hecataeus, who seem to have been given a *politeia* of their own, will have been Jewish mercenaries.[4] In terms of language, the 'Hellenization' of these Jewish garrison troops or cleruchs must have made fairly rapid progress. Only about twenty-five per cent of the names of Jewish military settlers mentioned in third-century papyri are Semitic; all the rest are already Greek. A few double names indicate a transitionary stage.[5] In reality, this percentage is even smaller, as Jewish bearers of Greek names can only be recognized by the addition *ioudaios*, which can by no means be taken for granted. This process of 'Hellenization' took place quickly because in the early Hellenistic period the cleruchs were not settled in homogeneous ethnic groups, but mixed, and garrisons had a great variety of manpower. The proportion of Jewish names increases somewhat in the second century, since from the time of Ptolemy VI Philometor Jewish mercenaries were organized into independent units and gained considerable political significance under their own troop leaders; sometimes, as in Alexandria, they were even organized into independent *politeumata* (see p. 91 below). This increase in Jewish names is also a sign that Jewish national self-awareness had also increased as a result of their stronger political position in Egypt and in the home country of Palestine.[6] The Ptolemies seem to have installed larger numbers of Jewish mercenaries above all in Cyrenaica, where the freedom-loving Greek population of the city caused considerable difficulties to the regime;[7] they, too, organized themselves into *politeumata* and later formed a distinctive fourth force alongside 'Greek citizens', Libyans and *metoikoi*.[8] Even in Palestine we find a mixed military colony with Jewish and Macedonian cavalry on the other side of the Jordan, in Ammanitis. The contract for the purchase of a slave girl dated in the early summer of 259 BC names as witnesses a Jewish cavalryman, son of Ananias, with the gentilicum *Persēs*, and Greeks from Miletus, Athens, Colophon and Aspendos.[9] The Jewish cleruchs, who here had to protect the borders of the cultivated land against the Arabs, seem largely to have become 'Hellenized'. True, at a later date they fought as cavalry in the Maccabean revolt on the side of the orthodox believers against the Seleucids, but this may derive from their traditional attitude of support for the Ptolemies. Two of their officers, Dositheos and Sosipatros, have Greek names.[10]

The Seleucids also used Jewish auxiliaries. According to II Macc. 8.20, they played a decisive role in a battle of Antiochus I (?)

against the Galatians, and later, around 210 BC, Antiochus III settled 2,000 Jewish cleruchs from Babylonia and their families in Phrygia, in order to pacify this unruly territory.[11] When the number of mercenaries from Greece, Thrace and Asia Minor diminished in the second century because of the economic and political decline of the Ptolemaic monarchy, the proportion of Jews clearly increased. Among these Semites, the Jews were particularly important. Ever since the founding of the military colony of Leontopolis by the high priest Onias IV, who had escaped to Egypt, they had acquired more and more political and military significance in the Ptolemaic monarchy and also attained the higher echelons of command; they were able to maintain this position until the Roman conquest of the country after the battle of Actium.[12] Of course they could only achieve this position in a Hellenistic state because they were largely 'Hellenized' in language and life-style. Under Roman rule the political situation of the Jews grew considerably worse, both in Egypt and in Cyrenaica, in contrast to the situation, say, in Asia Minor or Greece. This may be one of the reasons for the suicidal rebellion of AD 116/17, which only involved the former sphere of Ptolemaic rule, Egypt, Cyrenaica and Cyprus.

In addition to Jewish mercenaries and military settlers, Jewish slaves, agricultural workers and craftsmen also increased the strength of Diaspora Judaism. By contrast, apart from Cowley Papyrus 81 we have no evidence for Jewish merchants in the early Hellenistic period. At that time the Jews were evidently still predominantly a peasant people. In the Hellenistic period Syria and Palestine seems to have been an important country for the export of slaves, not least to Egypt, where the enslaving of free labourers was prohibited by royal law and slaves were therefore much sought after. The Greeks in the country took the use of domestic slaves for granted, and did not want to change their ways. 'It appears from the Zeno papyri that most of the slaves in Ptolemaic Egypt, including no doubt Alexandria, were Syrians.'[13] Ptolemy II Philadelphus also enacted a law which prohibited the enslaving of the semi-free agricultural population of the province of 'Syria and Phoenicia' by the Ptolemaic military settlers and the Greek landowners.[14] However, despite strict controls, Greek business men did sell Semitic slaves abroad, evading duty and without an export licence.[15] The Zeno papyri often mention slaves from Syria (*sōmata apo Syriās*) and Syrian villages; among other things, *Syroi* worked as slaves or semi-free agricultural workers in Egyptian vineyards. It is sometimes difficult to distinguish the two groups. The translator of Gen. 49.15 probably had this social situation, in which it is no longer possible to draw a clear dividing line between slave labour and agricultural labour, in mind when he changed the description of Issachar as a 'slave employed in forced labour' (*mās-'ōbed*) into that of a peasant farmer (*anēr geōrgos*).[16] To take one example, we find two slave girls with the names 'Ioana' and 'Anas', i.e. Joanna and Hanna, in the household of Apollonius, the minister of finance. These may well have been Jews. Zeno himself bought a number of slaves in Palestine; two of them, Idumaeans, ran away and returned to their old master. Four young Palestinian slaves, two of whom were presumably Jews, were sent with a eunuch as mentor by the Jewish magnate Tobias to Apollonius.[17] We can understand how such Semitic house slaves would soon become assimilated to their Greek environment. Here the references in the papyri are supplemented by literary evidence: in connection with Agatharcides, Pseudo-Aristeas and Josephus report that in his capture of Jerusalem (mentioned on pp. 18f. above) Ptolemy I Soter took most of the prisoners to Egypt as slaves. According to Pseudo-Aristeas they became the property of the soldiers and were ransomed by Ptolemy II Philadelphus.[18] Even if the details of the *Letter of Aristeas* are exaggerated, they must at least have a historical nucleus. It is therefore wrong to play off against it the account in Pseudo-Hecataeus to the effect that many Jews voluntarily emigrated to Egypt at the invitation of a high priest Hezekiah.[19] The one does not exclude the other, and both accounts have their tendentious exaggerations.

That Jewish slaves were sold to Greece and the Aegean is already clear from the threat against the Phoenician and Philistine slave dealers in Joel 4.4–8, which is probably as early as the fourth century (see p. 19 above). Even in the fourth century BC we find the name 'Anna' on a tombstone in Athens, and this could be a reference to a Jewish slave. It would be the earliest evidence so far for Jews in Europe.[20] A little later, an inscription from the early third century about the emancipation of the Jew Moschus son of Moschion, because of the incubation dream granted to him in the temple of the god Amphiaraus in Oropus in Attica, gives us more information. Evidently the Jewish slave 'in the nation far off' (Joel

4.8) had become assimilated to the Gentile environment.[21] We find Phoenician intermediaries in the coastal region, who hoped to make a business out of trading with Jewish slaves, in connection with Nicanor's attack on rebellious Jews in II Macc. 8.11. At the same time there are increasing accounts of the emancipation of Jewish slaves in Greece: a Jewish slave whom his masters had simply called *ioudaios* (*ioudaios to genos ioudaiōn*) was freed in Delphi in 163/162 BC. From the same period (between 170 and 157/56) we have the emancipation of a Jewess Antigone with her daughters Theodora and Dorothea.[22] Here the names of the two girls were an unmistakable acknowledgment of the one God of Israel. It is certainly no coincidence that the Greek name we find most frequently among Diaspora Jews is Dositheos; Theodotus, Theodorus were also favourites. We find Dositheos, 'God gives', almost only among Jews.[23]

In addition to Jewish military settlers and slaves we also come up against individual free Jewish wage-earners. For example, about the middle of the third century BC we find two Jewish vintners in the Zeno archive, Alexander and Samuel, who became tenants of a vineyard belonging to Zeno, but worked here without success. Among other free Jewish workers we find a shepherd, a man in charge of the guard-dogs, and a brickmaker (or despatch man) who will not work on the sabbath.[24] Of course, these examples are hardly representative of Ptolemaic Egypt generally. They are limited to Zeno's activities in the newly-founded estate of Philadelphia in the Fayum, which tended to collect a large number of people of different nationalities looking for work, because it was always short of labour.[25] As a rule the Jewish wage earners and leaseholders were dependent on Greek landlords and employers. In addition, we have some reports of Jewish peasants and shepherds from the third and second centuries, also from the Fayum. Philadelphus had opened up this area again and resettled it – not least with foreign immigrants. One of the villages there was called 'Samareia', presumably because it had originally been founded by Samaritans and Jews; later, however, it had a mixed population of Jews, Macedonians and Cilicians. One Cilician officer even established a gymnasium in Samareia.[26] In the third century BC, Jews and Greeks lived side by side as two special ethnic groups in the village of Psenyris in the Fayum. By contrast, there is no mention of Egyptians. Possibly here too the settlers were specifically military.[27]

The Jewish cleruchs certainly had the highest standard of living compared with other professions. They received portions of different sizes from the royal estates, and these could pass over into the possession of their families. They include officers, above all in the second century; some of them own considerable tracts of land.[28] The extent of their economic activity emerges from the relatively large number of private contracts, all of which are in Greek. Here we come up against that milieu in which there is a ready acceptance of Greek language and civilization, in order to maintain and improve social status. One document which illustrates the close contacts between Jews and Greeks is a list from the second century BC, presumably of members of a military unit, in which Jews and Macedonians are mixed.[29] At a later date, Jewish members of such units could even be called 'Macedonians'. There was a detachment of Jewish Macedonians even in Alexandria.[30] The social interchanges between Jews, Egyptians and Greeks (or Graeco-Egyptians) in Upper Egypt are illuminated by a large number of receipts for taxes on ostraca, mostly from the second century BC. Here we come across individual, very rich Jewish tax farmers like Sabbataios, the man in charge of taxation on ferries over the Nile, and Simon, son of Iazarus, who paid a number of talents as 'fish tax' into the royal bank and at the same time deposited grain as a recipient of taxation, though he was unable to write.[31] As this last point is mentioned specially, we must regard it as an exception for a man of this standing.

We have least information about early Hellenistic Alexandria, for in the delta and at the coast no papyri have been preserved. We have first to reject as unhistorical bias Josephus' claim that Alexander had already settled Jewish mercenaries there and given them the same rights as the Macedonians (see p. 161, n. 1). On the other hand, we cannot exclude the possibility that the high priest Hezekiah mentioned by Pseudo-Hecataeus emigrated to Alexandria and succeeded in securing for the Jews there a special status as an ethnic minority guaranteed by royal decree. In this connection Pseudo-Hecataeus speaks of a 'written constitution' (*politeia gegrammenē*) and explicitly states that this Hezekiah 'was intimately familiar with us'; this probably means that he had close contacts with Greeks and that Greek customs were well known to him.[32] However, far-reaching legal autonomy, i.e. the formation of a separate *politeuma* (as attested by the Pseudo Letter of Aristeas) under the leadership of an ethnarch or genarch and concentration on a particular district of the town, will only have been granted in the second century through the special favour of Ptolemy VI, who was well disposed towards the Jews.[33] The fact that in the early Ptolemaic necropolis of Alexandria we find Aramaic and Greek inscriptions on Jewish tombs among Gentile graves accords with the cohabitation of Jews and Macedonians or Greeks in mixed military units and military settlements. Clermont-Ganneau already conjectured that these were the tombs of mercenaries.[34] We have a further pointer from the Tobiad romance of Josephus. According to this, Josephus, superintendent of tax-farming in Jerusalem, not only maintained a slave as agent in Alexandria to look after his great resources there, but also had good relationships with the Ptolemaic court.[35] His brother Solymius had the ambition to marry off his daughter to a prominent Jew in Alexandria, just as at a later date Marcus Alexander, the son of the Jewish alabarch and nephew of Philo, married Berenice, the daughter of king Agrippa I.[36] Greek education was a basic requirement for Jews in such an influential position. Since we find relatively rich Jewish tax farmers even in Upper Egypt, we may assume that there was an even larger rich Jewish business community in Alexandria; we may know nothing about it simply because of our lack of information about early Alexandrian Judaism generally. Sources are more abundant only when we come to the Roman period. By and large, the Jews in Egypt, as in Palestine, were not particularly prosperous; they tended more to belong to the lower and middle classes.[37] Josephus still stresses that the Jews are not a people of merchants, but a people of peasants.[38]

Obviously the danger of complete assimilation to the Greek world was strongest among the upper classes. However, we have very little evidence of this. The only known example from an early period is Dositheos son of Drimylos, who according to III Maccabees saved the life of king Ptolemy IV Philopator before the battle of Raphia when the renegade Theodotus attempted to murder him (see p. 36 above). 'By birth he was a Jew, but later he apostatized from the Law and departed from ancestral beliefs.' He presumably held the office of *hypomnēmatographos* as early as 240 BC; i.e., he was one of the two directors of the royal secretariat. In 225/4 he accompanied Ptolemy III Euergetes on a journey to Egypt and in 222 BC he appears as a priest of Alexander and the divinized

Ptolemies.[39] One might compare his career in some respects with that of the Tobiad Joseph in Ptolemaic Judaea; the difference is that the Diaspora Jew Dositheos in Alexandria became completely assimilated to his Greek environment in the interest of his career at court, whereas at least externally, Josephus in Jerusalem kept to the Jewish tradition. The interesting thing in his exceptional case is that even in the second half of the third century a Jewish apostate with a Greek education could attain a high position at the court of Ptolemy in a way which was impossible in principle for Egyptians of the time. A parallel from Roman times would be the apostate Tiberius Julius Alexander, another nephew of Philo and brother of Marcus Alexander, who succeeded in becoming prefect of Egypt. The only evidence for a mixed marriage between a Jew and a Gentile in the Ptolemaic period is uncertain. In a petition to the king, a 'Helladote, daughter of Philonides' makes a complaint about her Jewish husband Jonathan, to whom she is married 'in accordance with [the law of] the Jewish comunity'. The text is not completely certain, and even the origins of the wife are obscure. If the way in which the papyrus has been reconstructed is correct, this is the only mention of the Jewish Law in documents from Egypt relating to the Jews.[40] This means that in the external forms of legal life as expressed in the papyri, the Jews had adapted themselves completely to Hellenistic law. This development is partially hinted at even in the Septuagint, and Philo takes it completely for granted. Even the titles of the divinized rulers are not omitted in the official documents. Thus not only the Greek language, but also Greek law governed the professional and economic life of the Jewish settlers in Egypt. Here, too, could be found the principle expressed by Babylonian teacher Mar-Samuel in the third century AD: 'The law of the state is the (valid) law.'[41]

The Hellenization of the Diaspora in Ptolemaic Egypt

It is amazing how quickly the Jews in Ptolemaic Egypt gave up their familiar Aramaic and adopted Greek. We have extraordinary little Aramaic and Hebrew evidence from Hellenistic times compared with that in Greek.[1] Though Aramaic continued to be spoken in the private sector – because of constant immigration from Palestine into Egypt, Aramaic never died out there completely – Greek became the dominant official language, not only in dealings with the Hellenistic environment but even in the Jewish communities themselves. The Jewish inscriptions and papyri and the new Jewish-Hellenistic literature including the Septuagint are overwhelming evidence for this fundamental shift.[2] This victory of the Greek language affected all social strata, from the Jewish aristocracy in Alexandria to the day-workers and slaves in the Chora. True, we have a few references to Jewish illiterates,[3] but even these will have understood and spoken Greek. By contrast, Jews will hardly have been interested in Demotic Egyptian. We have no clear evidence that they ever learnt it.[4] That means that they attempted to attain a higher social status by adopting the language of the new masters. I have already referred to the dominant use of Greek names among Jewish military settlers even in the third centurn (see p. 86 above). How unconcerned they were emerges from the fact that about a third of these names are of a theophoric Gentile character. Among the Jews of Egypt we find the names Apollonius, Artemidorus, Diosdotus, Demetrius, Dionysius, Diophantus, Heracleia and Heracleides, Hermaios, Hermias and others.[5] The name Simon was a particular favourite, as in Palestine, because here the Semitic and Greek forms came very close.[6] However, all this does not necessarily denote a break with ancestral tradition. On the contrary, Jewish worship, the spiritual centre of the Jewish community, was probably also held in Greek from the first half of the third century onwards. It is probable that mercenaries and military settlers with a good social standing played an important role in the formation and organization of the Jewish communities. As they were in constant contact with the Greeks, at the same time they were most concerned with the use of Greek. Other ethnic groups of soldiers formed cultic communities in the form of *politeumata* or *koina*.[7] Thus the Jews in the service of the Ptolemaic state presumably had a special interest in the introduction of the new language into worship and in the translation of the Torah into Greek. One indication of the connection of the translation of the Septuagint with the Jewish military settlers in Egypt could be the fact that the term *ṭaph*, which really means children (and old people) unable to walk, is usually translated *aposkeuē*, a new formation which in Polybius, Diodore and the papyri principally means baggage and all the other movable possessions of a soldier. This sociological background would also explain why Ptolemy II Philadelphus encouraged the translation of the Jewish Law. This is the historical nucleus of truth in Pseudo-Aristeas. The religion and religious rights of a particular group of his mercenaries and military settlers could not remain a matter of indifference to so foresighted a king, who was interested in so many things.[8] This also explains the fact that the synagogue inscriptions which have come down to us from Ptolemaic times – all of them in Greek – almost all begin with a dedication to a Ptolemy. The development of the new form of Jewish worship in Greek would hardly have been conceivable without the positive tolerance, indeed support of the Ptolemaic kings. However, it is striking that while in two cases the synagogue inscriptions – in contrast to the numerous dedications of pagan places of worship – contain the cultic title, they never have the designation *theos*.[9] A comparable phenomenon is the 'Hellenization' of the worship of the Idumaean god 'Qos-Apollo' in Idumaean military settlements of the second and first centuries BC. Our evidence for this is the inscriptions from Idumaean cultic associations in Hermopolis Magna and Memphis. Whereas the Idumaeans offered bloody sacrifices 'according to ancestral law' to 'Qos Apollo' even in a foreign land, and sang hymns to him 'in a foreign language',[10] in the Egyptian Diaspora the Jewish cult took on a new form which was almost revolutionary in antiquity: it became a purely verbal form of worship and consisted of prayer (*proseuche*), which probably included the singing of hymns, the reading of the Law and its interpretation. This non-sacrificial, verbal form of worship with a strongly ethical stamp must have looked to the world of the time very like a philosophy. It is no coincidence that the earliest Greek accounts, like those of Theophrastus, Hecataeus, Megasthenes, Clearchus of Soloi and even Strabo (or his informant, perhaps Posidonius), depict the Jews and their lawgiver Moses as barbarian philosophers.[11] Jewish apologists down to Philo and Josephus could take up this point and declare that the ethical monotheism proclaimed in the Jewish *proseuchai* was the true philosophical religion.[12] The new design-nation for the building in which the worship was held, *proseuche*, is at the same time an indication of this new form of worship. The word itself is a new coinage by the Septuagint.[13] We find the first *proseuchai*, i.e. the first synagogues, in inscriptions from the time of Ptolemy III Euergetes (246–222 BC).[14] In the synagogue in-scriptions we find as the official designation for the God of Israel the title *theos hypsistos*, a Greek interpretation of the 'God of heaven' from Persian times. This then becomes the official designa-tion of the Jewish God throughout later antiquity.[15] By contrast, Kyrios, the *qᵉre* (the spoken substitute) for the tetragrammaton in Jewish worship, had been quite incomprehensible to the Greeks as a designation for God. Iao, the transcription of the Jewish divine name in the Septuagint, was probably not used in public in Egypt any more than in Palestine. That is why this – secret – divine name found its way into Jewish syncretistic magic.[16] At a later date – probably under Palestinian influence – Iao was in turn replaced by the tetragrammaton in Old Hebrew or square writing, or even by the *qᵉre*, Kyrios, though this became really widespread in the manuscripts only in the post-Christian period.[17]

The astonishingly literal translation of the Pentateuch is essen-tially evidence for the faithfulness of the Jews to the 'ancestral Law'. The translators were men with an exceptional command of the *koine* of early Hellenistic Egypt, and presumably they had practical experience of translation, whether in the liturgy or in legal affairs and matters of state. So the Septuagint has no rhetorical polish of any kind. Rather, it is a solid, 'craftsmanlike' translation, of the kind that we also find in legal documents and contracts. Its unique terminology derives from this translation, which is literal without being slavish. There is still dispute as to whether a spoken

'Jewish Greek' underlies the translation.[18] We cannot speak of the influence of Hellenistic philosophy.[19] The most consequential 'interpretation' is the translation of Yahweh's definition of himself in Ex. 3.14, 'I am who I am', with *ego eimi ho ōn*: 'When the "Seventy" Platonized the Lord himself . . . they interpreted words which, obscure in the original, called for some elucidation when rendered into Greek.'[20] Philo later regards *ho ōn* as the only adequate designation for God. It was also a move towards universalism when *ṣᵉbā'ōt* or *šadday* was translated *pantokratōr* or *kyrios tōn dynameōn* in the Septuagint. The designation *pantokratōr* had also been applied to individual Greek deities, like Hermes,[21] and the Greek audience saw the *dynameis* as the powers of the cosmos rather than the angels as the heavenly court of Yahweh. Thus from the beginning the God of the Greek Bible was without qualification a universal God, who did not tolerate any comparable powers and forces beside him. This was a new feature in antiquity and laid the foundations for an encounter with the philosophical 'monotheism' of the Greeks from the time of Xenophanes, which was often critical of religion. By appealing to the one true God, Hellenistic Jews could take over themes from the philosophical criticism of religion right down to Euhemerism, and use them to counter the polytheism of their surroundings. Generally speaking, we find that the Septuagint carefully tones down offensive anthropomorphisms;[22] there are a very few faint allusions to Greek mythology;[23] the geographical picture of the world is modernized;[24] some passages take political account of the Ptolemies;[25] and on points of detail the Law of Moses is assimilated to legal practice obtaining in Egypt.[26] The conservative attitude of the translators encouraged the composition of the legend contained in Pseudo-Aristeas, that the seventy-two translators had all been Palestinian Jews. Of course the author takes it for granted that these Palestinians had had a perfect Greek education.[27] The fact that the lascivious Canaanite nature religion is sometimes described in terms taken from the mysteries (specifically the Dionysian mysteries) indicates religious controversies; this polemical tendency is then taken further in Wisdom and in Philo.[28] On the other hand, Ex. 22.27, *theous ou kakologēseis*, is interpreted to mean a renunciation of polemic against strange gods.[29] Their status as a minority required the Jews to be somewhat restrained towards the very different religions of their environment. An anti-Jewish attitude grew up both among the 'Greek' citizens of Alexandria and among the Egyptians of the Chora, by the latest, from the second century on.[30] The tendency to update or to Hellenize – this latter above all in Proverbs and Job – becomes considerably stronger in the prophetic writings and hagiographies which were probably only translated in the second century. At the same time, alterations with a markedly 'anti-Hellenistic' tendency increased. Thus the Philistines are made 'Hellenes', and in the book of Esther, which was presumably translated in Jerusalem, Haman the Agagite is made into a Macedonian.[31]

The remnants of early Jewish Hellenistic literature show even more strongly than the Septuagint translation the considerable Greek education of their authors and the fusion of Jewish and Greek thought. It demonstrates the high degree of 'Hellenization' of the leading classes of the Jewish Diaspora in Egypt. 'The Jews as a whole were on a higher cultural level than the Egyptians, and, as the surviving works of Jewish-Greek literature of the third and second centuries show, the Greek culture which they acquired was of a superior quality.'[32] Some fragments of Jewish Hellenistic writers from the Ptolemaic period have been preserved for us by Alexander Polyhistor, the Roman collector of rarities (*c.* 105–*c.* 49 BC). They probably all date from the second and third centuries BC. It is striking that none of the works are anonymous or pseudonymous – in contrast to the Palestinian literature, apart from Ben Sira; all the authors write under their own names. That means that, like the Greeks from the seventh and sixth centuries BC onwards, they have an idea of a 'spiritual heritage' which was not to be found in the Palestine of the time.[33] Granted, in Egypt too we largely find traditional anonymous and pseudepigraphic literature, but this had more of a popular character and was tied to certain forms taken over from Palestine: the Novelle, the apocalypse and wisdom writing. While the themes of the new Jewish Hellenistic writers serve to glorify their own 'sacred history', the literary form of their words is completely adapted to Greek standards. Demetrius the chronographer, writing at the time of Ptolemy IV Philopator (222–205), produced a strictly academic, chronographical historical work which demonstrates the extreme age of Jewish religion and at the same time seeks to solve exegetical difficulties by the method of *aporiai kai lyseis*.[34] By contrast, Artapanus wrote an imaginative, historical-aretalogical romance which made Joseph and Moses 'first inventors' and the Jewish lawgiver, as Hermes-Thoth or 'Musaeus', the father of Orpheus, not only the inventor of writing and literature, but even the founder of Egyptian (and indirectly also Greek) religion.[35] Ezekiel the tragedian described the exodus from Egypt in the form of a drama and in the language of Aeschylus and Euripides. However, for him the all-powerful fate of the Greeks is replaced by the providence of the God of Israel, who directs the course of history.[36] It is quite possible that this drama was performed in Jewish communities, especially as the *proseuchai* often had large courtyards: in Berenice (Cyrenaica) the community even had an amphitheatre at their disposal.[37] Others, like the Samaritan Theodotus and the older Philo, depicted the history of the people of God or the holy cities of Shechem and Jerusalem in the form of an epic with archaic hexameters.[38] The Jewish Sibyl uses the same form;[39] its original text, which dates from about 140 BC, proclaimed coming judgment and the kingdom of God to the Greek world in the language of Homer and in imitation of political *vaticinia ex eventu* as we meet them in Lycophron's *Alexandra*.[40] It also gave an interpretation of the whole of world history. The author puts the whole work on the lips of a daughter-in-law of Noah, who is said later to have migrated to Greece and to have been identical with the earliest Erythrean Sibyl. Here the classical form was used for manifestly anti-Hellenistic polemic: Hesiod's *Theogony* was 'demythologized' in a euhemeristic way; he turned the Titans and gods of Olympus into primal kings who brought war to the earth after Noah. It was possible to unmask Homer, the greatest of the Greek poets, as a dangerous liar. This pseudepigraphical combination of Homeric language and the content of Jewish apocalyptic had a tremendous effect. It was continually imitated right down to the Middle Ages, and the combination of world history and salvation history which it presented, along with the book of Daniel, had a decisive influence on Western philosophy of history.[41] In addition to the Sibyl we find other 'apologetic' forgeries which confess the one god of Israel in Greek garb. They include quotations from the Greek tragedians and comic poets, alleged verses of Pythagoras, the didactic poetry of Pseudo-Phocylides, the fragments of Pseudo-Hecataeus, and many others.[42]

The extant fragments of Aristobulus, preserved by Eusebius, have a philosophical and apologetic character.[43] Aristobulus presumably worked in the time of Ptolemy VI Philometor (180–145) as an advisor on Jewish affairs to the king, who was well disposed towards the Jews. In his work we find the first beginnings of an allegorical reinterpretation of offensive passages in the Pentateuch, along with the claim that Pythagoras and Plato had already known the Law of Moses. In Philo this argument was then developed into the theme of the theft of the Greeks. To establish that Jewish philosophy was the true philosophy, he quotes not only a forged Testament of Orpheus,[44] but also partially forged verses of Homer and Hesiod, which stress the significance of the number seven in connection with the seventh day; he also uses the beginning of Aratus' *Phainomena*. The verses, forged and authentic, probably in turn go back to an anthology of Jewish-Pythagorean origin. The divine wisdom is identical with the number seven, and as the primal light forms the basic structure of the world. Here for the first time the Old Testament revelation is associated with Greek philosophical argument to form a system which ventures an attempt at a spiritual synthesis. The aim of this early Jewish thinker was not assimilation, but a genuine integration of the challenge presented in the superior thought of the Greeks. We may well assume that from his time down to that of Philo there was a Jewish philosophical school tradition in Alexandria,[45] the aims of which were later continued both by the Christian gnostics and by the catechetical schools of Pantaenus, Clement of Alexandria and Origen. These Jewish Hellenistic traditions in fact only come down to us through the latter. Rabbinic Judaism later repudiated and rejected Jewish Hellenistic literature. The *Letter of Aristeas*,[46] which was composed a little later, combines the most varied Hellenistic forms of literature into an apologetic writing which is aimed in two directions. On the one hand it defends Greek education and culture and loyalty towards the Ptolemaic royal house against the radical Jewish nationalism which had been aroused by the Maccabean wars, while on the other it attacks those who despise the Jewish people and their Law. This double approach was probably typical of the Jewish upper class in Alexandria with their Greek education. The allegorical interpretation which had already been begun by Aristobulus is developed still further in the *Letter of Aristeas* to serve as an apology for the Law. Outwardly the work is a fictitious romance in the form of a letter, into which have been incorporated a travel account, learned dialogue and above all a royal symposium which in turn contains a pattern of conduct for the king. A certain 'neo-Pythagorean' influence is noticeable in the interpretation of the Law given by Aristobulus and Pseudo-Aristeas, and then later in Philo. It might be pointed out in this connection that as early as the third century BC the Alexandrian writer Hermippus connected Pythagoras with the Jews and that the neo-Pythagorean writing of Pseudo-Ekphantos and then the philosopher Numenius in the second century BC could draw on the Jewish account of creation. The latter even believed that Plato was dependent on Moses.[47]

Jason on Cyrene wrote a historical work which described the most recent past, namely the unsuccessful Hellenistic attempt at reform and the Maccabean rebellion – presumably down to the death of Judas Maccabaeus. It is thoroughly academic in style and belongs to the genre of solemn historical writing so popular in the Hellenistic period.[48] An unknown epitomator then cut down the work from five books to one, so-called II Maccabees.

The aim of this early Jewish Hellenistic literature from Alexandria with its wealth of literary forms and coupled with that, its single-minded tendency to glorify the Jewish people, its divinely guided history, its Law and its truly philosophical religion, was less the conversion of other believers than the satisfaction of the literary needs of the growing Jewish upper class in Alexandria itself. They were no longer satisfied with the traditional Jewish edificatory literature, although bit by bit this was being translated into Greek. The best example of such translation work is the prologue by the nephew of Ben Sira, who translated the latter's wisdom book into Greek.[49] By contrast, this literature, like the Septuagint, was virtually unnoticed by non-Jews.[50] The one exception here is possibly the Sibylline writings. Magical and astrological 'secret literature' of Jewish provenance may have had an even stronger external influence. Antiquity saw Moses not only as the great lawgiver but even more as the arch-magician.[51] Pseudepigraphical astrological writings of Jewish origin were also in circulation.[52] Interest in Jewish writing outside Judaism itself only increased at the time of the empire, above all from the second century AD onwards, under Christian, neo-Pythagorean and Hermetic influence.

Thus in Egypt, and here especially in Alexandria, the Jewish Diaspora developed an extraordinarily lively spiritual life. At least the upper classes acquired an often astonishing rhetorical and philosophical education – going beyond a knowledge of Greek, which was taken for granted. That means that they gained access to the educational institutions of the Greek world, the Greek school, the gymnasium and advanced study in rhetoric and philosophy. Jewish names appear later on lists of ephebes both in Cyrenaica and in Asia Minor.[53] Philo of Alexandria, with his extensive education, was certainly not the only Jew who had had a universal *enkuklios paideia*. His complex interpretation of the texts of the Pentateuch from the perspective of 'general learning' certainly presupposes an earlier tradition at this very point. The way towards such an education was probably taken by the upper classes in the Jewish Diaspora in Alexandria as early as the third century BC. It is clear from the numerous completely Hellenized epitaphs and inscriptions from Leontopolis, which date from the late-Ptolemaic or early Roman period, that Hellenistic education was not limited to a small circle in the Egyptian capital: with few exceptions, the names are the only thing to indicate Jewish tombs.[54] Here we learn about the death-bringing Moira, Hades with its everlasting darkness, and the gloomy descent to Lethe. For the Jewish official Abramos, who had led two Jewish *politeumata* and is praised for his wisdom, the poet has only the timeless, conventional wish: 'May the earth rest lightly on you for ever!'[55]

Despite this completely external 'Hellenization', which was not just limited to language and literary education, but covered large areas of daily living, the Jewish Diaspora did not become unconditionally assimilated to its Hellenistic environment. Jews might undergo the customary gymnasium education, make the acquaintance of Homer and classic poetry, and pursue other rhetorical and philosophical studies; they might visit the theatre and games, maintain business contacts with non-Jews and even embark on successful careers in the administration of the Ptolemaic state, but they did not adopt Greek polytheistic religion. They kept the sabbath holy, avoided unclean food and went to services in the synagogue in which a rhetorically polished lecture, fashioned in the form of the diatribe, increasingly came to occupy the central position, alongside prayers and hymns, and made the educated Jew feel that he was a representative of the true philosophy.[56] It was in a similar, well-educated milieu that, for example, the young Pharisee Paul of Tarsus acquired his masterly rhetorical style, in which rabbinic exegesis and popular philosophy are combined with an apocalyptic view of the world. An education of this kind could be given even through Greek-speaking schools in Jerusalem. Of course the scope for movement differed from place to place. Pseudo Aristeas, for example, makes the courtier Aristeas explain Jewish belief in God in the following way. 'These worship the same Lord and Creator of all things whom all men worship. We simply give him another name, Zeus and Dis. In this way the men of old expressed the fact that the one by whom all things are given life and created is himself the director and creator of all things.'[57] Here the author makes use of the Stoic etymology of Dis from *dia* and Zeus from *zēn*. By contrast, in his version of the Testament of Orpheus and in the quotation from Aratus, Aristobulus substitutes *theos* for the name of Zeus and expressly stresses: 'As is appropriate, we have given our interpretation by removing the words "Dis" or "Zeus" as they appear in the poems, because by meaning they refer to God, and that is why we have expressed them in that way . . . For all philosophers are agreed that people must have sacred concepts of God, but that is something about which our school of philosophy (*hairesis*) is most urgent.'[58] Here we find signs of a controversy within Judaism over the degree to which it is possible to transfer pagan divine names to the true God. That critical distinctions of this kind were necessary is evident not only from the Greek and Roman attempts to identify the God of Israel with other gods, e.g. Dionysius, Sabazius or Jupiter,[59] but also from the fact that two Jews in the Ptolemaic period attached two inscriptions to the pan-temple of ar-Ridīsīya near Apollinopolis (Edfu) in Upper Egypt in which they give thanks to God (*theou eulogia* or *eulogei ton theon*), one for rescue from drowning at sea. A certain Lazarus even boasts that he has made the journey to the Paneion three times.[60] For non-Jews, it seemed even more natural to identify the God of the Jews with a known divine figure, as the real name of the Jewish God, Iao, was kept secret. Lucan therefore talks of an '*incertus deus*'.[61] Dionysus above all seems to have lent himself to identification with the God of the Jews. That this attempt at identification was widespread is clear not only from Plutarch, Cornelius Labo and the later compiler Johannes Lydus, but even from Tacitus' protest: 'However, their priests used to perform their chants to the flute and drums, crowned with ivy, and a golden vine was discovered in the Temple; and this has led some to imagine that the god thus worshipped was Pater Liber, the conqueror of the East. But the two cults are diametrically opposed. Liber founded a festive and happy cult; the Jewish belief is para-doxical and degraded.'[62] It is quite possible that after his victory at Raphia, Ptolemy IV Philopator, a fervent worshipper of Dionysus, attempted to initiate upper-class Jews in Egypt into the mysteries of Dionysus through threats and promises, as he himself took their God to be a kind of Semitic Dionysus.[63] Some decades later, radical Jewish reformers, hand in hand with king Antiochus IV and pagan military settlers, attempted to change the worship of Yahweh on Mount Zion into the cult of Zeus Olympius/Baal Shamem, as outsiders felt that this must be one and the same God of heaven.[64] However, an overwhelming majority of Jews in the Diaspora and in the home country resisted this temptation. The legendary III Maccabees affirms: 'However, most stood firm with noble souls and did not apostatize from their religion.'[65] Thus there is no more authentic evidence for Jewish-pagan syncretism in the pre-Roman Hellenistic period than there is from Egypt. In my view, the development of a 'Jewish gnosticism' of which there is so much talk today was possible only in the Roman period, after Philo. By contrast, we have no sources at all for the Ptolemaic era.[66] There was a real fusion between Jews and pagans only in the sphere of magic and astrology, which proved to be of increasing interest to Egyptians, Jews and Greeks from the second century BC and penetrated to all levels of the populace.

Mt. Angel Abbey Library
St. Benedict, Oregon 97373

The Hellenization of the Diaspora outside Egypt

We have very little information about the early-Hellenistic Diaspora outside Egypt and its 'Hellenization'. Apart from Joel 4.6, with its polemic against the sale of Jewish slaves to the Greeks, Isa. 11.11f. and above all 66.19 are the only references in late prophetic prediction to a Jewish emigration into the Aegean: Greece and Asia Minor. The texts may come from the fourth or the beginning of the third century. They are matched by some inscriptions from Greece from the fourth and third centuries BC (see pp. 88f. above and p. 106 below) which specifically relate to Jewish slaves.

We hear no more of the fate of the two thousand Babylonian Jews in Phrygia whom Antiochus settled, along with their families, to pacify the province he had regained, while he went on his anabasis to the Eastern provinces (212–205).[1] A few years later, after the battle of Magnesia in 190 BC, this area came under the rule of the Attalids of Pergamum. As we have a large number of Jewish inscriptions from the interior of Asia Minor, from Phrygia and Lydia, from Roman times, we may assume that these cleruchs formed the backbone of the Diaspora in Asia Minor.[2] An epitaph from Hierapolis in Phrygia speaks of the *katoikia* of the Jews living in Hierapolis. This designation, which is unusual for a synagogue community, could go back to the Jewish military settlers.[3] An earlier list of givers from Iasos in Ionia, dating from the second century BC, mentions a Nicetas son of Jason of Jerusalem (*Hierosolymitēs*) who gave one hundred drachmae for the feast of the Dionysia. On this Schürer rightly comments: 'The support of a pagan festival by a Jew recalls similar happenings in Jerusalem before the beginnings of the Maccabean revolt.'[4] We do not know whether this Nicetas was still really a Jew and whether he made his contribution to the festival of Dionysus voluntarily, or under compulsion. In the pre-Roman period pressure on Jews seems to have been stronger on the west coast of Asia Minor than, say, in Ptolemaic Egypt. Even before Marcus Agrippa, round about 13 BC, the Ionian cities asked of the Jews living among them that, 'If the Jews really belonged to them, they should also worship their gods.'[5] An accusation by the rhetorician Apollonius Molon (Rhodian ambassador to Rome in 81 BC), that 'the Jews do not accept people who have other views about God',[6] is on similar lines. On the other hand, after the successful fight for freedom against the Seleucids in Judaea, the good political relationships between the new Jewish state and Rome also benefited the Jews in the Aegean and Asia Minor. This is demonstrated, for example, by the decree of the Pergamenes at the time of Hyrcanus I (135–104 BC), which finally refers to the friendship between Abraham and the forefathers of the Pergamenes. This is evidently a legend with a purpose, which recalls the affinity between Jews and Spartans (see pp. 116 below) and which perhaps arose among the groups of military settlers who had come to Magnesia under the rule of the Pergamene empire.[7] The Noah coins from Apameia in Phrygia, with their representation of the departure from the ark after the flood, may also go back to a local Jewish saga from Hellenistic times. It is striking here that the ark is depicted in the form of a shrine for the Torah.[8] The considerable expansion of the Jews even in Asia Minor and the Aegean in the second half of the second century BC is evident, *inter alia*, from the letters which were written in 142 or 139 BC by a Roman consul in favour of the Jewish *ethnos* to a series of city states and territories in the Aegean and Asia Minor, asking them to hand over fugitive Jewish Hellenists to the high priest Simon.[9] A little later, the earliest synagogue so far excavated is evidence that there was a large and flourishing Jewish community in the trading port of Delos.[10] The two tablets of curses from the mortuary island of Rheneia, which date from the same period, and ask God to take vengeance for the murder of two Jewish girls, are not only the first epigraphical evidence for the Septuagint, but also show how angels played a particular role in the spirituality of these Diaspora Jews.[11]

There seem already to have been connections between Jerusalem and Sparta in the pre-Maccabean period. This is the only explanation of the fact that after an abortive attempt at rebellion, the inaugurator of the Hellenistic reform after 175, the high priest Jason, son of Simon the Just, from the ancient family of the Oniads, deposed and accursed, finally arrived in Sparta by way of Egypt and ended his life there. This exceptional choice of location is probably connected with the belief of Jewish Hellenists that there was an archaic affinity between Jews and Lacedaimonians through Abraham. Jason would hardly have fled there had he not had acquaintances or friends to go to.[12] At round about the same period we also find Jewish epitaphs in Athens.[13] Jewish slaves are, however, to be found a good deal earlier in Attica, even in the fourth and third centuries BC (see pp. 88f. above). As early as the first half of the third century BC, Clearches of Soloi reported the meeting of Aristotle with a Jew from Jerusalem who had had a Greek education: 'he was a Hellene not only in his language but also in his soul'. This encounter, which must have taken place as early as 340 BC, should probably be relegated to the realm of fable, but we can infer from it that Clearchus, who came from Cyprus, had himself come across such Jews.[14] He reflects the interest of the Aristotelian school in 'barbarian philosophy' which we also find in the fragment of Theophrastus on the Jews and in Megasthenes. Here the Jews were associated with the Indian gymnosophists and Brahmans.[15] In Asia Minor, where the Jews were much more in the minority than they were in Egypt, we may suppose that under the rule of the Attalids Jewish syncretistic amalgams developed in which, say, Phrygian Sabazius was identified with the *kyrios sabaōth* of the Jews. This would explain the remarkable note of Valerius Maximus that round about 139 BC the Praetor Cornelius Hispalus had expelled from Rome the Jews who wanted to introduce the cult of Jupiter or Iovis Sabazius. However, this report might also derive from a simple confusion of the names Iao Sabaoth and Iovis Sabazius.[16] Although there is evidence of the cult of Zeus or *theos hypsistos* in Asia Minor, Macedonia, Thrace and Egypt, and also in the Bosphorus empire, and of the widespread worship of the *theos aggelos*, sometimes identified with Zeus *hypsistos*, in Roman Asia Minor,[17] we need not always suppose Jewish influence, although cross-fertilization is quite possible.[18] Thus, for example, it is striking that the *theos hypsistos* inscriptions which are obviously Jewish (because they come from the synagogues) often date from the pre-Christian, Hellenistic period, whereas the pagan cult of the 'supreme God' only really began to flourish in the Roman empire.

We find a further point of contact with syncretistic amalgams of Judaism and paganism in connection with the observance of the sabbath, which despite all the polemic could also prove attractive for non-Jews.[19] Thus in Phrygia there is isolated evidence for the cult of a *theos Sabathikos*. A verse inscription calls him 'the greatest God' (*megistos hyparchōn*) 'who possesses the world' (*tou katechontos ton kosmon*).[20] Two inscriptions in Western Cilicia date from the same period, that of Augustus: they are evidence of a cultic association of the *Sabbatistai*, which worshipped a *theos Sabbatistēs* under the leadership of a *synagogeus*.[21] On the other hand, the Sabbatheion in Thyateira may have been a synagogue.[22] At the same time we find in Naucratis in Egypt a *synodos Sambatikē*, which probably practised a similar cult.[23] There is also clear Jewish influence in the *synodos peri theon hypsiston* in Tanis at the mouth of the Don, where 'worshippers of the supreme God' (*sebomenoi theon hypsiston*) had gathered together. By contrast, in other cities in this region these 'godfearers' were directly connected with the Jewish synagogue community.[24] Particularly in Asia Minor, this syncretistic evidence continues down to the sect of the Hypsistarians in the fourth century AD.[25] It is very probable that Jewish pagan amalgams of this kind, which suddenly emerge at the beginning of the Christian era, had already begun to develop in pre-Christian, Hellenistic times. We should look for their place of origin in Asia Minor rather than in Egypt itself. In Asia Minor, too, for the first time groups of sympathetic non-Jews, the so-called 'godfearers', may have come into being, not fully adherents of Judaism, but associated with the synagogue community. Paul's mission to the Gentiles proved particularly successful here. In the first century AD, the Roman satirists accept them as part of the scene, and so does Luke, who may well have been one of them.[26]

We should not, of course, overestimate these syncretistic marginal groups. And at the same time we should ask whether they were pagan associations who allowed themselves to be influenced by Judaism, or whether paganized Jews played the decisive role. Presumably the first of the alternatives was the case. A Jew who broke with the Law is hardly likely to have turned to a semi-Jewish cult; he will have become completely assimilated to his Hellenistic environment. Even outside Egypt, Diaspora Judaism of the Hellenistic period shows an astonishing capacity to resist the temptation of real assimilation, the surrender of the distinguishing mark of Jewish faith, its bond with the Law and the one God. On the contrary, it demonstrated its strength by carrying on an active mission. On the other hand, it can be shown that the Diaspora communities who had an independent tradition from before the Maccabean period – for example in Egypt, Cyrenaica, Asia Minor and the Aegean, adopted a freer attitude towards Hellenistic culture than those communities which only came into being after the Maccabean revolt with a marked influx from Palestine, as for example in Rome and Italy. The role of Alexandria as the centre of a Hellenistic Jewish pattern of education was unique here and unrivalled in the rest of the ancient world. We can see evidence of the difference I have just described, for example, by comparing the Jewish epitaphs from Leontopolis about the beginning of the Christian era with the numerous Jewish inscriptions in Rome from the Christian era, or by comparing Jewish literature from Alexandria up to the time of Philo with the work of Josephus, the Hellenized Palestinian Jew, who wrote in Rome.

It is strange that we know almost nothing at all about the early development of Diaspora Judaism in the area which had the largest Jewish population in the Christian era, namely in Syria and Phoenicia. Josephus reports of the Jews in Antioch that, like those in Alexandria, they had enjoyed *isopoliteia* from the foundation of the city. In reality this will only have been a special corporation law for the Jewish community there.[27] In the sources, the community appears for the first time at the time of the Hellenistic reform. Thus it is said to have been enraged by the murder, by Andronicus, of the high priest Onias III, who had taken refuge in the sanctuary of the temple of Apollo and Artemis in Daphne.[28] Evidently no offence was taken at the fact that the Jewish priest had looked for sanctuary in a pagan temple. As far as one can see, the community was not troubled during the forcible reform attempt in Jerusalem under Antiochus Epiphanes. The anti-Jewish measures taken by the king and the radical reformers were evidently limited to Palestine. As a royal foundation, under the 'kings succeeding Antiochus' the great synagogue in Antioch received some of the vessels plundered by Antiochus Epiphanes from the Temple in Jerusalem. In this connection Josephus speaks of a *hieron*. Now that Jerusalem had become increasingly remote from the Seleucid empire, perhaps there was an attempt here to create a rival sanctuary – as in Leontopolis or in 'Irāq al-Amīr ('Arāq el-Emīr) in

Transjordania.[29] The legend of the martyrdom of a Jewish mother and her seven sons was later cherished in the Jewish community there. It is possible that the tractate known as IV Maccabees was written there – but of course only in Roman times.[30] However, Antioch, unlike Alexandria, never won independent significance as a centre of Jewish-Hellenistic culture and literature. The Seleucids never succeeded in making their capital an intellectual centre even remotely comparable with Alexandria. Presumably – though in view of the state of the sources this can be no more than a conjecture – the 'Hellenization' of the Jews in Syria and Phoenicia went on at a slower pace than in Egypt, since here the Jewish population found strong support in the fact that they spoke Aramaic. On the other hand, the Canaanite that was spoken in Phoenician cities was akin to Hebrew. However, in the Roman period, Greek became fully established even here, at least in the larger cities and among the upper class.[31] The same is true of large areas of Palestine, above all in the coastal regions. As there had long been a variety of contacts between the heart of Judaism in Palestine, the Phoenician coastal cities and the Syrian metropolises in the north, like Damascus, Apameia and Antioch, the internal development of Judaism in Syria must in any case be seen in close connection with the home country itself. Connections between Palestine and Syria were stronger than with Alexandria, above all from the beginning of the Seleucid rule. This is further confirmed by the course of the earliest Christian mission, which found its first Gentile Christian centre in Antioch, rather than in Alexandria.

The Influence of Hellenistic Civilization in Jewish Palestine down to the Maccabean Period

It was in Palestine that the Jews made the acquaintance of the Macedonians and Greeks in the time after Alexander's expedition. Not only did they discover them as a cultural force; they were also confronted with their absolute military and political superiority. Even more markedly than under Persian rule the Jews now became the passive object of history and were the helpless victims of the changing configurations of power in Syria and Palestine during the struggle of the Diadochoi. The fact that they are either not mentioned at all in the Greek sources of the time, or only appear on the periphery (Agatharcides and Hecataeus of Abdera), only shows their political impotence. The renewal of prophetic prediction in the early 'apocalyptic' of the anonymous author of Deutero-Zechariah[1] or the Isaiah apocalypse shows that under the impact of the cruelty of war and the arrogance of the new rulers, God's intervention to save his people was a matter of intense expectation. Now the Greeks could take the place of the traditional opponents, the Assyrians and the Babylonians, as the eschatological enemies of the people of God.[2] That means that the first stage was not cultural encounter but polemical confrontation, which is continued in the image of the cruel and godless 'fourth kingdom' of later apocalyptic. The emigration of Jews to Egypt under the rule of Ptolemy I Soter, reported by Pseudo-Hecataeus, will – as Pseudo-Aristeas suggests – have largely been the result of external compulsion (see pp. 19f. above). By contrast, the writings of the Chronicler show that what made an impression was above all the military power of the Macedonians and the fortresses built by the Ptolemies, along with their agriculture based on large estates;[3] at the same time, the greater harshness of the foreign rule led to a picture of the past painted in ideal colours, with a heightened contrast between good and evil.

Whereas the destruction of Samaria and the foundation of a Macedonian military colony considerably reduced the political and economic supremacy of their northern fellow-countrymen akin in descent and religion (see p. 8f, above), the specifically Jewish region of the old Persian sub-satrapy of Yehud suffered no ill consequences from the foundation of Graeco-Macedonian military colonies on the coastal plain and in Transjordania.[4] The great trade routes by-passed Jerusalem, and the zeal with which the Phoenician coastal cities adopted Greek language and Greek ways of life – at least outwardly – need not necessarily have been imitated immediately in the hill-country of Judaea. However, once political conditions had been stabilized at the beginning of the third century BC, a turning point will have come. The new ruler Ptolemy I Soter was concerned to further military and economic development in the newly-won bulwark formed by Palestine, a policy in which he was followed by his no less brilliant son Ptolemy II Philadelphus; in the wake of this, Palestinian Judaism, which was conservative simply by virtue of its geographical setting, could no longer escape the spirit of the new age. The small area of the Jewish territory around Jerusalem and the relative poverty of the population compared with the rich Phoenician and Palestinian coastal cities should not blind us to the fact that there was a vigorous intellectual life in the various Jewish wisdom schools in the country, stimulated not least by the growing Jewish Diaspora in Egypt, Babylonia and Syria. Since, as we saw, the Jews adopted the Greek language and a Greek way of life relatively quickly in Egypt, because they came as military settlers, merchants, craftsmen, peasants or slaves, this influence will in turn have had an effect on the home country through those who returned.[5] The fragments of the Jewish literature of the fourth and third centuries as they have come down to us in the late works of the Old Testament canon and in the apocrypha, show a great variety of content and literary forms; nor was this literature all religious in character: some of it took the form of secular *belles lettres*.[6] Even though we must be very careful about arguing for 'Hellenistic influence' in this early period, here at least we come up against an intellectual climate that was prepared to be stimulated and influenced in a number of ways; in particular some tendencies in the development of Jewish wisdom and also in apocalyptic made them particularly open to such an encounter with Greek ideas.[7] In the papyrus documents connected with the journey to Palestine made by Zeno as agent of Apollonius the finance minister in 259 BC, we find a great many contacts between Greek officers, officials, merchants and adventurers, and the local Semitic inhabitants, including Jews. The Ptolemaic administration sought to administer its colony just as strictly and exploit it with just as much thoroughness as the Egyptian mother country itself. Greek agents and 'excisemen' visited every last village for this purpose. The numerous garrisons and military colonies which had to protect the frontier province against the Seleucids in the north and the Arabic tribes in the East, and against inner unrests, were ethnically mixed and furthered the process of economic and cultural integration. Jerusalem, too, seems to have had a permanent garrison with which the Jewish population had to live. In addition there were regular contacts with the numerous armies which crossed Palestine and, say in winter, were billeted among the local population in the villages. It was probably contacts of this kind which made young Jews, too, want to be mercenaries so that they could enjoy the same privileges as the foreign soldiers. Between the death of Alexander the Great and the Roman conquest by Pompey (323–63 BC), Morton Smith counts 'at least 200 campaigns fought in or across Palestine'.[8] One difference from Egypt, where the native aristocracy no longer had a role, was that the Ptolemaic officials and military forces were prepared to work in close collaboration with the local upper classes in the province and to allow them to have a share in its produce.[9] Thus we find a mixed Macedonian-Jewish military colony in Ammanitis in Transjordania commanded not by a Greek but by the Jewish magnate Tobias, whose family controlled the area even in Persian times and whose predecessors had once caused Nehemiah very great difficulties.[10] According to Josephus he was the brother-in-law of the high priest. Zeno paid a visit to his citadel in Ammanitis with great success, and he later appears in correspondence with Apollonius and the king in Alexandria, treating them almost as his equals. He sends the king rare animals for his zoo, and provides Apollonius with young slaves. In this correspondence he also proves himself to be a very liberal Jew. Of course he has a Greek secretary. As commander of a Ptolemaic unit with

Macedonian subordinates he himself must also have been capable of both speaking and writing Greek.[11]

According to the Tobiad romance in Josephus, his son Joseph became a figure of great political and economic significance in Jerusalem – presumably under Ptolemy III Euergetes. Not only did he become *prostatēs*, representative of the Jewish *ethnos* to the Ptolemaic kingdom, but he also succeeded in securing for himself supervision of tax collection throughout the whole province of 'Syria and Phoenicia', as he had particularly good connections with the royal house. He forcibly overcame individual Hellenistic cities which sought to resist the new tax authority. He maintained a permanent agent in Alexandria who administered his gigantic fortunes and kept relations happy by sending 'gifts' to the court and royal officials. We may take it for granted that this Joseph was thoroughly Hellenized and also brought up his sons in Greek ways. That is the only explanation for his rapid rise. His youngest son, Hyrcanus, later became supreme commander of the family possessions in the Ammanitis including the Ptolemaic military settlement, where he 'levied tribute from the barbarians' (*kākei dietriben phorologōn tous barbarous*); in other words, he subjected the Nabataean and Arabian tribes there. His brothers continued to have great political influence in Jerusalem.[12] Their descendants became the protagonists of the radical Hellenistic reform which followed the accession of Antiochus IV Epiphanes in 175 BC.[13] Through the Tobiad family in particular, remote and retrograde Jerusalem was introduced to a new, luxurious life-style which was certainly in conflict with the strict principles of ancient Israelite tradition and which Koheleth describes tersely and aptly: 'Feasts are held at will, and wine gladdens life, and money answers everything.'[14]

The gradual invasion of Hellenistic civilization is also clear from the appearance of Greek names. In Phoenician territory we find numerous Greek names and Graeco-Semitic double names as early as the third century. We find a vivid mixture of Phoenician, Idumaean, Jewish and Greek names in the Phoenician colony of Marisa, founded in the middle of the third century. It was the chief centre in Idumaea, only about twenty-five miles south-west of Jerusalem and in a cultural milieu which had already been fully Hellenized.[15] There was also presumably a Sidonian colony of the same kind, in Samaritan Shechem (Sikima). Individual fragments of inscriptions of Greek names have also been found there.[16] Goodenough's verdict on the tombs of Marisa may also be applied to Shechem, and indeed to large areas of Palestine at the beginning of the second century: 'It seems reasonable to suppose that we have here a picture of the sort of syncretizing Hellenization against which, as it affected Jews, the Maccabees revolted. Had syncretism gone on in this way among the Jews, Judaism would probably be now as little known as the other religions of the ancient Levant.'[17]

We find Greek names even among 'conservative' Jews in Palestine: the fathers of the delegates sent to Sparta or Rome by the Maccabaeans Jonathan and Simon, Numenius, son of Antiochus, Antipater, son of Jason, and Alexander, son of Dorotheos, will all have been born at the end of the third century BC.[18] The second son of the high priest Simon the Just appears under the name Jason. He displaced his conservative brother Onias III and in 175 became the real power behind the Hellenistic reform, which sought to transform Jerusalem into a Greek *polis*. With royal consent, and to the general approval of the aristocracy of Jerusalem, he established a gymnasium alongside the Temple and had the sons of the high-born educated there as ephebes.[19] However, after a few years he had to give way to the even more radical brothers, Menelaus, Lysimachus and Simon, from the priestly family of Bilga, who were closely associated with the Tobiads. After an unsuccessful attempt at rebellion, Jason fled via Petra and Egypt to his supposed relatives in Sparta.[20] According to rabbinic accounts, because of this the priestly order of Bilga was later excluded from service at sacrifices 'for all time', allegedly because the daughter of a priest, Miriam, had married a Greek officer and had desecrated the altar in the Temple. Evidently at the time of the reform the members of this order had been unconditionally in favour of assimilation. In his enumeration of the priestly orders, Eleazar Kalir still calls them 'the Greek order'. There are a few other indications of Jewish mixed marriages in early Hellenistic Palestine.[21] There was even free love. Meleager of Gadara in Transjordania complains in an epigram that his beloved Dema is warming herself with a Jewish lover on the cold sabbath.[22] The otherwise unknown Antigonus of Socoh, who according to Pirqe Aboth 1.3 received the Law from Simon the Just and rejected the expectation of reward as slavish, was probably also a contemporary of Jason and Menelaus. At a later date he was made the spiritual father of the Sadducees. The only two officers of the Maccabean cavalry from Transjordania, presumably from the cleruchy of Tobias and Hyrcanus, to be mentioned by name are called Dositheos and Sosipatros.[23] John, from the priestly family of Haqqoṣ, who negotiated with Antiochus III about 200 BC (see p. 42 above), called his son Eupolemus. Under Judas Maccabaeus he became leader of the first embassy in Rome and composed what was presumably a historical work about the Jewish kings in Greek.[24] Under the Hasmonaeans this predilection for Greek names and Greek culture continued in the upper class, despite all the resistance from the circles faithful to the Torah. It is striking that we find foreign names equally among the advocates of the Hellenistic reform and their Maccabean opponents. A large number of the seventy-two elders of the Letter of Aristeas, who come to Alexandria to translate the Torah, have Greek names like Theodosius, Theodotus, Theophilus, Dositheus and Jason. The author of the letter evidently took this for granted.[25]

Even more important than the Greek names of individual translators is the fact that the author also takes it for granted that the seventy-two Jewish scholars from Palestine 'not only had a thorough knowledge of Jewish literature but also had a thorough knowledge of Greek'.[26] That means that at about the middle of the second century BC the author thought it quite possible that educated Palestinian Jews could have a perfect knowledge of Greek. As early as the first half of the third century BC, Clearchus of Soloi presupposes that Jews from Jerusalem had a Greek education.[27] Furthermore, one of the foundations of the political success of the various Jewish delegations, first in Antioch and then in Sparta and Rome, was that their members could speak and write perfect Greek.[28]

The same is true of communications with Diaspora Judaism in Egypt, Asia Minor and the Aegean, where the knowledge of Aramaic had quickly been lost. If the Temple in Jerusalem wanted to maintain and develop its significance as the religious centre of Judaism in the Hellenistic world, it had to keep in touch with the communities there. The pilgrims who came to the feasts in Jerusalem from the West brought their Greek mother tongue to Jerusalem.[29] The various documents in Greek from the second century BC in Josephus and in Maccabees indicate an experienced Greek chancery in the Temple. The Hasmoneans later attempted quite deliberately to strengthen the religious and political influence of the Jerusalem sanctuary on the Diaspora, and to this end even encouraged the dissemination of nationalistic Jewish literature in the Greek-speaking Diaspora and probably also its translation into Greek. Herod gladly continued this policy, and even more markedly than the Hasmoneans made himself the political advocate and protector of Diaspora Judaism. Under him Jerusalem became even more of a Greek-speaking city – at least as far as the upper classes were concerned.[30]

We find the first slight traces of the influence of Greek in Koheleth, in Ben Sira and with the musical instruments in the book of Daniel. They are then extraordinarily numerous in later Jewish rabbinic literature.[31] Literary Hebrew and Aramaic as we find them, say, in the writings of the Qumran library, give the impression of being almost artificially pure in comparison with the spoken idioms of later Talmudic literature. This suggests that foreign words had found their way into the vernacular substantially earlier, a fact which is now also confirmed by the Aramaic copper scroll of Qumran.[32]

The establishment of a gymnasium with ephebes in Jerusalem in 175 BC would have been unthinkable had not the knowledge of Greek and in some respects of Greek literature not already been widespread among the Jerusalem aristocracy at this time. This also presupposes the existence of a Greek elementary school – presumably on a private basis – in the Jewish capital.[33]

A further indication of the penetration of Greek thought into Jerusalem is the claim that the Jews were related to the Spartans through Abraham, which presumably arose as early as the third century BC among circles which were well-disposed towards the Greeks. The starting point is the letter from the Spartan king Areus to the high priest Onias II. As king Areus I was killed at Corinth in 265 BC, in the Chremonidean war, and the initiative in questions of affinity is hardly likely to have come from the Spartans, this letter may be a forgery. The Phoenicians similarly appealed to their affinity with the Greeks through Cadmus; according to Hecataeus the ancestors of the Greeks once emigrated from Egypt with the Danaeans under the leadership of Cadmus at the time when Moses set out for Palestine. According to the Jewish historian Cleodemus Malchus, Heracles married a granddaughter of Abraham in Libya. In Asia Minor the Pergamenes called attention to the former friendship of their ancestors with

Abraham. Whereas the Romans claimed that they were descended from fugitives from Troy, various cities in south-western Asia Minor claimed to be Lacedaemonian colonies. A letter from the people of Tyre to Delphi, preserved on an inscription, calls the Delphians 'kindred'.[34] According to E. Bickerman, this sort of thing was regarded as an 'entrance ticket into European culture',[35] i.e. into the community of the Hellenes. Constructions of this kind in the third century thus served as an ideological preparation for the transformation of Jerusalem into a Greek *polis* after 175 BC. It is striking that even Jonathan the Maccabee referred to this Jewish Hellenistic legend in his attempt to strike up a political alliance with the Spartans, which certainly went against his hatred of the Greeks and the national self-consciousness of his Hasidic compatriots. It is evident here that the Hasmoneans did not really slow down the 'process of Hellenization' in Palestinian Judaism, but in fact continued it as soon as they themselves came to power.[36] The assertion of an affinity between the Jews and the Spartans may of course also be connected with the conservative attitude of both peoples towards their law given on the one hand by Moses and on the other by Lycurgus, along with their xenophobia and their pride in their military past.

Higher, literary Greek education also gradually began to find a footing in Palestine. Thus for example in Gaza and Sidon we find two extensive verse inscriptions in impeccable form from the period round about 200 BC. The one from Gaza is the epitaph of two Ptolemaic officers and members of their family;[37] the one from Sidon is in honour of the suffete Diotimus for his victory in the pan-Hellenic Nemean chariot race in Argos. The poem lays special emphasis on the mythological affinity between Argives, Thebans and Phoenicians.[38] A graffito from one of the tombs of Marisa contains a skilful erotic poem in the genre of the Locrian hymn.[39] The fortress of Gadara in Transjordania was a special seedbed of Greek culture. Strabo, who in fact confuses Gadara with Gazara (Gezer), which had become Jewish in the Maccabean period,[40] mentions four famous writers who come from this city, remote from all other centres of ancient culture: 'Philodemus the Epicurean, Meleager, Menippus the satirist ʹand Theodorus the Rhetorician from our days'.[41] Menippus was presumably born towards the end of the fourth century and is said to have been sold as a slave to Sinope, in Pontus in Asia Minor. We might conclude from this that he was descended, not from new Greek settlers, but from Syrians, were not the theme of slaves and celebrated literary figures quite so widespread. This would in that case be an example of the degree to which even then Semites could become assimilated to Greek culture. Later he became a citizen of Thebes. According to Diogenes Laertius, who calls him a 'Phoenician', he became the pupil of the Cynic Metrocles. He is the creator of the polemic philosophical genre of the satire. The new stylistic form combining prose and poetry which he introduced evidently has Semitic roots. A later Syrian, Lucian of Samosata, then completely transformed the Greek satire, with reference to Menippus. Meleager, the creator of the Greek Anthology, was born in the middle of the second century and educated in Tyre, where the 'Phoenician school', which was significant for Greek lyric poetry, developed under Antipater of Sidon (about 170–100 BC). Meleager himself called his native city 'Assyrian Attica', and a later epitaph gives it the honorific title *chrēstomousia*.

In the second century BC, significant philosophers like the Stoic Boethus of Sidon and the Epicurean Zeno of Sidon taught in Phoenician cities. Meleager and the younger Philodemus were both marked by Epicurean *joie de vivre*. Ashkelon, too, became an intellectual centre alongside Gadara in the second century BC and produced a series of significant philosophers and writers.[42] Of course the intellectual development of Hellenistic Palestine suffered a severe blow as a result of Jewish-Hasmonean and Arabic-Iturean expansion. Almost all the Palestinian poets and philosophers emigrated to the West, especially to Italy. The papyrus library of Herculaneum, some of which survives, goes back to the Epicurean Philodemus of Gadara. How far the lively intellectual milieu of the Phoenician cities, as of individual Greek settlements, like Gadara, extended its influence into the Jewish world must remain an open question. However, events during the Hellenistic reform show that the Hellenists in Jerusalem thought it particularly important to have good contacts with the Phoenician cities, as centres of Hellenistic civilization. Because of that, the citizens of the newly founded *polis* of Antiocheia in Jerusalem participated in the quinquennial festivals in Tyre which had been founded by Alexander, under the aegis of the high priest Jason. However, at that time they did not dare give directly to the Tyrian god Heracles Melkart the three hundred drachmae which the high priest had provided for a sacrifice, so the money was used to equip ships.[43] Even the pro-Maccabean Jewish Palestinian 'historian' Eupolemus still tells proudly how Solomon had once sent king Syron of Tyre a golden pillar which Syron had erected in 'the temple of Zeus', i.e. of the Phoenician Baal Shamem; this report is also confirmed by Tyrian historians.[44] Thus for example the Phoenician 'historians' Laitos and Menander reported that Solomon had married the daughter of the Phoenician king when king Menelaus of Sparta visited Tyre after the capture of Troy.[45] Such elaborations of their own national history made it possible for Phoenicians and Jews on the one hand to stress their connection with superior Greek culture while at the same time pointing to the greater antiquity of their own tradition, which made them teachers of the Greeks. On a similar level is the assertion of Meleager of Gadara that Homer had been a Syrian, 'since in accordance with the customs of his homeland he never has the Achaeans eating fish, although the Hellespont is full of them'.[46] The Hellenistic-type designation of Jerusalem as Hierosolyma, which appears for the first time in Hecataeus and in the Zeno papyri, but only late on in the Septuagint and in Hellenized authors,[47] may well be more than a fortuitous piece of nomenclature; it may be a deliberate Greek interpretation made by earlier Jewish Hellenistic circles which is connected with Homeric tradition. The first part of the word, *hiero-*, showed the holy city, like Hiera- or Hieropolis in Phrygia or like the Syrian Hierapolis-Bambyce or the various *Hierai-kōmai* in Asia Minor, to be a temple city. This corresponds with the report of Polybius quoted by Josephus (*Antt.* XII, 136): 'The Jews who live around the sanctuary (*hieron*) called Hierosolyma . . .' On the other hand, the second half of the word, -solyma, connects the inhabitants with the 'famed people of the Solymians' (*Solymoisi . . . kydalimoisi*), already mentioned by Homer in *Iliad* VI, 184, a people who, according to Eratosthenes (Pliny, *Historia Naturalis* V, 127), no longer existed. As Homer, *Odyssey* V, 283, also speaks of 'mountains of Solymi' in the vicinity of Ethiopia, in his account of the antiquity of the Jewish people in *Contra Apionem*, Josephus can describe its inhabitants, who according to a poem of Choïrilos of Samos were part of Xerxes' army, as Jews (*Contra Apionem* I, 173f.); Pseudo-Manetho also calls the later inhabitants of Hierosolyma *Solymitai* (*Contra Apionem* I, 248, cf. 241). The fourth Sibylline oracle (115, 126) and Philostratus in his *Vita Apollonii*

(6, 29) also similarly call Jerusalem simply Solyma; Tacitus (*Histories* 5, 2, 3) finally gives the ancient reader an illuminating explanation for this: 'Others (*alii*) attribute a glorious origin (*clara . . . initia*) to the Jews. The Solymians, a race celebrated in the poems of Homer, called the capital which they founded Hierosolyma, taking up their own name.' The *alii* is presumably a reference to Hellenistic Jews. The Greek interpretation of the holy city along these lines was surely meant to heighten its significance in Greek eyes. Thus the alteration of the name follows the same line as the alleged affinity to the Spartans.

Alexander Polyhistor has preserved for us fragments of a Jewish-Samaritan historical work which praises similar tendencies and which was presumably written in Palestine after the conquest by the Seleucids, but before the outbreak of the Maccabean revolt. According to this, Enoch, whom the Greeks call Atlas, received the secrets of astrology from the angels and handed them down to posterity. Abraham, 'who surpassed all men in nobility and wisdom', then brought them at God's command to the West and first taught the Phoenicians, and later the Egyptian priests in Heliopolis. This is a deliberate reversal of the biblical pattern of Abraham's journeying. As later, in the Sibylline writings, the pagan gods are devalued in a euhemeristic way and made to serve the greater glory of the Jews through the theme of the 'first inventor' (*prōtos heuretēs*). The Samaritan origin of the history emerges from the stress on the 'city sanctuary of Hargarizim', as the place where Abraham 'received gifts' from the priest-king Melchizedek.[48]

The spirit of the new age and indeed the direct influence of Greek thought can even be found in some parts of Hebrew wisdom literature. This is true above all of the book Koheleth, which is puzzling in so many ways, and in which earlier scholars traced the influence of Greek philosophy. The work was probably written in the third century, in Jerusalem, under the Ptolemies; to some degree it has an aura of the early Hellenistic enlightenment.[49] This is already evident from certain linguistic affinities. Thus terms for destiny which Koheleth is fond of using, like *miqreh*, death, and *ḥeleq*, man's due portion, recall Greek *moira* and *tychē*. The often-recurring 'under the sun' was regarded as another Graecism. It was supposed that a Greek equivalent of the decisive term *hebel*, nothingness, was *typhos*; *'āśāh tōb* represented the Greek *eu prattein* or *eu drān*, while *tōb 'ašer yapeh* was thought to be the well-known *kalos kāgathos* or *to kalon philon*.[50] There are also Greek parallels to the stress on time as a term for destiny. Other features are the impersonal conception of God, restraint towards prayer and worship, the complete absence of Jewish history with the exception of the disputed mention of Solomon at the beginning, the omission of the tradition about the Law, and above all the almost fatalistic notion that man is the victim of his fate and that the only thing for him to do is to enjoy his portion as long as he may. In particular, this invitation to *carpe diem* and the conception that after death 'the breath of man ascends on high' has a wealth of Greek parallels.[51] A comparison with the Greek gnomic tradition shows that Koheleth must have been acquainted with it. The question remains open whether he knew it from oral tradition or in a literary form. Presumably both were available. Parallels can be produced from Greek poetry and popular philosophy for almost every verse.[52] It should, however, be stressed that Koheleth combined these new stimuli coming from outside with traditional Jewish, Eastern wisdom teaching, with which he is engaged in a critical discussion, to produce a coherent work with a character all of its own and a considerable degree of artistic skill. Presumably his provocative work, which above all broke with the old pattern of a just connection between act and consequence brought about by God, and thus raised doubts as to God's righteousness and goodness, was later revised and toned down by another hand.[53]

Another wisdom teacher is Ben Sira, who presumably lived a generation or two later than Koheleth, whose work he knew and used. In contrast to Koheleth, he does not hide behind a mysterious *nom de plume*, and is the first writer in Hebrew literature to give his own name. This too is a sign of a new age.[54] Awareness of the nature of intellectual originality now also found its way into Palestinian Judaism. Furthermore, the author openly presents himself as a 'wise man' and a 'scribe' who invites the young into his 'school' and – in contrast to the earlier wisdom of a Job or a Koheleth – deliberately takes his place in the tradition of the salvation history of Israel. Perhaps he was one of the 'temple scribes' mentioned in the decree of Antiochus III. Sometimes he speaks with the claim of prophetic authority and includes the interpretation of the prophetic writings in his task as a scribe.[55] More than that, however, for him the Torah given by God on Sinai is central; he boldly identifies it with the pre-existent wisdom which God poured out on all creation.

At God's bidding, this primal and universal wisdom found its dwelling place on Mount Zion in Jerusalem: here the mediating form of wisdom, which by virtue of its universality could be compared with the Platonic world-soul and the Stoic Logos, is exclusively connected with Israel, God's chosen people, and his sanctuary. In the hymn to wisdom in chapter 24, the centrepiece of his work, Ben Sira follows Prov. 8.22ff. by taking over aretalogical forms known to us from the Egyptian Isis aretalogies and which were perhaps used in Palestine in honour of Phoenician-Canaanite Astarte.[56] Here we have a characteristic which distinguishes him markedly from Koheleth. However, he uses new 'Hellenistic' forms and material just as much as Koheleth, not to criticize the traditional religious heritage of Israel but to defend it in the contemporary intellectual struggle. Thus he attacks the wicked men and apostates, i.e. the Hellenists among the Jewish aristocracy, who want to forsake the Law;[57] those who deny free will, who make God himself responsible for their failure, and above all those who doubt the justice of God's recompense. He defends the purposefulness of the world and God's providence and justice with Stoic arguments; that is, he tries to develop something like a theodicy in terms of popular philosophy. Like Chrysippus, he argues that the evil in the world is there for the just punishment of sinners.[58] Ben Sira can describe the relationship of God to the world in almost pantheistic-sounding formulas: 'and the sum of our words is: "He is the all" '.[59] While on the one hand he takes up themes from the social preaching of the prophets, by attacking the exploitation of the poor by the rich landowners,[60] on the other hand he can value riches, is familiar with the etiquette of Greek meals, defends consultations with doctors and praises the reputation and the political significance of the wise man who travels to foreign lands on behalf of the great.[61] Like Koheleth, he also knows Greek gnomic literature,[62] but does not glorify the wisdom and the heroes of alien peoples; his praise is reserved for the Torah and the great men of God from the sacred history which reaches from Adam and Enoch to his contemporary, the high priest Simon the Just,[63] whose sons he warns about division:[64] round about 180 BC, when he was finishing his book, the Hellenistic reform was already casting a shadow forward. The eschatological prayer, with its petition for liberation from the Gentile yoke, clearly shows that he was very critical of alien Seleucid rule. However, with the caution of a wise man, he knows how to disguise his criticism, and this prayer, too, is set in the framework of an almost universalist philosophical concept of God. It begins with the petition, 'Have mercy upon us, O Lord, the God of all . . .' and ends, 'and all who are on the earth will know that thou art the Lord, the God of the ages.'[65] There has been much discussion as to whether Ben Sira was pro-Hellenist or anti-Hellenist, but this is to pose a false alternative.[66] It must be viewed in the light of the divided historical situation in Judaea in the pre-Maccabean period. Furthermore, a distinction needs to be made between a Hellenistic-type form and the basically xenophobic tendency.[67] Ben Sira was a religious conservative, a Jewish *sōper* (scribe), faithful to the Torah and thinking in nationalistic terms, who believed that he had an obligation to ancestral tradition but was nevertheless more influenced than he was aware by the spirit of his time, i.e. the thought-world of Hellenism. However, in addition there can be no doubt that he was consciously an opponent of the Hellenistic reformers in the city and that if he was still alive to experience events after 175 BC he would have been on the side of the Maccabees and certainly not on that of Jason, Menelaus, Alcimus or the Tobiads. In him we find that spirit which we later meet again among the early Sadducees, who were also conservative, nationalistic Jews, put up bitter resistance against the Romans and Herod's seizure of power, and yet did not despise Hellenistic civilization and its resources, supporting the transformation of Judaea into a 'Hellenistic' monarchy which was brought about by the Hasmoneans.

To conclude, it is also important to consider the opposition movement of the Hasidim[68] which began to organize itself shortly before, or at the beginning of, the Hellenistic reform. The influence of the new age can be seen even in those who rejected the spirit of Hellenism with particular vehemence; indeed, it can be seen here above all. That is true of the free form of organization which they adopted, that of the religious association, which was later adopted by the *yaḥad* (*koinon*) of the Qumran Essenes and the *ḥᵃbūrōt* of the Pharisees:[69] we must understand it as the sign of a new religious individualism which rested on the free decision – the 'conversion' – of the individual. Other signs of the spirit of a new age are many of their religious views, which have been recorded above all in the apocalyptic literature, produced from their circles. The Essenes, of course, vigorously rejected Gentile, Hellenistic civilization. However, they in particular show signs of varied influence from this alien spirit of the age and therefore their teaching was especially suitable for a philosophical and apologetic *interpretatio graeca*.[70] It would be wrong to see the *hasidim*, moulded by apocalyptic thought, as being in conscious opposition to Jewish wisdom or to the Temple cult.[71] In reality the division of the people ran through the priests and Levites as well as through the scribes. A new phenomenon in hasidic apocalyptic was the claim it raised to special revelations of divine wisdom. Here the concept of the secret took on central theological significance.[72] A 'higher wisdom' appeared alongside the wisdom handed down by tradition, which was received through a special revelation, through dreams and visions, through journeys to heaven and hell, through the appearances of angels and through inspiration. Here we find the same forms of revelation as in the Hellenistic world; to some degree the same 'religious *koinē*' is spoken.[73] The heyday of Jewish apocalyptic, from the second century BC, which then quickly spilled over to the Diaspora in the form of the Sibylline oracles, runs parallel to the renewal of a 'religion of revelation' in the Hellenistic world. Of course it began there rather later, and reached its climax only from the second century AD onwards, in the time of the Empire. A further essential point was the emergence of the individual's hope of overcoming death, along with the conception of the judgment of the dead. The development of a future hope beyond death then in turn exercised an essential influence on burial customs and the form of tombs, which underwent a particularly intensive development in the late Hellenistic and Roman period. In Palestine this expectation assumed the typically Jewish form of the physical resurrection from the dead; alongside it, certainly under Greek influence, there developed the idea of the immortality of the soul, which was influential above all in the Diaspora. However, both were variable and could be combined. The development of a hope beyond death is closely connected with the question of theodicy, which was raised especially as a result of persecution. In Greece the hope of immortality, the expectation of a judgment of the dead and the conception of places of reward and punishment for the dead were very much older. We must not rule out influence from here on early Jewish apocalyptic. This is especially true of the idea of astral 'immortality' and future hope for the wise teachers, which we find as early as the end of the book of Daniel.[74] Lastly, mention should also be made of the concept of the unity of world history, which is closely bound up with the idea of world kingdoms; this developed in the controversy with the Hellenistic monarchies. The imminent kingdom of God will soon make an end to the overwhelming arrogance of the world empire. The imagery of the four metals of successively inferior quality as symbols for the world kingdoms in Nebuchadnezzar's dream recalls the four metals in Hesiod's picture of the ages of the world, which had a decisive influence on ancient historical thinking.[75] The notion of universal mission to be found, with its eschatological proviso, in Greek-speaking primitive Christianity, and the thinking of Paul in particular, both of which represent something completely new in the history of religion, are a last consequence of the universalist, Hellenistic, apocalyptic conception of the one *oikoumenē*, the unity of the inhabited, civilized world. On the other hand, Jewish and Iranian apocalyptic in turn influenced ancient poetry. The best example of this is Virgil's Fourth Eclogue.[76]

Thus the adoption of Hellenistic civilization, its language, its literature and its thought, by ancient Judaism and the conflict which resulted is a complex development involving a great deal of tension. The development in Palestine differed only partially from that in the Diaspora; it affected almost all strata and groups of the population and involved both the political and economic and the intellectual and religious spheres. The reactions of individual classes and groups was also very different. The aristocracy proved to be most open to the new life-style and the education that went with it; this upper class was also particularly threatened with assimilation. However, the opposition too, the Hasidic apocalypticists or the Jewish Hellenistic apologists, all of whom wanted to preserve the ancestral heritage intact, did not escape the influence of the thought of the new age in this political and intellectual struggle. Precisely by accepting new ideas and working intensively with them, ancient Judaism acquired the inner strength to pull itself out of the morass of alien and seductive civilization and even in a different garb and in connection with new forms of thought and expression to preserve the traditional religious heritage and to remain true to its divine task in history. Thus by and large we may term Judaism of the Hellenistic Roman period, both in the home country and the Diaspora, 'Hellenistic Judaism'.[77] The Christian theologian in particular may see this Hellenistic-early Roman history of ancient Judaism in the home country of Palestine and in the Diaspora as a real preparation for the gospel. It is no coincidence that Eusebius took up so many Jewish Hellenistic fragments from the Diaspora and Palestine in his work which bears this name.

ABBREVIATIONS

AAB	Abhandlungen der königlich Preussischen (after 1945/46 Deutschen) Akademie der Wissenschaften zu Berlin
AAG	Abhandlungen der Göttinger Akademie der Wissenschaften
AAMz	Abhandlungen der Akademie der Wissenschaften . . ., Mainz
AGG	Abhandlungen der Gesellschaft der Wissenschaften, Göttingen
AGSU	Arbeiten zur Geschichte des Spätjudentums und Urchristentums
BA	*The Biblical Archaeologist*
BASOR	*Bulletin of the American Schools of Oriental Research*
BBB	Bonner Biblische Beiträge
BhAPF	Beihefte zum Archiv für Papyrusforschung
BZ	*Biblische Zeitschrift*
BZAW	Beihefte zur Zeitschrift für die Alttestamentliche Wissenschaft
CAH	*The Cambridge Ancient History*
CBQ	*Catholic Biblical Quarterly*
CC	Corpus Christianorum
CIG	Corpus Inscriptionum Graecarum
CIJ	Corpus Inscriptionum Judaicarum
CPJ	Corpus Papyrorum Judaicarum
CRAI	*Comptes Rendus de l'Académie des Inscriptions et Belles-Lettres*
EPROER	Etudes preliminaires aux religions orientales dans l'empire romain
FGrHist	Fragmente der Griechischen Historiker, ed. F. Jacoby
FRLANT	Forschungen zur Religion und Literatur des Alten und Neuen Testaments
GCS	Die Griechischen Christlichen Schriftsteller der ersten 3 Jahrhunderte
GOF	Göttinger Forschungen
HAT	Handbuch zum Alten Testament
HAW	Handbuch der Altertumswissenshaft

HTR	*Harvard Theological Review*
HUCA	*Hebrew Union College Annual*
ICC	International Critical Commentary
IEJ	*Israel Exploration Journal*
IG	Inscriptiones Graecae
JBL	*Journal of Biblical Literature*
JEA	*Journal of Egyptian Archaeology*
JHS	*Journal of Hellenic Studies*
JQR	*Jewish Quarterly Review*
JR	*Journal of Religion*
JSJ	*Journal of the Study of Judaism*
JSS	*Journal of Semitic Studies*
JTS	*Journal of Theological Studies*
LXX	Septuagint (Greek translation of the Septuagint)
MusHelv	*Museum Helveticum*
NF	Neue Folge (New Series)
OGIS	Orientis Graeci Inscriptiones Selectae, ed. W. Dittenberger
OTS	*Oudtestamentische Studien*
PAAJR	*Proceedings of the American Academy for Jewish Research*
PCZ	*Zenon Papyri*, ed. C. C. Edgar
PG	*Patrologia Graeca*, ed. J. P. Migne
PL	*Patrologia Latina*, ed. J. P. Migne
PRECA	*Paulys Realencyclopädie der classischen Altertumswissenschaft*
PSI	Pubblicazioni della Società Italiana, Papiri Greci et Latini
QDAP	*Quarterly of the Department of Antiquities in Palestine*
RAC	*Reallexikon für Antike und Christentum*
RB	*Revue Biblique*
RechSR	*Recherches de Science Religieuse*
RheinMus	*Rheinisches Museum für Philologie*
REG	*Revue des Etudes Grecques*
REJ	*Revue des Etudes Juives*
RHPR	*Revue d'Histoire et Philosophie Religieuses*
SAB	Sitzungsberichte der Deutschen (Preussischen) Akademie der Wissenschaften zu Berlin
SAH	Sitzungsberichte der Heidelberger Akademie der Wissenschaften
SB	*Sammelbuch griechischer Urkunden aus Ägypten*, ed. F. Preisigke, F. Bilabel and E. Kiessling
SBS	Stuttgarter Bibelstudien
SC	Sources Chrétiennes

ScrHier	*Scripta Hierosolymitana*
SEG	Supplementum epigraphicum Graecum
SupplNovTest	Supplements to *Novum Testamentum*
SVF	Stoicorum Veterum Fragmenta
TDNT	*Theological Dictionary of the New Testament*, ed. G. Kittel and G. Friedrich
TU	Texte und Untersuchungen
VT	*Vetus Testamentum*
WdF	Wege der Forschung
WMANT	Wissenschaftliche Monographien zum Alten und Neuen Testament
ZAW	*Zeitschrift für die Alttestamentliche Wissenschaft*
ZDPV	*Zeitschrift des Deutschen Palästina-Vereins*
ZNW	*Zeitschrift für die Neutestamentliche Wissenschaft*
ZPapEp	*Zeitschrift für Papyrologie und Epigraphik*
ZThK	*Zeitschrift für Theologie und Kirche*

BIBLIOGRAPHY

Abel, F.-M., 'Alexandre le Grand en Syrie et en Palestine', *RB* 43, 1934, 528–45; *RB* 44, 1935, 42–61.

———, *Géographie de la Palestine* I, II, Paris ³1967.

———, *Histoire de la Palestine depuis la conquête d'Alexandre jusqu'à l'invasion arabe* I, II, Paris 1952.

———, 'La Syrie et la Palestine au temps de Ptolémée Ier Soter', *RB* 44, 1935, 559–81.

Bengtson, H., *Griechische Geschichte von den Anfängen bis in die römische Kaiserzeit*, HAW III/4, Munich ⁴1969.

———, *Die Strategie in der hellenistischen Zeit* I–III, Münchener Beiträge zur Papyrusforschung und antiken Rechtsgeschichte 26, 32, 36, Munich 1937–52, revised impression 1964–67.

Berve, H., *Das Alexanderreich auf prosopographischer Grundlage* I, II, Munich 1926.

Bi(c)kerman(n), E. J., *Chronology of the Ancient World*, London 1968.

———, 'La Coelé-Syrie. Notes de Géographie historique', *RB* 54, 1947, 256–68.

———, *From Ezra to the Last of the Maccabees*, New York 1962.

———, *Der Gott der Makkabäer*, Berlin 1937.

———, *Institutions des Séleucides*, Bibliothèque archéologique et historique 26, Paris 1938.

———, 'The Septuagint as a Translation', *PAAJR* 29, 1959, 1–39.

Braun, R., *Kohelet und die frühhellenistische Popularphilosophie*, BZAW 130, Berlin 1973.

Braunert, H., *Binnenwanderung*, Bonner historische Forschungen 26, Bonn 1964.

Deissmann, A., *Light from the Ancient East*, London 1910.

Delcor, M., *Le Livre de Daniel*, Paris 1971.

Denis, A.-M., *Fragmenta Pseudepigraphorum quae supersunt Graeca*, Leiden 1970.

———, *Introduction aux Pseudépigraphes grecs d'Ancien Testament*, Leiden 1970.

Feldman, L. H., 'The Orthodoxy of the Jews in Hellenistic Egypt', *Jewish Social Studies* 22, 1960, 215–37.

Fraser, P. M., *Ptolemaic Alexandria* I–III, Oxford 1972.

Frey, J.-B., *Corpus Inscriptionum Iudaicarum* I, II, Rome 1936–52.

Gager, J. G., *Moses in Greco-Roman Paganism, JBL* Monograph Series 16, Nashville and New York 1972.

Hadas, M., *Hellenistic Culture. Fusion and Diffusion*, New York 1959.

Harmatta, J., 'Irano-Aramaica (Zur Geschichte des frühhellenistischen Judentums in Ägypten)', *Acta Antiqua* 7, 1959, 337–409.

Hengel, M., 'Anonymität, Pseudepigraphie und "Literarische Falschung" in der jüdisch-hellenistischen Literatur', in *Pseudepigrapha* I, Entretiens sur l'antiquité classique XVIII, Vandoeuvres-Genève 1972, 229–329.

——, *Judaism and Hellenism*, London and Philadelphia 1974.

——, 'Proseuche und Synagoge. Jüdische Gemeinde, Gotteshaus und Gottesdienst in der Diaspora und in Palästina', in *Tradition und Glaube*, Festschrift for K. G. Kuhn, Göttingen 1971, 157–84.

——, 'Die Synagogeninschrift von Stobi', *ZNW* 57, 1966, 145–83.

——, 'Zwischen Jesus und Paulus. Die "Hellenisten", die "Sieben" und Stephanus', *ZThK* 72, 1975, 151–206.

Jones, A. H. M., *The Cities of the Eastern Roman Provinces*, Oxford ²1971.

Jüthner, J., *Hellenen und Barbaren*, Das Erbe der Alten, NF VIII, Leipzig 1923.

Kahrstedt, U., *Syrische Territorien in hellenistischer Zeit*, AGG, philosophisch-historische Klasse, NF XIX 2, Berlin 1926.

Kippenberg, H. G., *Garizim und Synagoge*, Religionsgeschichtliche Versuche und Vorarbeiten 30, Berlin and New York 1971.

Launey, M., *Recherches sur les armées hellénistiques* I, II, Bibliothèque des Écoles françaises d'Athènes et de Rome 169, Paris 1949–50.

Lenger, M.-T., *Corpus des Ordonnances des Ptolemées*, Academie royale de Belgique, Memoires LXI, 3, Brussels 1964.

Marböck, J., *Weisheit im Wandel*, BBB 37, Bonn 1971.

Middendorp, T., *Die Stellung Jesu ben Siras zwischen Judentum und Hellenismus*, Leiden 1973.

Mørkholm, O., *Antiochus IV of Syria*, Classica et Mediaevalia, Diss. VII, Copenhagen 1966.

Niese, B., *Geschichte der griechischen und makedonischen Staaten* I–III, reprinted Darmstadt 1963.

Peters, J. P. and Thiersch, H., *Painted Tombs in the Necropolis of Marissa*, London 1905.

Peremans, W., *Vreemdelingen en Egyptenaaren in Vroeg-Ptolemaeisch Egypte*, Louvain 1943.

Pfister, F., *Alexander der Grosse in den Offenbarungen der Griechen, Juden, Mohammedaner und Christen*, AAB 1956, Schriften der Sektion Altertumswissenschaft, Heft 3.

——, 'Eine jüdische Grundungsgeschichte Alexandrias', SAH, phil-hist.Kl. 1914, 11.

Préaux, C., *L'économie royale des Lagides*, Brussels 1939.

——, *Les Grecs en Égypte d'après les archives de Zénon*, Brussels 1947.

Reinach, T., *Textes d'auteurs grecs et romains relatifs au Judaïsme*, Paris 1895, reprinted Hildesheim 1963.

Rostovtzeff, M., *Dura-Europos and its Art*, Oxford 1938.

——, *The Social and Economic History of the Hellenistic World*, Oxford 1941.

Schalit, A., *König Herodes*, Studia Judaica IV, Berlin 1969.

——, (ed.), *The World History of the Jewish People* VI, *The Hellenistic Age*, Jerusalem 1972.

Schmitt, H. H., *Untersuchungen zur Geschichte Antiochos' des Grossen und seiner Zeit*, Historia Einzelschriften 6, Wiesbaden 1964.

Schürer, E., *Geschichte des jüdischen Volkes im Zeitalter Jesu Christi* I–III, Leipzig 3,41901–9.

Schürer, E., Vermes, G. and Millar, F., *The History of the Jewish People in the Age of Jesus Christ* I, Edinburgh 1973; II, Edinburgh 1979.

Seibert, J., *Alexander der Grosse*, Erträge der Forschung 10, Darmstadt 1972.

——, *Untersuchungen zur Geschichte Ptolemaios' I*, Münchener Beiträge zur Papyrusforschung und antiken Rechtsgeschichte 56, Munich 1969.

Sellers, O. R., 'Coins of the 1960 Excavation at Shechem', *BA* 25, 1962, 87–96.

Sevenster, J. N., *Do You Know Greek?*, SupplNovTest 19, Leiden 1968.

Smith, Morton, *Palestinian Parties and Politics that Shaped the Old Testament*, New York and London 1971.

Speyer, W., 'Barbar A/B', *Jahrbuch für Antike und Christentum* 10, 1967, 251–67.

Stern, M., *Greek and Latin Authors on Jews and Judaism* I, *From Herodotus to Plutarch*, Jerusalem 1974.

Tarn, W. W. and Griffith, G. T. *Hellenistic Civilization*, Cleveland and New York 31961.

Tcherikover (Tscherikower), V., *Hellenistic Civilization and the Jews*, New York 1961.

——, 'Die hellenistischen Städtegründungen von Alexander dem Grossen bis auf die Römerzeit', *Philologus Supplement* XIX, Vol. 1, Leipzig 1927, 1–216.

——, 'Palestine under the Ptolemies', *Mizraim* 4/5, 1937, 7–90.

Tcherikover, V. A. and Fuks, A., *Corpus Papyrorum Judaicarum* I–III, Cambridge, Mass. 1957–64.

Thissen, H.-J., *Studien zum Raphiadekret*, Beiträge zur klassischen Philologie, Heft 23, Meisenheim am Glan 1966.

Treu, K., 'Die Bedeutung des Griechischen für die Juden im römischen Reich', *Kairos* 15, 1973, 123–44.

Uebel, F., *Die Kleruchen Ägyptens unter den ersten sechs Ptolemaern*, AAB, Klasse für Sprachen, Literatur und Kunst 1968, 3, Berlin 1968.

Vatin, C., *Recherches sur le mariage et la condition de la femme mariée a l'époque hellénistique*, Bibliothèque des Écoles françaises d'Athènes et de Rome 216, Paris 1970.

Walter, N., *Der Thoraausleger Aristobulos*, TU 86, Berlin 1964.

Weinberg, S. S., 'Tel Anafa: The Hellenistic Town', *IEJ* 21, 1971, 86–109.

Welles, C. B., *Royal Correspondence in the Hellenistic Period*, New Haven and London 1934.

Welten, P., *Geschichte und Geschichtsdarstellung in den Chronikbüchern*, WMANT 42, Neukirchen-Vluyn 1973.

Westermann, W. L., Keyes, C. W. and Liebesny, H., *Zenon Papyri II*, Columbia Papyri Greek Series No. 4, New York 1940.

Will, E., *Histoire politique du monde hellenistique (323–30 avant J.-C.)* I, II, Nancy 1966–67.

GENEALOGIES

The following three genealogies are based on those to be found in H. Bengtson, *Griechische Geschichte von den Anfängen bis in die römische Kaiserzeit*, HAW III, 4, Munich [4]1969, 569-71, and in the *Lexicon der Alten Welt*, Zurich-Stuttgart 1965, 173f., 2475f., 2759f. (H. H. Schmitt).

1. THE ANTIGONIDS

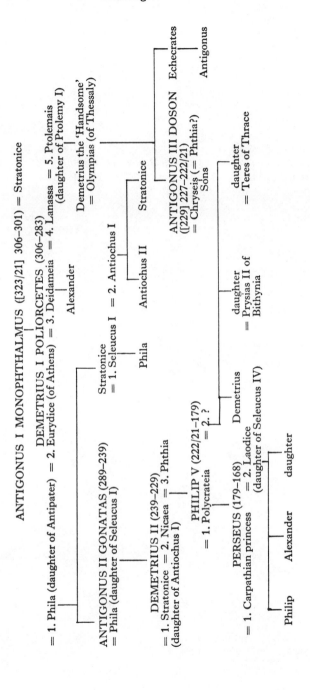

2. THE PTOLEMIES (to Ptolemy VIII)

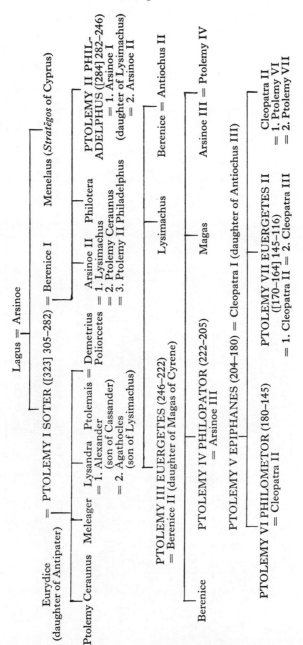

3. THE SELEUCIDS (to Antiochus IV)

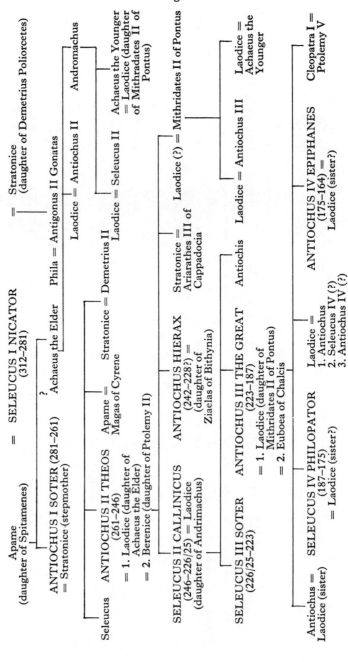

NOTES

Chapter 1

1. See the survey in Smith, *Palestinian Parties*, 149f.
2. Diodore XVI, 41–45; F. Kienitz, *Die politische Geschichte Ägyptens vom 7. bis 4. Jh.*, Berlin 1953; Smith, *Palestinian Parties*, 59f., 156f.
3. D. Auscher, 'Les Relations entre la Grèce et la Palestine avant la conquête d'Alexandre', *VT* 17, 1967, 8–30; Smith, *Palestinian Parties*, 57ff.; S. S. Weinberg, 'Post-Exilic Palestinian-Archaeological Report', *Proceedings of the Israel Academy of Sciences and Humanities* IV, 1971, 78–97; Hengel, *Judaism and Hellenism* I, 32–35. There is a survey of literature on the minting of coins in Syria and Phoenicia in the period before Alexander in G. Le Rider, 'Les ateliers monétaires de la côte syrienne, phénicienne, palestinienne . . .', in *Congresso Internazionale di Numismatica, Roma 11–16 Settembre 1961*, *Vol. I Relazioni*, Rome 1961, 69–71.
4. Arrian II, 11, 10; Curtius Rufus III, 13, 1ff.; IV, 1, 4; Plutarch, *Alexander* 24. For the following see Abel, 'Alexandre le Grand'; id., *Histoire de la Palestine* I, Paris 1952, 1–22; F. Schachermeyr, *Alexander der Grosse*, Vienna 1973, 206ff., 211ff.; V. Tcherikover, in A. Schalit (ed.), *World History* VI, 56ff.
5. Diodore XVII, 40, 2f.; Arrian II, 16, 7f.; Curtius Rufus IV, 2, 2f.
6. Schachermeyr, *Alexander*, 215.
7. O. Eissfeldt, 'Tyros', in *PRECA*, 2. R. VII, 1948, 1887–90.
8. Diodore XVII, 46, 4; Arrian II, 24, 5f.; Curtius Rufus IV, 4, 17; H. Volkmann, *Die Massenversklavungen der Einwohner eroberter Städte in der hellenistisch-römischen Zeit*, AAMz 1961, no. 3, 62, 112.
9. Justin, *Epitome* XVIII, 3, 19; and on this Tcherikover, 'Städtegründungen', 68f.; Eissfeldt, 'Tyros', 1895. For the revival of Tyre see H. Seyrig, 'Sur une prétendue ère tyrienne', *Syria* 34, 1957, 93–8; cf. Le Rider, 'Ateliers monétaires', 71f.
10. U. Rappaport, 'Gaza and Ascalon in the Persian and Hellenistic Periods in Relation to their Coins', *IEJ* 20, 1970, 75f.
11. Arrian II, 25, 4–27, 7; Curtius Rufus IV, 6, 7–30; Diodore XVII, 48; Plutarch, *Alexander* 25.

12. Hegesias, FGrHist 142 F 5, quoted by Dionysius Halicarnassus, *De comp. verb.* 18; Curtius Rufus, IV 6, 26–29. W. W. Tarn, *Alexander the Great* II, Cambridge 1948, 265–70, doubts the historicity of this action because of his tendency to idealize Alexander. But cf. already Abel, 'Alexandre le Grand', 47f. For the origins of Batis see E. Merkel in F. Altheim and R. Stiehl, *Die Araber in der Alten Welt* I, Berlin 1964, 170ff.; he differs from Tarn in seeing him as an Arab, rather than an Iranian.

13. Arrian III, 27, 7, and on this Abel, 'Alexandre le Grand', 48. The report of the permanent destruction (Strabo XVI, 2, 30) refers to Alexander Jannaeus, Josephus, *BJ* (= *Bellum Judaicum*) I, 87; *Antt.* (= *Antiquities*) XIII, 358ff.

14. Jones, *Cities*, 234; see pp. 65f., 75f. Schachermeyr, *Alexander*, 216, refers to the heroic defence of other Semitic cities like Carthage, Jerusalem, Hatra and Palmyra in antiquity against their later Roman conquerors.

15. Arrian II, 25, 4; 20.4f.; Curtius Rufus IV, 2, 24; Plutarch, *Alexander*, 24; cf. Abel, 'Alexandre le Grand', 543f.

16. Curtius Rufus IV, 1, 5; 2, 1; cf. H. Willrich, *Juden und Griechen vor der makkabäischen Erhebung*, Göttingen 1895, 14ff.

17. *Hist. nat.* XII, 25, 117, and Tcherikover, *Hellenistic Civilization*, 422 no. 31: 'The sentence *Alexandro Magno res ibi gerente* may be interpreted as referring to Alexander's stay in Syria as a whole.'

18. Tcherikover, 'Städtegründungen', 75f., 143; Jones, *Cities*, 237f., cf. n. 39 below.

19. Josephus, *Antt.* XI, 302–47. The earlier literature, including the rabbinic parallels, can be found in R. Marcus, *Josephus*, Loeb Classical Library VI, 1958, Appendix C, 512–32, and Seibert, *Alexander der Grosse*, 103–7, 271–4; cf. also Tcherikover, *Hellenistic Civilization*, 41–50; id., in A. Schalit (ed.), *World History* VI, 57ff., 311f.; Kippenberg, *Garizim*, 44–57; A. Alt, *Kleine Schriften . . .* II, Munich ³1964, 357f.

20. A. Büchler, 'La Relation de Josèphe concernant Alexandre le Grand', *REJ* 36, 1898, 1–26.

21. Op. cit., 45, 420 n. 17 (quot.).

22. *Ps. Kallisthenes Rezension Γ Buch 2*, ed. H. Engelmann, Beiträge zur klassischen Philologie 12, Meisenheim am Glan 1963, 216–30 = chs. 24–28.

23. Hengel, *Judaism and Hellenism* I, 61; see the large number of Hellenistic-type representations on the seal impressions in the documents from the death cave of Wādi Dāliya: see F. M. Cross, 'Papyri of the Fourth Century . . .', in *New Directions in Biblical Archaeology*, ed. D. N. Freedman and J. C. Greenfield, New York 1969, 47.

24. Josephus, *Antt.* XI, 310.

25. *Antt.* XI, 325.
26. Thus still Tcherikover, *Hellenistic Civilization*, 44, 419 n. 12.
27. F. M. Cross, 'The Discovery of the Samaria Papyri', *BA* 26, 1963, 110–21; id., 'Aspects of Samaritan and Jewish History in Late Persian and Hellenistic Times', *HTR* 59, 1966, 201–11; id., 'Papyri', 41–62; Kippenberg, *Garizim* 44.
28. IV, 28, cf. Abel, *Histoire* I, 11, and Hengel, *Judaism and Hellenism* I, 15, against Tcherikover, *Hellenistic Civilization*, 420 n. 13.
29. Josephus, *Antt.* XI, 321, 345.
30. Josephus, *Contra Apionem* I, 192, 200; cf. *Antt.* XI, 339.
31. *bYoma* 69a and in the scholion on *Megillat Taanit*, see H. Lichtenstein, 'Die Fastenrolle', *HUCA* 8/9, 1931/32, 339; and on this Tcherikover, *Hellenistic Civilization*, 48: 'the town's mention in the tale is purely a matter of convention'.
32. Josephus, *Antt.* XI, 338; cf. Antiochus III, *Antt.* XII, 142, 150, see p. 43 below; Arrian I, 17, 4; 18, 2; VII, 20, 1; Strabo XVI, 1, 11 (C 741). Cf. Curtius Rufus IV, 7, 5 on Egypt.
33. *Antt.* XI, 340ff.; see the rabbinic versions mentioned in n. 31 above.
34. Curtius Rufus IV, 8, 9f.
35. There is a German translation of the Chronicle, which has been preserved in Armenian, in J. Karst, GCS 20, Leipzig 1911, 197; however, see 199 on the year 296/5 BC: 'those who had settled there from Perdicca' (see below pp. 13f.). Cf. Jerome's version, ed. R. Helm, GCS 47, Berlin 1956, 123, 128; the passages from the Byzantine historians are also given on p. 365.
36. See n. 27 above: cf. also P. W. Lapp on the further investigation of the death cave, *RB* 72, 1965, 405–9.
37. Thus Ps. Hecataeus, who according to Josephus, *Contra Apionem* II, 43, is exaggerating: 'Because of the friendliness and fidelity shown to him by the Jews, he gave them the territory of Samaria as a tribute-free possession.' According to I Macc. 11.34, towards 145 BC Demetrius II gave the Jews three Samaritan districts. It is possible that Demetrius is merely confirming an earlier frontier. It is striking that the Wādi Dāliya near Jericho, with its cave of refuge, lies in what later became Jewish territory. Perhaps Alexander had already put this under Jerusalem.
38. Isa. 24.10; 25.2; 26.5f.; 27.10; by contrast, see the expansion of all the frontiers in 26.15.
39. K. Elliger, 'Ein Zeugnis aus der jüdischen Gemeinde im Alexanderjahr 332 v. Chr.', *ZAW* 62, 1949/50, 63–115; M. Delcor, 'Les allusions à Alexandre le Grand dans Zach. IX, 1–8', *VT* 1, 1951, 110–124.
40. According to E. Stern, 'The Dating of Stratum II at Tell Abu

Hawam', *IEJ* 18, 1968, 213–19, the second phase of the settlement of Tell Abū Hawām near Haifa and the old Acco, Šikmona and Stratum I of Megiddo were destroyed in connection with the siege of Tyre.

41. For Gerasa see H. Seyrig, 'Alexandre le Grand, fondateur de Gérasa', *Syria* 42, 1965, 25–28. A coin from Capitolias (Bēt Rās) north of Gerasa calls Alexander the *genarchēs* of the city: id., *Syria* 36, 1959, 66.

42. Kippenberg, *Garizim*, 56.

43. G. E. Wright, *Shechem*, New York and Toronto 1965, 170–85; cf. O. E. Sellers, 'Coins of the 1960 Excavation at Shechem', *BA* 25, 1962, 87–96, and the stimulating account in E. Bickerman, *From Ezra to the Last of the Maccabees*, 41ff.

44. R. J. Bull and G. E. Wright, 'Newly Discovered Temples on Mt Gerizim in Jordan', *HTR* 58, 1965, 234–7; R. J. Bull and E. F. Campbell Jr, 'The Sixth Campaign at Balatah (Shechem)', *BASOR* 190, 1968, 17f., and the short note by E. F. Campbell Jr, *BASOR* 204, 1971, 4.

45. Strabo XVI, 2, 2 (C 749); Josephus, *Antt.* XVII, 20; XVIII, 85; Sir. 50.25f.; see Hengel, *Judaism and Hellenism* II, 18 n. 156; Bickerman, *From Ezra*, 43f.; against Alt, *Kleine Schriften* II, 403f.

46. So Abel, *Histoire* I, 13; Berve, *Alexanderreich* II, 108f. differs. Cf. A. B. Bosworth, 'The Government of Syria under Alexander the Great', *CBQ* 23, 1973, 46–64.

47. Jones, *Cities*, 236f.

48. Rostovtzeff, *Social and Economic History* I, 129f.; see also the hoards of Alexander coins in Byblos and Galilee; A. R. Bellinger, *Berytus* 10, 1952/53, 37–49; and J. Baramki, *QDAP* 11, 1945, 86–90; Abel, *Histoire* I, 15ff.

49. W. Schmitthenner, 'Über eine Formveränderung der Monarchie seit Alexander d. Gr.', *Saeculum* 19, 1968, 31–46.

50. Abel, *Histoire* I, 13; Berve, *Alexanderreich* 60, 259, differs somewhat. Cf. also Tcherikover in, A. Schalit (ed.), *World History*, 311f. n. 21.

51. Pfister, 'Eine jüdische Gründungsgeschichte Alexandrias'; id., *Alexander d. Gr.*; M. Simon, 'Alexandre le Grand, Juif et Chrétien', *RHPR* 21, 1941, 177–91; I. J. Kazis (ed.), *The Book of the Gests of Alexander of Macedon*, 1962; G. Cary, *The Medieval Alexander*, 1956.

52. Dan. 11.3, cf. 8.5–21; Ethiopian Enoch 90.2; IV Sib. 87–96, and on this Justin, *Epitome* XII, 16, 9–11.

53. Dan. 11.4, cf. 8.8, 22f.

54. Dan. 7.7.

55. I Macc. 1.1–4.

56. Cf. Dan. 8.10 and II Macc. 9.10 on Antiochus IV Epiphanes. For the divinization of Alexander see Seibert, *Alexander*, 192ff.; Schachermeyr, *Alexander*, 242ff., 525ff., 595ff. For the conflict which the Jews

had with the ruler cult, see M. Hengel, *Die Zeloten*, AGSU 1, Leiden
²1976, 103ff.; id., *Judaism and Hellenism* I, 518ff., see also index, II,
326 s.v.

Chapter 2

1. Arrian II, 6,6: for this reason he was in command of the prisoners
under Alexander. Cf. further Seibert, *Untersuchungen*, 27ff., and R. M.
Errington, 'From Babylon to Triparadeisos', *JHS* 90, 1970/71,
49–77.

2. Arrian, *De reb. succ. Alex.*, FGrHist 156 F 9, 25; Diodore XIII,
28, 1; Abel, *Histoire* I, 24: 'ce . . . véritable temple ambiant'.

3. Will, *Histoire* I, 35ff.

4. For the designation 'Coele Syria' see Bickerman, 'Coelé-Syrie';
K. Galling, *Studien zur Geschichte Israels im persischen Zeitalter*,
Tübingen 1964, 201ff., differs.

5. Diodore XVIII, 43, cf. Appian, *Syr.* 43; Seibert, *Untersuchungen*,
129.

6. Diodore XVIII, 73, 2.

7. Diodore XIX, 57–59; 61.5. Cf. Tcherikover in A. Schalit (ed.),
World Hist. VI, 64.

8. Diodore XIX, 80; Justin, *Epitome* XV, 1, 6–9; Plutarch, *Demetrius*
6. For the site of the battle see Abel, 'Syrie', 567–75; cf. Seibert,
Untersuchungen, 162ff.

9. Bickerman, *Chronology*, 71ff.

10. Diodore XIX, 93, 2; Plutarch, *Demetrius* 6, 3. The place 'Myus'
cannot be identified. It will be on the upper part of the Orontes; cf.
R. Dussaud, *Topographie historique de la Syrie antique et médiévale*,
Paris 1927, 410.

11. Diodore XIX, 93, 5–7.

12. F.-M. Abel, 'L'expédition des Grecs à Pétra en 312 av. J.-C.',
RB 46, 1937, 373–91; R. Dussaud, *La pénétration des Arabes en Syrie
avant l'Islam*, Paris 1955, 21ff.; Hengel, *Judaism and Hellenism* I, 37f.

13. F. Jacoby, PRECA VIII, 1913, 1540ff. (quot. 1540); FGrHist
154 T 6 = Diodore XIX, 110, 1–3.

14. Tcherikover, 'Städtegründungen', 69–81; id., *Hellenistic
Civilization*, 90–116, esp. 105f.; Jones, *Cities*, 237f. At least Pella is the
Hellenization of an earlier Semitic name: in the Egyptian sources from
the nineteenth century BC *phr*, in the Talmud *peḥal*, in Arabic *faḥil*.
Arṣūf could be connected with the semitic God *Rešef-Mikal*, who was
identified with Apollo on Cyprus.

15. Hengel, *Judaism and Hellenism* I, 14f.

16. Schalit, *König Herodes*, 186f.

17. Hengel, *Judaism and Hellenism* I, 20ff.; Jones, *Cities*, 240. In
Diodore XIX, 95, 2, Jerome of Cardia speaks of *tēs Idoumaiās eparchiās*.

18. Diodore XX, 73, 74, 76; F.-M. Abel, 'Les Confins de la Palestine et de l'Égypte sous les Ptolémées', *RB* 48, 1939, 219–33.
19. Hengel, *Judaism and Hellenism* I, 6.
20. *Contra Apionem* I, 214.
21. Bickerman, *From Ezra*, 46f.
22. In Porphyry, *De Abstinentia* II, 26 (Nauck 155); see also Reinach, *Textes*, 7f.; Stern, *Authors* I, 8ff.
23. In Clement of Alexandria, *Strom.* I, 72, 4 = FGrHist 715 F 3; Reinach, *Textes*, 13; Stern, *Authors* I, 45ff.
24. Diodore XL, 3 = FGrHist 264 F 6; cf. Reinach, *Textes*, 14ff.; Stern, *Authors* I, 20ff.
25. Cf. Hengel, 'Anonymität', 301ff.
26. *Contra Apionem* I, 186–9.
27. L. Y. Rahmani, 'Silver Coins of the Fourth Century BC from Tel Gamma', *IEJ* 21, 1971, 158–60. The substitution of *hphh* for the earlier reading *yhd* does not exclude a reference to the high priest Hezekiah from Ps. Hecataeus. His departure to Egypt was probably caused by tensions in Jerusalem. Furthermore, we may assume that Alexander and the Diadochi simply continued the Persian system of administration: see A. Kindler, *IEJ* 24, 1974, 75f.
28. Kindler, *IEJ* 24, 1974, 73–6 and D. Jeselsohn, *IEJ* 24, 1974, 77f. For the *yehud* coins generally and in particular for the god on the winged wheel see the work by my pupil H. Kienle, *Der Gott auf dem Flugelrad*, GOF VI, 7, Wiesbaden 1975, with a detailed bibliography.
29. *Contra Apionem* I, 208–11; *Antt.* XII, 5f.; cf. also Appian, *Syrian Wars*, 50.
30. Ps. Aristeas 4, 12ff. 23. The contrast with Ps. Hecataeus, see n. 27 above and p. 88 below, is probably connected with the fact that in 312 BC the 'high priest Hezekiah' went into voluntary exile in Egypt.
31. *Hellenistic Civilization*, 56f., against Abel, *Histoire* I, 31.
32. Hengel, *Judaism and Hellenism* I, 15ff., 41ff.; see pp. 85f.
33. Hengel, *Judaism and Hellenism* I, 42.
34. Cf. I Chron. 12.9,25; II Chron. 11.12; 12.35; 14.7; 25.5; fortification and siege engines: II Chron. 26.9, 14ff., cf. also the economy of the royal domains, v.10; the rejection of the mercenaries from the northern kingdom in the war against the Seirites of Sela (Petra), 25, 6ff. For Hellenistic influence on Chronicles see Welten, *Geschichte und Geschichtsdarstellung*, 106ff., 110ff., 199ff. For the work of the Chronicler and Hellenistic historiography see Bickerman, *From Ezra*, 11–31. For the tradition of the 'holy war' see M. Hengel, *Die Zeloten*, AGSU 1, Leiden ²1975, 277ff.
35. Welten, *Geschichte und Geschichtsdarstellung*, 201; Hengel, *Judaism and Hellenism* I, 17f.

Chapter 3

1. Polybius V, 86, 10.
2. Hengel, *Judaism and Hellenism* II, 3 n. 4.
3. Eusebius, *Chronicle of Jerome*, ed. Helm, GCS 47, 127f., cf. 369; on this Hengel, *Judaism and Hellenism* II, 3 n. 2; Will, *Histoire* I, 73, 79f.; see 65f. below.
4. Diodore XXI, 1, fr. 5; Polybius V, 67, 4–10; Hengel, *Judaism and Hellenism* II, 3 n. 1.
5. Hengel, *Judaism and Hellenism* II, 4 n. 12.
6. For the term see Bickerman, 'Coelé-Syrie', 256–60; Tcherikover, *Hellenistic Civilization*, 423 n. 36.
7. H. Seyrig, 'Aradus et sa pérée sous les rois Séleucides', *Syria* 28, 1951, 206–20; Jones, *Cities*, 238f.
8. Will, *Histoire* I, 115.
9. H. Volkmann, 'Ptolemaius', in *PRECA* XXIII, 2, 1959, 1646; Will, *Histoire* I, 121ff.
10. W. W. Tarn, 'Ptolemy II and Arabia', *JEA* 15, 1929, 9–25; H. Kortenbeutel, *Der ägyptische Sud- und Osthandel in der Politik der Ptolemäer und römischen Kaiser* (phil. Diss.), Berlin 1931. For Palestine see Hengel, *Judaism and Hellenism* I, 14, 15, 37f. Cf. also F. Altheim and R. Stiehl, *Die Araber in der Alten Welt* I, Berlin 1963, 65–79: Ptolemaeans and Nabataeans.
11. D. Lorton, 'The Supposed Expedition of Ptolemy II to Persia', *JEA* 57, 1971, 160–4. Theognis XVII, 86, says that Ptolemy 'cut off' a bit of 'Phoenicia, Arabia and Syria'.
12. *Polyaenus* IV, 15; *PCZ* 59006; cf. M. Rostovtzeff, *Caravan Cities*, Oxford 1932, 95ff., and Will, *Histoire* I, 128f.; Tcherikover, 'Palestine', 34ff. For the *pompé* see Athenaeus V, pp. 196ff., according to Kallixenos of Rhodes.
13. Against U. Kahrstedt, *Syrische Territorien in hellenistischer Zeit*, AGG NF XIX, 2, Berlin 1926, 23f., and Will, *Histoire* I, 209, 215. *PCZ* 59251 does not say that Sidon was the first city south of the (new) frontier. For example, PSI 495 mentions a Ptolemaic garrison in Tripolis. Cf. Tcherikover, 'Palestine', 81 n. 51. The first Ptolemaic city on the coast was Orthosia.
14. Basic details in Tcherikover, 'Palestine'; id., *Hellenistic Civilization*, 60ff.; papyri relating to the Jews have been collected in V. A. Tcherikover and A. Fuks, CPJ I, 115–46. Cf. Abel, *Histoire* I, 60–71; Hengel, *Judaism and Hellenism* I, 7, 21f., 39ff., 47f, 267ff.
15. W. W. Tarn, *JHS* 46, 1926, 162: 'The Zenon papyri exhibit a country which might never have heard of battles, with its finance minister seemingly anxious only about his new apple trees.'
16. For the route of his travels see S. Mittmann, 'Zenon im Ostjordan-

land', in *Archaeologie und Altes Testament*, Festschrift K. Galling, Tübingen 1970, 199–210.

17. For Ptolemaic economic policy see Préaux, *L'économie*; Rostovtzeff, *Social and Economic History* I, 255–422; for its relationship to foreign policy see Will, *Histoire* I, 148–78, and ibid., 155 on monetary policy. For the role of Alexandria in economics see Fraser, *Ptolemaic Alexandria* I, 132–88.

18. Tarn and Griffith, *Hellenistic Civilization*, 179.

19. Hengel, *Judaism and Hellenism* I, 19ff., 35ff., 39ff.

20. PER 24552 gr (= SB 8008); text with bibliography and commentary in Lenger, *Corpus*, 37ff., nos. 21/22.

21. Rostovtzeff, *Social and Economic History* I, 351ff.; Hengel, *Judaism and Hellenism* I, 39f., 43ff., 46f. For Bet 'Anat see id., *ZNW* 59, 1968, 11ff., 23ff.

22. L. A. Geraty, *Third Century BC Ostraca from Khirbet el Kom*, Phil. Diss. Harvard Divinity School 1972; summary *HTR* 65, 1972, 595f. Cf. the summary report by J. S. Holladay, *IEJ* 21, 1971, 175ff.; *RB* 78, 1971, 593ff.

23. Hengel, *Judaism and Hellenism* I, 20.

24. Bengtson, *Strategie* III, 166ff.; Hengel, *Judaism and Hellenism* I, 20ff. For Marisa see *PCZ* 59015 and on it Tcherikover, 'Palestine', 40ff., and *Hellenistic Civilization*, 65f. There is a detailed commentary in F.-M. Abel, 'Marisa dans le Papyrus 71 de Zénon . . .', *RB* 33, 1924, 566–74.

25. Tcherikover, 'Palestine', 81 n. 56.

26. M. Avi-Yonah, 'Scythopolis', *IEJ* 12, 1962, 123–34. Cf. Schürer, *Geschichte des jüdischen Volkes* II, 56, 171.

27. Tcherikover, 'Städtegründungen', 65ff.

28. Pseudo-Skylax, ch. 87; Strabo XVI, 2, 27 (758); Pliny the Elder, *Historia Naturalis* 5, 75ff. and G. Hoelscher in *PRECA* XXII, 1, 1953, 271f. Alt, *Kleine Schriften* II, 386 n. 3, refers to a Berenice both on the Golan plateau and in the coastal plain. Here he conjectures 'edges of a domain'.

29. S. S. Weinberg, 'Tel Anafa: The Hellenistic Town', *IEJ* 21, 1971, 86–109.

30. Jones, *Cities*, 239ff.; Abel, *Histoire* I, 51ff.; Tcherikover, *Hellenistic Civilization*, 90ff.; id., 'Palestine', 44f.

31. Hengel, *Judaism and Hellenism* I, 70f.; see p. 65 below.

32. Hengel, *Judaism and Hellenism* II, 37 n. 373; cf. A. Kriesis, *Greek Town Building*, Athens 1965, 71ff. For the foundation sagas see Hengel, *Judaism and Hellenism* II, 172, n. 27; Schürer, Vermes and Millar, *History* II, 29–52; S. A. Cook, *The Religion of Ancient Palestine*, London 1930, 153–225.

33. For the distinction between *polis* and *ethnos* see Bickerman, *Institutions*, 141ff., 164ff., and above, p. 142 n. 45.

34. See the decree of Ptolemy II relating to the scheduling of native slaves, n. 20 above. Lenger, *Corpus*, 43, no. 22, lines 17ff. on the soldiers and other settlers living with native wives. See pp. 61ff. below.

35. *PCZ* 59003; 59076; 59075 = V. A. Tcherikover and A. Fuks, CPJ I, 118ff., 125ff., nos. 1, 2, 4, 5; Hengel, *Judaism and Hellenism* I, 15, 22f., 47f., 268ff.

36. *PCZ* 59015; see n. 24 above; *PCZ* 59018 = V. A. Tcherikover and A. Fuks, CPJ I, 129f., no. 6.

37. P. Lond. 1948 and PSI 554, and on them M. Hengel, 'Das Gleichnis von den Weingärtnern Mc 12, 1–12 im Lichte der Zenonpapyri und der rabbinischen Gleichnisse', *ZNW* 59, 1968, 11–16, 23ff.

38. Hengel, *Judaism and Hellenism* I, 38f., 41ff., 48ff.

39. Peters and Thiersch, *Painted Tombs*; Hengel, *Judaism and Hellenism* I, 43f., 62ff.; II, 195 n. 233.

40. A. Pridik, *Berenike, die Schwester König Ptolemaios III. Euergetes*, Acta et commentationes Universitatis Tartuensis B. Humaniora XXXV/ XXXVI, Dorpat 1935; Will, *Histoire* I, 213ff.

41. H. Volkmann, in *PRECA* XXIII, 2, 1959, 1655.

42. The main source is P. Petrie II, no. 46, and III, no. 144 = FGrHist 160. The author of this account of the war is Ptolemy III or his brother Lysimachus. See also the Adulis inscription, OGIS 54, and Polyaenus. VIII, 50; Will, *Histoire* I, 223ff.; Volkmann, *PRECA* XXIII, 2, 1959, 1669ff. differs.

43. Eusebius, *Chronicle* (ed. Karst, GCS 20, 118), for 242/1 BC (according to FGrHist 260 F 32, from Porphyry).

44. Justin, *Epitome* XXVII, 2,5–9, cf. Dan. 11.9.

45. *Contra Apionem* II, 48.

46. Dan. 11.5–9, and see the commentary by Jerome, Migne *PL* 25, 1884, 559ff. = CC 75A, 1964, 899ff., who in turn draws on Porphyry, *Adversus Christianos*, FGrHist 260 F 33–61.

47. A. Segré, 'The Ptolemaic Copper Inflation 230–140 BC', *American Journal of Philology* 63, 1942, 174ff.; Sellers, 'Coins', 92; Hengel, *Judaism and Hellenism* I, 27f., 44f., and the statistics on coins, II, 208f.

48. Josephus, *Antt*. XII, 158–236. Cf. J. A. Goldstein, 'The Tales of the Tobiads', in *Christianity, Judaism . . .*, Studies for Morton Smith, 1975, III, 85–123, which stresses the historical value of the reports, but proposes another chronology.

49. *Antt*. XII, 224. See Rostovtzeff, *Social and Economic History* I, 349; II, 1400 n. 132; Tcherikover, *Hellenistic Civilization*, 130ff.; Hengel, *Judaism and Hellenism* I, 27f., 268ff.; Schürer, Vermes and Millar, *History* I, 140 n. 4; 149f. n. 30.

50. Quoted in Josephus, *Antt*. XII, 136; cf. Sib. 3. 213f. For other details about Jerusalem see Hengel, *Judaism and Hellenism* I, 53f.

51. Josephus, *Antt*. XII, 224.

52. Braun, *Kohelet*; Hengel, *Judaism and Hellenism* I, 115–28.
53. Rostovtzeff, *Social and Economic History* I, 350.
54. The text of this passage is not completely certain. For the whole passage see E. Bickerman, *Four Strange Books of the Bible*, New York 1967, 141–67. Hengel, *Judaism and Hellenism* I, 50ff.; see pp. 120f. below.
55. II Chron. 26.10; cf. also the list of royal functionaries in I Chron. 27.25ff.
56. E. Bammel, *ptōchos*, *TDNT* 6, 888–902.

Chapter 4

1. Seleucus I was murdered in 281 and Seleucus III Soter in 223; Antiochus II Theos died in 246 in his forties, in uncertain circumstances.
2. Schmitt, *Untersuchungen*, 2ff.
3. Polybius V, 42,5–9. For the passages from Polybius in the following section see F. W. Walbank, *A Historical Commentary on Polybius* I, Oxford 1957.
4. V, 34; H. Volkmann, in *PRECA* XXIII/2, 1959, 1679ff.; for the date see A. E. Samuel, *Ptolemaic Chronology*, Münchener Beiträge zur Papyrusforschung . . . 43, Munich 1962, 106ff. Cf. Porphyry according to Jerome in Dan. 11.13, Migne *PL* 25, 1884, 562 = CC 75A, 1964, 907: '(*Antiochos*) *qui, contempta Philopatoris Ptolemaei ignavia* . . .'
5. Polybius V, 45,5–46,5. For the site of Gerrha and Brochoi see R. Hachmann (ed.), *Bericht über die Ergebnisse der Ausgrabungen in Kamid el-Loz (Libanon) in den Jahren 1966 und 1967*, Saarbrücker Beiträge zur Altertumskunde 4, Bonn 1970, 84f.
6. Polybius V, 58–61,2; cf. Abel, *Histoire* I, 74ff.
7. Polybius V, 40,1–3; 61,3–62,6.
8. Polybius V, 66,67; Will, *Histoire* II, 25ff.
9. Polybius V, 68,6. Cf. Josephus, *Antt*. XVI, 361 = *BJ* I, 539, and B. Spuler, 'Platanos 3', in *PRECA* XX/2, 1950, 2338f.
10. Polybius V, 70,1–11; Hengel, *Judaism and Hellenism* I, 8f.
11. Polybius V, 70,12; Kamus = Kamōn, Judg. 10.5; Judith 4.4(?); Josephus, *Antt*. V, 254; Abel, *Géographie* II, 412; Gephrus = Ephron: I Macc. 5.46; II Macc. 12.27; id., *Géographie* I, 318f.; in V, 71, 2 Polybius speaks of the district of Galatis, i.e. the biblical Gilead.
12. Polybius V, 71,1–3; Niese, *Geschichte* II, 378.
13. Polybius V, 71,4–10; cf. Mittmann, 'Zenon', 208f.
14. Polybius V, 71, 11; cf. the same terminology in II Macc. 15.1.
15. III Macc. 1.3, and on this Tcherikover and Fuks, CPJ I, 230ff., no. 127; cf. Polybius V, 81.
16. Polybius V, 79, 9,12; 85,4. The 'Syrians' in 85.10 are probably identical with 'those sought out from the whole kingdom and armed in Macedonian fashion', 79,4.

17. Polybius V, 82–86; W. Peremans, 'Notes sur la bataille de Raphia', *Aegyptus* 31, 1951, 214ff.

18. Cf. Porphyry/Jerome in Dan. 11.12, loc. cit.: '*omnem Antiochus amisit exercitum et, per desertum fugiens, paene captus est.*'

19. Polybius V, 86,9.

20. Polybius V, 87; Thissen, *Studien*, 19, 60ff., §§23–25.

21. Polybius V, 107, 1–3, and on this Thissen, *Studien*, 62, on the basis of §25 of the decree of Raphia.

22. Polybius V, 86,11; the decree of Raphia: Thissen, *Studien*, 15, §15f.: 'He went through the other places which were in his kingdom. He went into the temples which were there. He made burnt offerings and drink offerings, in that all the people who were in the cities received him . . .'

23. Marisa: F. J. Bliss and R. A. S. Macalister, *Excavations in Palestine 1898–1902*, London 1902, 62f., supplemented by C. Clermont-Ganneau, *CRAI* 1900, 535–41; Joppa-Jaffa: B. Lifschitz, 'Beiträge zur palästinischen Epigraphik', *ZDPV* 78, 1962, 82f.; inscription of the hipparch Dorymenes from the neighbourhood of Tyre, *Supplementum Epigraphicum Graecum* VII, no. 325, and on it Polybius V, 61,9.

24. Thissen, *Studien*, 19, §26; Polybius V, 87,6 speaks of three months.

25. III Macc. 1.8–2.24; V. A. Tcherikover, 'The Third Book of Maccabees as a Historical Source of Augustus' Time', *ScrHier* 7, 1961, 1–26. Bibliography in J. Tondriau, 'La Dynastie Ptolémaique et la religion dionysiaque', *Chronique d'Egypte* 25, 1950, 310ff.

26. Dan. 11.10–12, and on it Jerome, *PL* 25, 1884, 561f. = CC 75A, 1964, 905–7.

27. Justin, *Epitome* XXX, 1,6.

28. Will, *Histoire* II, 32ff.

29. For the problem, see S. K. Eddy, *The King is Dead*, Lincoln 1961, 290ff.; there is a new edition of the potter's oracle in L. Koenen, 'Die Prophezeiungen des "Töpfers" ', *ZPapEp* 2, 1968, 178–209.

30. Josephus, *Antt.* XII, 186–22, 228–36, quot. 224, 229; see Hengel, *Judaism and Hellenism* I, 269–76.

31. Josephus, *Antt.* XII, 228f.; Tcherikover, *Hellenistic Civilization*, 80f., 154.

32. Sirach 50.4.

33. T. Reekmans, 'Economic and Social Repercussions of the Ptolemaic Copper Inflation', *Chronique d'Égypte* 24, 1949, 324–42; H. Volkmann, 'Ptolemaios IV. Philopator', *PRECA* XXIII/2, 1959, 1690; see p. 147 n. 47 above.

34. III Macc. 2.25ff.; Volkmann, 'Ptolemaios IV Philopator', *PRECA* XXIII/2, 1959, 1689, see p. 103 below.

35. Schmitt, *Untersuchungen*, 92ff.

36. Josephus, *Antt.* XII, 147–53; A. Schalit, 'The Letter of Antiochus III to Zeuxis regarding the Establishment of Jewish Military Colonies in Phrygia and Lydia', *JQR* NF 50, 1960, 289–318; E. Olshausen, 'Zeuxis', *PRECA* 2. Reihe X, 1972, 383f. The authenticity of this letter, which was defended by A. Shalit and others, is now doubted by I.-D. Gauger, *Beiträge zur jüdischen Apologetik*, Cologne and Bonn 1977, 3–19.

37. II Macc. 8.20; Hengel, *Judaism and Hellenism* I, 16.

38. Schmitt, *Untersuchungen*, 104ff.; Bickerman, *Institutions*, 236ff., 247ff.; F. Taeger, *Charisma* I, Stuttgart 1957, 314ff.

39. Will, *Histoire* II, 99f.; Schmitt, *Untersuchungen*, 237ff. For the dating see Samuel, *Ptolemaic Chronology*, 108ff.

40. Niese, *Geschichte* II, 577ff.; H. Volkmann, 'Ptolemaios V. Epiphanes', *PRECA* XXIII/2, 1695. For the dating, M. Holleaux, 'La chronologie de la 5e Guerre de Syrie', *Études d'épigraphie et d'histoire grecques* III, Paris 1942, 318–35.

41. Polybius XVI, 22a; 18,2; Josephus, *Antt.* XII, 130f.; XIII, 150f.; Justin, *Epitome* XXXI, 11f.

42. Josephus, *Antt.* XII, 135 = Polybius XVI, 39,1.

43. Dan. 11.14; Tcherikover, *Hellenistic Civilization*, 77ff.

44. *In Dan.*, *PL* 25, 1884, 562 = CC 75A, 1964, 908: '*Iudaea . . . in contraria studia scindebatur, aliis Antiocho, aliis Ptolemaeo faventibus.*'

45. Polybius XVI, 18f., following Zeno of Rhodes, see F. W. Walbank, *A Historical Commentary on Polybius* II, Oxford 1967, 523ff.

46. Jerome, *In Dan.*, *PL* 25, 1884, 563 = CC 75A, 910: '*donec, fame superatus, Scopas manus dedit et nudus cum sociis dimissus est.*' Porphyry and Jerome are right in connecting Dan. 11.15 with the siege of Sidon and not with that of Gaza.

47. Josephus, *Antt.* XII, 133, 136, 138. Jerome, loc. cit.: '*quod praesidium Scopiae in arce Hierosolymorum, annitentibus Judaeis, multo tempore oppugnaverit.*'

48. Loc. cit.: '*. . . et, optimates Ptolemaei partium secum abducens, in Aegyptum reversus est.*'

49. Josephus, *Antt.* XII, 129f., 139.

Chapter 5

1. Josephus, *Antt.* XII, 138–44; E. J. Bickerman, 'La charte séleucide de Jérusalem', *REJ* 100 = nos. 197/8, 1935, 4–35; Abel, *Histoire* I, 88–93; R. Marcus, in *Josephus* VII, Loeb Classical Library, London 1961, 743ff., 751ff.; Tcherikover, in A. Schalit (ed.), *World History* VI, 81ff.

2. *Antt.* XII, 145f.; E. Bickerman, 'Une proclamation séleucide relative au temple de Jérusalem', *Syria* 25, 1946/48, 67–85; Marcus, in *Josephus* VII, Loeb Classical Library, London 1961, 701ff.

3. Y. H. Landau, 'A Greek Inscription found near Hefzibah', *IEJ* 16, 1966, 54–70, and on it J. and L. Robert, 'Bulletin Épigraphique', *Revue des Études Grecques* 83, 1970, 469ff. no. 627.

4. II Macc. 4.11; cf. I Macc. 8.17. This Eupolemus is perhaps identical with the Jewish historian, fragments from whom have been preserved in Alexander Polyhistor: Hengel, *Judaism and Hellenism* I, 92ff.; see p. 115 below. Cf. now B. Z. Wacholder, *Eupolemus. A Study of Judaeo-Greek Literature*, New York 1974.

5. V. A. Tcherikover, 'Was Jerusalem a "Polis"?', *IEJ* 14, 1964, 61–78; Walbank, *Commentary* II, 546f. on Polybius XVI, 39,4.

6. Hengel, *Judaism and Hellenism* I, 25ff.

7. *Antt.* XII, 143: *atelesin einai.* For three years' freedom from taxation with the same formula in connection with a *synoikismos* see the letter of Antigonus to Teos, C. B. Welles, *Royal Correspondence in the Hellenistic Period*, New Haven and London 1934, 18, no. 34, lines 70f.

8. Hengel, *Judaism and Hellenism* I, 28f.

9. Bickerman, *Gott der Makkabäer*, 50ff.

10. II Macc. 4.9,19, see below, pp. 123f.

11. P. Herrmann, 'Antiochos der Grosse und Teos', *Anadolu* 9, 1965, 29–160.

12. Hengel, *Zeloten*, 219f.

13. Hengel, *Zeloten*, 204ff.

14. Hengel, *Judaism and Hellenism* I, 52f., 271f.

15. Polybius V, 65,3; OGIS I, 376, no. 230; Bengtson, *Strategie* II, 161ff., also presupposes it behind II Macc. 3.5.

16. Landau, 'Greek Inscription', 66 n. 15.

17. Josephus, *Antt.*, XII, 234ff., with an obviously wrong dating. See Hengel, *Judaism and Hellenism* I, 272f., 275.

18. Bickerman, *Institutions*, 170ff., on the local dynasts.

19. 'Städtegründungen', 70f., 175; *Hellenistic Civilization*, 101f., following A. Schlatter, *Zur Topographie und Geschichte Palästinas*, Stuttgart 1893, 314ff. One of the places could be identical with the Hellenistic settlement of Tell 'Anafa, which has been excavated very recently. See p. 26 above.

20. Polybius XVI, 27,5; Justin, *Epitome* XXX, 1,2; M. Holleaux, *CAH* VIII, 1954, 165f. For the new Roman orientation eastwards see H. H. Scullard, *Roman Politics 220–150 B.C.*, Oxford 1973, 89ff.

21. Livy, XXXV, 13; Polybius XVIII, 51,10; XXVIII, 20,9; Appian, *Syrian Wars* 5; Josephus, *Antt.* XII, 154f.; E. Cuq, 'La condition juridique de la Coelé-Syrie au temps de Ptolémée V Epiphane', *Syria* 8, 1927, 143–62; contrast Bengtson, *Strategie* II, 161 n. 2: 'an invention of Josephus'; Will, *Histoire* II, 161ff.

22. Livy XXXVII, 40; Appian, *Syrian Wars* 31 (according to Polybius).

23. Will, *Histoire* II, 185–93; A. H. MacDonald, 'The Treaty of Apamea', *Journal of Roman Studies* 57, 1967, 1–8. For Scipio's policy towards the East see Scullard, *Roman Politics 220–150 B.C.*, Oxford 1973, 128ff.

24. Hengel, *Judaism and Hellenism* I, 10f., 102f.; Mørkholm, *Antiochus*, 22–37, 'The Seleucid Kingdom after Apamea'.

25. Will, *Histoire* II, 200ff.

26. II Macc. 3; Polybius XXX, 26,9, cf. XXXI, 4,9; Hengel, *Judaism and Hellenism* I, 280f.

27. The high priest Onias again had close connections with Hyrcanus in Ammanitis, who was sympathetic to the Ptolemies, II Macc. 3.11; Hengel, *Judaism and Hellenism* I, 271.

28. Dan. 11.18f.

29. Text following A. Bentzen, *Daniel*, HAT I, 19, Tübingen ²1952, 80, and J. A. Montgomery, *A Critical and Exegetical Commentary on the Book of Daniel*, ICC, Edinburgh 1964, 442ff. (*bal-liḥyah* = LXX *en horkōi*).

30. Sir. 11.34; 13.2–20; 34.24,27 etc.; Hengel, *Judaism and Hellenism* I, 136ff.

31. 50.23f.; Hengel, *Judaism and Hellenism* I, 133f.

32. 15.11–17; 16.17–23; 41.8f.; Hengel, *Judaism and Hellenism* I, 141ff., 150ff., see below, pp. 121ff.

33. 24.23; Hengel, *Judaism and Hellenism* I, 160ff.; Marböck, *Weisheit*.

34. 36.1f., 9, 12, 17. The conjecture by T. Middendorp, *Die Stellung Jesu ben Siras zwischen Judentum und Hellenismus*, Leiden 1973, 125ff., that Sir. 36.1–17 was only added in the Maccabean period, is unjustified. However, he has valuable insights into the political and social setting, 137ff.; see my review in *JSJ* 5, 1974, 83–87. Num. 24.17 underlies 36.12(a). M. Segal, *Sepher Ben Sira' haš-šalem*, Jerusalem 1958, 227, sees Antiochus III as the 'head', while A. Caquot, 'Ben Sira et le Messianisme', *Semitica* 16, 1966, 48f., conjectures that there is a reference to the Aetolian Scopas. However, it can hardly be demonstrated that the poem was composed in the year 200. The saying could be directed against any Hellenistic ruler.

Chapter 6

1. Hengel, 'Anonymität', 252ff., 304.

2. Hengel, *Judaism and Hellenism* I, 3.

3. C. Préaux, 'Réflexions sur l'entité hellénistique', *Chronique d'Égypte* 40, 1965, 133ff.; Hengel, *Judaism and Hellenism* I, 1ff.

4. I, 6 (329C): *diallaktēs tōn holōn*.

5. I, 4 (328B).

6. Cf. Trajan in Pliny the Younger, *Ep.* X, 97, on the rejection of the anonymous denunciation: *nec nostri saeculi est*. A comparison with the

writing *De fortuna Romanorum* shows how much at the same time Plutarch had the Roman government in mind; see R. Flacellière, in *Mélanges J. Carcopino*, Paris 1966, 367–75, especially on chs. 2 and 13.

7. V. Martin, 'La politique des Achéménides', *MusHelv* 22, 1965, 38ff.: Ahuramazda has 'given all the kingdoms of the world into the hand' of the Great King. F. Wehrli, review of H. C. Baldry, *The Unity of Mankind in Greek Thought*, *Gnomon* 38, 1966, 643 = *Theoria und Humanitas*, Zürich and Munich 1972, 174.

8. Hengel, *Judaism and Hellenism* I, 180ff.

9. See the survey of literature by Seibert, *Alexander*, 207ff. A. Daskalakis, *Alexander the Great and Hellenism*, Saloniki 1966, gives a positive account of the idea of world empire and Hellenization. Schachermeyr, *Alexander*, 227ff., 319ff., 479ff., 487ff. rightly stresses Alexander's unbounded concern for power as a last motive.

10. A. Daskalakis, *The Hellenism of the Ancient Macedonians*, Saloniki 1965.

11. Seibert, *Alexander*, 186ff., 300ff.

12. On this see G. Delling, 'Philons Enkomion auf Augustus', *Klio* 54, 1972, 183. For the terminology *hellēnizein* and *hellēnismos* and the *hellēnistai* of Acts 6.1ff. see my study 'Zwischen Jesus und Paulus', *ZThK* 72, 1975, 166ff.

13. Libanius, *Orationes* 11, 103 (Foerster I, 469f.) on Seleucus I as a founder of cities: *all'hellēnizōn dietelese tēn barbaron*. Elsewhere *hellēnizein* means 'speak impeccable Greek' and transitively, 'translate into Greek'. See also p. 159 n. 131 below and *ZThK* 72, 1975, 167 n. 55.

Chapter 7

1. Jüthner, *Hellenen und Barbaren*; Speyer, 'Barbar'; H. Schwabl, 'Die Hellenen-Barbaren-Antithese im Zeitalter der Perserkriege', in *Grecs et Barbares*, Entretiens sur l'antiquité classique VIII, Vandoeuvres-Genève 1962.

2. H. E. Stier, *Die geschichtliche Bedeutung des Hellenennamens*, Arbeitsgemeinschaft für Forschung des Landes Nordrhein-Westfalen 159, Cologne 1970, 20.

3. Op. cit., 22ff.

4. Speyer, 'Barbar', 255f., 263f. The verdict of Pentheus on the successes of Dionysus among the barbarians, who all do homage to him, is typical: *phronousi gar kakion Hellēnōn polu*, Euripides, *Bacchae* 483.

5. *De prov. cons.* 5,10; Livy XXX, 39, 8 (following Polybius?); Josephus, *BJ* VI, 42; Tacitus, *Histories* 5,8,2; cf. Euripides, *Iphigeneia in Aulis* 1400f.; *Helen* 276; Speyer, 'Barbar', 253. For Philostratus see *Vit. Apoll.* VIII, 7,12 (I, 319f.). Cf. already the picture of the Phrygian-

Trojan slaves in Euripides: *Orestes* 1505ff.; *Andromache* 155ff., 173ff., 243, 261ff.; *Hecuba* 1199f. On the situation in the Roman Empire cf. A. N. Sherwin-White, *Racial Prejudice in Imperial Rome*, Cambridge 1967.

6. Aristotle, *Politeia* I, 2 (1252b), quoted Euripides, *Iphigeneia in Aulis* 1400; Plutarch, *De fortuna aut virtute Alexandri* I, 6 (329B); Jüthner, *Hellenen und Barbaren*, 25ff.; Speyer, 'Barbar', 256. Roman imperialism took over this thesis of Aristotle, see W. Capelle, *Klio* 25, 1932, 107ff.

7. Aristotle, *Politeia* I, 5 (1254a).

8. Xenophon, *Hellenica* II, 1,15,19; cf. Agesilaus VII, 5f.

9. 245c/d. For the rejection of mixed marriages see Euripides, *Medea* 591f.

10. XXXI, 29, 15; cf. already Isocrates, *Panegyricus* 181f., 184; Plato, *Republic* V, 470c: *polemious physei einai*; *Menex.* 242d: the Greeks fight each other until one side wins, but against barbarians until they have been annihilated. Polemic against the barbarians continues in Roman times, see e.g. Philostratus, *Vita Apollonii* VIII, 7,8 (I, 313, 7ff. Kayser): *polemiōtatous ontas kai ouk enspondous tōi peri hēmās genei* and the letter to Domitian, *Ep.* 21 (I, 350).

11. Cf. E. Schütrumpf, 'Kosmopolitismus oder Panhellenismus?', *Hermes* 100, 1972, 9ff.; Polybius XI, 5,6 (cf. XI, 4–6); also V, 104; IX, 37ff., and on this H. H. Schmitt, *Hellenen, Römer und Barbaren. Eine Studie zu Polybios*, Wissenschaftliche Beilage zum Jahresbericht 1957/58 des Humanistischen Gymnasiums Aschaffenburg, 3f. For Philo see *de Josepho* 29f.; cf. *Opif.* 3, 142; *Conf.ling.* 106; *Spec.leg.* 2, 165ff.; *Mig. Abr.* 59. See also M. Hammond, *City State and World State in Greek and Roman Political Theory until Augustus*, New York 1966.

12. Herodotus V, 22; cf. Daskalakis, *Hellenism*, 97ff.

13. Hengel, *Judaism and Hellenism* I, 66f.

14. Rostovtzeff, *Social and Economic History* III, Index s.v. 'intermarriage'; C. Vatin, *Recherches sur le mariage et la condition de la femme à l'époque hellénistique*, Bibliothèque des Écoles françaises d'Athènes et de Rome 216, Paris 1970, 132ff.

15. Livy XXXVII, 54, 18ff., following Polybius.

16. Rostovtzeff, *Dura Europos*, 21f. Vatin, *Recherches sur le mariage*, 136ff.

17. *Annals* VI, 42,1; cf. Plato, *Ep.* 353a; *Laws* 692c/693a; Polybius III, 58,8; Plutarch, *Timoleon* 17,2 (244) and G. Walser, *Rom, das Reich und die fremden Völker*, Basler Beiträge zur Geschichtswissenschaft 37, 1951, 71. For Seleuceia on the Tigris cf. Pliny the Elder, *Historia naturalis* VI, 122: *libera hodie ac sui iuris Macedonumque moris.*

18. Euagoras 20,47 (pp. 14,28f., van Horst).

19. Josephus, *Antt.* XVIII, 372ff.

20. Quoted from his history by Josephus, *Antt.* XIV, 115.

21. Josephus, *Contra Apionem* II, 68–72: *Iudaei, Graeci, multitudo Aegyptiorum.* The mercenaries seem to have been the basis of the Jewish element in the population. Polybius XXXIV fr. 14 = Strabo XVII, 1, 12 (797): Egyptians, mercenaries, citizens; cf. Fraser, *Ptolemaic Alexandria* I, 61ff., 76ff.

22. In *Kunst und Altertum* V, 1925, 1–82; reprinted in *Der Hellenismus in Mittelasien*, WdF XCI, 1969, 19–72; quot. 47f. For Isocrates and Erastosthenes, whose remarks were not common currency, see pp. 76, 68 below.

23. Braunert, *Binnenwanderung*, 54, 75ff.; Fraser, *Ptolemaic Alexandria* I, 70ff., 82ff.

24. Alexandria: *Antt.* XII, 8; XIV, 188; XIX, 281; *c. Ap.* II, 32, 38ff., 69, 71f. Cf. Tcherikover, CPJ I, 41, 61ff.; II, 29ff., 36ff. for the letter of Claudius; Antioch: *Antt.* XII, 119ff.; Caesarea: *BJ* II, 266ff., 284ff.; cf. A. N. Sherwin-White, *Racial Prejudice in Imperial Rome*, 86–101; Tcherikover, *Hellenistic Civilization*, 296–331.

25. Livy XXXVII, 54,22, on the Massilians: *mores et leges et ingenium sincerum integrumque a contagione accolarum servarunt*; cf. however also XXXVIII, 17,12; the *politeuma mikton* of Emporion is a special exception: Strabo III, 4, 8 (160). The 'Mixohellenes' in Olbia were a group apart from the 'full citizens'; see Vatin, *Recherches sur le mariage*, 144ff.

26. See n. 21 above, cf. Justin, *Epit.* XXXVIII, 8, 6f., and on this Braunert, *Binnenwanderung*, 77ff.; Fraser, *Ptolemaic Alexandria* I, 87ff., differs.

27. XXXVIII, 17,11; even Philo explains the superiority of the Greeks by the exceptional climate of their country: *De prov.*, in Eusebius *Praeparatio Evangelica* VIII, 14, 66, GCS 43,1, ed. Mras p. 477, cf. Speyer, 'Barbar', 256. According to Plato, *Republic* 435e, the Greeks are eager to learn while the Phoenicians and Egyptians are simply covetous, cf. *Timaeus* 24c and *Laws* 747c.

28. Arrian VII, 4, 4ff.; 12.2.

29. Antoninus Liberalis, *Met.* 39, ed. M. Papathomopulos, Paris 1968, 64f.; see Rostovtzeff, *Social and Economic History* II, 1071f.

30. Cf. Willrich, *PRECA* IV, 2, 1901, 2800f., and Stähelin, op. cit., XI, 1, 1921, 786f. Will, *Histoire* II, 342ff., 363ff.

31. See the *prostagma* of Ptolemy II concerning the seizure of cattle and slaves in 'Syria and Phoenicia', 260 BC: *SB* 8008; bibliography in Lenger, *Corpus des Ordonnances*, 37ff., no. 22 lines 17ff.

32. Vatin, *Recherches sur le mariage*, 32ff.; Fraser, *Ptolemaic Alexandria* I, 71ff.

33. Braunert, *Binnenwanderung*, 41ff., 72ff.; cf. A. Świderek, 'La société indigène en Égypte au IIIe siècle avant notre ère d'après les

archives de Zenon', *Journal of Juristic Papyrology* 7/8, 1953/4, 256: 'Il
semble pourtant qu'en général la situation d'un homme pauvre, fut-il
Égyptien, Grec, Syrien, Arabe ou d'une autre nationalité encore, était
presque la même.' It should be added that in Egypt poverty was the rule,
whereas among the Greeks it was the exception.

34. A. E. Samuel, 'The Greek Element in the Ptolemaic Bureaucracy',
in *Proceedings of the Twelfth International Congress of Papyrology*,
American Studies in Papyrology VII, Toronto 1970, 443–53. For being
bilingual see R. Remondon, 'Problèmes du Bilinguisme dans l'Égypte
Lagide', *Chronique d'Égypte* 39, 1964, 126–46, and the qualifications by
W. Peremans, 'Über die Zweisprächigkeit im Ptolemäischen Ägypten',
in *Studien zur Papyrologie und antiken Wirtschaftsgechichte*, Friedrich
Oertel zum 80. Geburtstag gewidmet, Bonn 1964, 49–60. For *philhellēn*
see the comic fragment cited by A. S. Hunt and J. G. Smyly, in P.Tebt
III, 703 (p. 71) = *Selected Papyri*, ed. D. L. Page, Vol. III, 1941, 466
no. 112; M. Rostovtzeff, *Social and Economic History* III, 1421 n. 212.

35. Tarn and Griffith, *Hellenistic Civilization*, 201; A. Świderek, 'La
société grecque en Égypte au IIIᵉ siècle av. n.è.d'après les archives de
Zenon', *Journal of Juristic Papyrology* 9/10, 1955/56, 365f.

36. C. B. Welles, 'The Egyptians under the First Ptolemies', in
Proceedings . . . (see n. 34), 505–10.

37. A. Świderek, 'A la cour alexandrine d'Apollonius le dioecète',
Eos 50, 1959/60, 81–9.

38. Rostovtzeff, *Social and Economic History* II, 1070ff.; Préaux,
'Reflexions'; id., *Grecs en Égypte*.

39. For the Roman period, M. Rostowzew, *Studien zur Geschichte des
römischen Kolonats*, BhAPF 1, 1910, reprinted Darmstadt 1970, 204ff.,
is still important.

40. M. Launey, *Recherches sur les armées hellénistiques*, Bibliothèque
des Écoles françaises d'Athènes et de Rome 169, 1, 2, Paris 1949/50, I,
535ff.; the statistics, I, 89ff., show clearly the increase in the Semitic
element.

41. Polybius X, 27, 3; Pliny, *Historia naturalis* VI, 117: *Macedones
eam in urbes congregavere propter ubertatem soli.* E. Meyer (see n. 22), 29.
For Antiochus IV see Hengel, *Judaism and Hellenism* I, 227f.; Mørkholm, *Antiochus*, 115ff.; Jones, *Cities*, 247ff.; see also p. 114 below.

42. Cf. the *Hellēnogalatai*, Diodorus V, 32, or the *Gallograeci*, Livy
XXXVIII, 17, 9, and the *mixhellēnes* among the Carthaginian mercenaries, Polybius I, 67, 7.

43. XIV, 5, 24f. (678/9). That Greek cities and barbarian peoples and
rulers existed side by side in Asia Minor is an old theme: see already
Euripides, *Bacchae* 17ff.: *migasin Hellēsi barbarois th'omou.*

44. Speyer, 'Barbar', 259f.

45. Schmitt, *Untersuchungen*, 7f.

46. *De fin.* II, 49; cf. *De div.* 1.84; see Jüthner, *Hellenen und Barbaren,* 137 n. 151. For the Jewish division into three see Paul, Rom. 1.14,16; Col. 1.13. Cf. Josephus, *BJ* 5,17; *Antt.* 4,12; 11,229; 16,177; Philo, *Vit. Mos.* 2,12,19ff.; *Praem. et poen.* 165; *Spec. leg.* 2,165ff.

47. Hengel, *Judaism and Hellenism* I, 71: about 200 BC the 'suffete' *dikastēs* Diotimus from Sidon is celebrated as victor in the Pan-Hellenic Nemean chariot race at Argos in a Greek verse inscription. Cf. p. 117 below.

48. W. Peremans and E. van 't Dack, *Prosopographia ptolemaica* VI, Studia Hellenistica 17, Louvain 1968, 95f., no. 15085. Cf. pp. 21f. above.

Chapter 8

1. W. L. Westermann, 'The Ptolemies and the Welfare of their Subjects', *American Historical Review* 4, 1937/8, 270–87. Préaux, *Grecs en Égypte.*

2. Antiphon in H. Diels and W. Kranz, *Die Fragmente der Vorsokratiker,* Zurich and Berlin [11]1964, II, 352f. fr. 44 B II, 10: 'By nature we are all created equal in every respect, barbarians and Greeks.' See E. Schütrumpf, 'Kosmopolitismus', *Hermes* 100, 1972, 20ff.

3. Diogenes: Diogenes Laertius VI, 63; cf. already Democritus in Diels and Kranz, *Die Fragmente der Vorsokratiker* II, 194 fr. 247.

4. For Zeno see M. Pohlenz, *Die Stoa,* Göttingen 1959, I, 22f.; II, 14; Epicurus in Clement of Alexandria, *Stromateis* I, 15, 67, 1 (GCS 52, p. 42, ed. Stählin and Früchtel).

5. Strabo I, 4, 9 (66/7). It seems to me that the interpretation of Eratosthenes' saying in H. Dörrie, 'Die Wertung der Barbaren im Urteil der Griechen . . .', in *Antike und Universalgeschichte,* Festschrift H. E. Stier, Münster 1972, 155ff., goes too far. He sees this as the 'birth certificate' of Hellenism and conjectures that Eratosthenes had both Aristotle's letter to Alexander and Alexander's negative reply.

6. *Greek Anthology* VII, 417, 419, translated by Beckby; cf. Hengel, *Judaism and Hellenism* I, 84ff.; see p. 118 below.

7. Cf. Ps. Plato, *Epinomis,* 986e–987d, on the barbarian origins of astronomy and the final comment: 'Whatever the Greeks may have received from the barbarians, they improved upon.' See O. Reverdin, 'Crise spirituelle et évasion', in *Grecs et Barbares* (see p. 153 n. 1 above), 103ff.; cf. Jüthner, *Hellenen und Barbaren,* 22ff.; J. Kerschensteiner, *Platon und der Orient,* 1945.

8. Speyer, 'Barbar', 258ff., 267, 269ff.; cf. also Philo, *Quod omnis,* 73ff., 94ff.

9. Reverdin, 'Crise spirituelle et évasion', in *Grecs et Barbares,* 97ff. Diodore, II 29, 4ff. praises Chaldaean 'philosophy' as opposed to Greek, presumably following Ctesias.

10. W. Speyer, 'Hekataios', *Der kleine Pauly* II, Stuttgart 1967,

cols. 980ff. For the excursus on the Jews see J. G. Gager, *Moses in Greco-Roman Paganism*, Nashville and New York 1972, 26–37.
   11. K. Thraede, 'Erfinder', *RAC* V, Stuttgart 1962, cols. 1242ff., 1247ff., 1268ff. This also includes the theme of the 'theft of the philosophers', which can be found from Philo onwards.
   12. For the hymn to Tyche see *Selected Papyri*, ed. D. L. Page, III, 1941, 432 no. 99; Pliny the Elder, *Historia Naturalis* II, 22; cf. C. Schneider, *Kulturgeschichte des Hellenismus* II, Munich 1969, 830ff. For the ruler cult see M. P. Nilsson, *Geschichte der griechischen Religion* II, Munich ²1961, 132–84, 200ff., 208ff.; Schneider, *Kulturgeschichte des Hellenismus* II, Munich 1969, 888ff., is more positive; his criticism of Nilsson on p. 905 seems to me to be unjustified. Nilsson was right in seeing this as a symptom of decline. Immediately before his description of *fortuna*, in one breath Pliny justifies the 'humanist religion' of the ruler cult and condemns traditional belief in the efficacy of the gods. Here he is still completely in the tradition of the Hellenistic environment.
   13. Cf. Fraser, *Ptolemaic Alexandria* III, 70, index s.v. Sarapis.
   14. W. W. Tarn and G. T. Griffith, *Hellenistic Civilization*, 338f.; cf. also Schneider, *Kulturgeschichte des Hellenismus* II, 876–87, and M. P. Nilsson, *The Dionysiac Mysteries of the Hellenistic and Roman Age*, Lund 1957; Fraser, *Ptolemaic Alexandria* I, 201ff.: 'Certainly no Olympian deity was so easily accommodated to the requirements of the Ptolemies as was Dionysus' (quot. 206).
   15. B. V. Head, *Historia Numorum*, reprinted London 1963, 819ff.; G. Le Rider, *Suse sous les Séleucides et les Parthes*, Paris 1965, 95, 99, 181, 192, 196f., 372, 423f.; R. H. McDowell, *Coins from Seleucia, on the Tigris*, Ann Arbor 1935, 218f.
   16. Plutarch, *Crassus* 564 = Euripides, *Bacchae* 1169ff., cf. W. W. Tarn, *CAH* IX, 1932, 611f.
   17. Schürer, Vermes and Millar, *History* I, 578.
   18. Josephus, *Antt.* XIII, 318; cf. Schürer, Vermes and Millar, *History* I, 217 n. 6.
   19. Schürer, Vermes and Millar, *History* I, 219ff.; L. Y. Rahmani et al., 'The Tomb of Jason', *Atiqot* 4, 1964, 1–10; cf. also Schalit, *König Herodes*, 11, 106, 167f.; 196–206; 405, 530f.
   20. H. Dörrie, *Der Königskult des Antiochos von Kommagene im Lichte neuer Inschriften-Funde*, AAG III, 60, Göttingen 1964, 53, 29ff.; cf. Strabo XIV 2, 5. H. Waldmann, *Die Kommagenischen Kultreformen* ... EPROER 34, Leiden 1973, index, s.v. p. 246.
   21. Dörrie, *Königskult*, 31–3.
   22. Jacoby, FGrHist 790; C. Clemen, *Die phönikische Religion nach Philo von Byblos*, Mitteilungen der vorderasiatisch-ägyptischen Gesellschaft 42,3, 1939; O. Eissfeldt, *Kleine Schriften* II, Tübingen 1963, 127ff., 130ff.; R. du Mesnil du Buisson, *Nouvelles études sur les dieux et les mythes de Canaan*, EPROER 33, Leiden 1973, 61ff., 70ff.

23. Jacoby, FGrHist 680; H. R. Schwyzer, *Chairemon* (philosophical dissertation), Bonn 1932; A. J. Festugière, *La Révélation d'Hermès Trismégiste I: L'astrologie et les sciences occultes*, Paris 1950, 28ff.

24. Rostovtzeff, *Social and Economic History* I, 272ff., on Syria and Egypt.

25. Tcherikover, *Hellenistic Civilization*, 26ff., 161ff.

26. Rostovtzeff, *Social and Economic History* II, 883, 1545, and Braunert, *Binnenwanderung*, 72f.

27. *Panegyricus* 50.

28. Speyer, 'Barbar', 265; cf. Jüthner, *Hellenen und Barbaren*, 34ff. For the relationship between Philip and Isocrates and the revival of the notion of pan-Hellenism directed against the Persians see G. Dobesch, *Der panhellenische Gedanke im 4. Jahrhundert v.Chr. und der 'Philippos' des Isocrates*, Vienna 1968.

29. Liddell and Scott, *A Greek-English Lexicon*, ⁹1940, 536. See n. 12 p. 153 above.

30. Strabo XIV, 2, 28 (662).

31. Westermann, Keyes and Liebesny (eds.), *Zenon Papyri* II, 16ff., no. 66. For interpretation see C. Préaux, *Chronique d'Égpyte* 40, 1965, 130 n. 1 against the editors.

32. J. F. Oates, A. E. Samuel and C. Bradford Welles, *Yale Papyri in the Reinecke Rare Book and Manuscript Library* I, American Studies in Papyrology II, New Haven and Toronto 1967, 122f., no. 46; cf. Rostovtzeff, *Social and Economic History* III, 1421 n. 212.

33. Hengel, *Judaism and Hellenism* I, 39.

34. II Macc. 4.13; cf. 4.10,15; 6.9: *metabainein epi ta hellēnika*; 11.24; IV Macc. 8.8. Elsewhere *hellēnismos*, as *aretē logou*, means a pure Greek style, see Diogenes of Babylon (*c.* 240–152 BC), SVF III, 214 no. 24 = Diogenes Laertius VII, 59, the distinction between *hellēnismos* and *barbarismos*; cf. M. Hengel, *ZThK* 72, 1975, 167 n. 55.

35. *barbaroi*: II Macc. 2.21; 4.25; 10.4 cf. 5.22; 15.2 and Speyer, 'Barbar', 266f.; *politai*: II Macc. 4.5; 5.6,8,23; 9.19; 14.8; 15.30. Cf. also *patris*, 4.1; 5.8 etc.

36. II Macc. 2.21; 8.1; 14.38; cf. IV Macc. 4.26.

37. Esther 8.17, according to the LXX version. By contrast, the L version has only *perietemnonto*, see R. Hanhart, *Esther*, Septuaginta ... VIII, 3, Göttingen 1966, 196f.; Josephus, *BJ* II, 454; cf. Paul's attack on Peter, Gal. 2.14.

38. Diogenes Laertius I, 33; cf. Speyer, 'Barbar', 257.

39. *Tos Ber.* 7.18 (Zuckermandel 16 = Billerbeck III, 611) par. *j.Ber.* 9.2.13b, lines 57ff. (Krotoschin). According to *bab. Men.* 43b the tradition is ascribed to R. Meir.

40. Strabo I 4.9 (67). According to the Greek view, the barbarians had no *nomoi*, see Speyer, 'Barbar', 256.

41. II Macc. 8.17; cf. H. Strathmann, *polis*, TDNT 6, 523ff.; Hengel, 'Synagogeninschrift von Stobi', 179f. Cf. J. Lebram, 'Der Idealstaat der Juden', *Josephus-Studien*, Festschrift O. Michel zum 70. Geburtstag, Göttingen 1974, 233–53.

42. Josephus, *Contra Apionem* II, 65, cf. Tcherikover, *Hellenistic Civilization*, 375ff.

43. Cf. the petition of the Ionian cities to Marcus Agrippa: 'If the Jews belong with them, they should also worship their gods' (Josephus, *Antt.* XII, 126).

44. Josephus, *Contra Apionem* II, 66f. Cf. later Julian, *Ep.* 89a (Bidez I, 2, 154f.), who charges the Greeks with having 'forgotten the ancestral laws' to which the Jews remain faithful. However, he blames the Jews for 'not worshipping other gods', but 'in barbarian arrogance' worshipping only their own god, though all that is at stake is a difference in names.

45. E. Sandvoss, 'Asebie und Atheismus im klassischen Zeitalter der griechischen Polis', *Saeculum* 19, 1968, 312–29.

46. Josephus, *Antt.* XVI, 59.

47. Josephus, *Contra Apionem* II, 148; this charge is also made by Apion, *Contra Apionem* II, 135, and Celsus, Origen, *Contra Celsum* IV, 31. See Stern, *Greek and Latin Authors* I, 154f. For the theme of superstition see 547. For a general account of antisemitism in the ancient world see J. N. Sevenster, *The Roots of Pagan Antisemitism in the Ancient World*, Leiden 1975.

48. See Hengel, *Judaism and Hellenism*, index s.v. 'Inventor', II, 311; Josephus, *Contra Apionem* II, 293.

49. *Pro Flacco* 28, 67; Apuleius, Florida I, 6; Reinach, *Textes*, 336. Further examples in Speyer, 'Barbar', 262. Tacitus, *Hist.* V, 5, speaks of the *Iudaeorum mos absurdus sordidusque*. Julian the Apostate still accused the Jews of having a 'wretched and barbaric form of legislation': see Cyril, *adv. Iul.*, PG 76, 837D. Cyril countered this charge by referring to the unique antiquity of Mosaic legislation. Alexander Polyhistor already derived Jewish legislation from a woman named Moso, see Stern, *Greek and Latin Authors* I, 163, no. 52, presumably in order to mock them.

50. Josephus, *Contra Apionem* II, 165.

51. The concept appears only in the early Christian tradition, see the Kerygma Petrou in E. Hennecke, W. Schneemelcher and R. McL. Wilson, *New Testament Apocrypha* II, London 1965, 100 = Clement of Alexandria, *Stromateis*, VI, 5, 41, GCS 52, ed. Stählin, cf. Letter of Diognetus 1.1.

52. The triad of Jew, Greek and barbarian (with Scythian as the furthest extreme) is hinted at in Col. 3.11. See also pp. 154f., notes 19, 21.

53. For anti-Judaism see R. Rémondon, 'Les Antisémites de

Memphis', *Chronique d'Egypte* 35, 1960, 244–61; J. Yoyotte, 'L'Égypte ancienne et les origines de l'antijudaïsme', *Revue de l'Histoire des Religions* 163, 1963, 133–43; J. G. Gager, *Moses in Greco-Roman Paganism*, *JBL* Monograph Series 16, Nashville and New York 1972, 16 n. 4 (bibliography); D. Rokeaḥ, 'Jews and Their Law in the Pagan-Christian Polemic in the Roman Empire', *Tarbiz* 40, 1970/71, 462–71 (Hebrew); Fraser, *Ptolemaic Alexandria* I–III, see index s.v. 'Antisemitism', III, 7; Sevenster, see n. 47 above.
54. Tcherikover, *Hellenistic Civilization*, 264f.
55. Cf. Hengel, *Zeloten*, 296–318.

Chapter 9

1. Josephus, *Contra Apionem* I, 192ff.; II, 35, 42, 71f.; *Antt.* XI, 321, 339, 345; XII, 8. Hengel, *Judaism and Hellenism* II, 11 n. 84. The only unhistorical parts are Josephus' reports of the *isopoliteia* granted by Alexander to the Jewish military settlers in Alexandria. See Fraser, *Ptolemaic Alexandria* I, 54f.
2. According to the new version by J. Harmatta, 'Irano-Aramaica', *Acta Antiqua* 7, 1959, 337–409; see p. 338, col. A line 10.
3. Ps. Aristeas 13; see p. 19 above. According to Diodore XIX, 85,4, Ptolemy I arranged the distribution of eight thousand prisoners of war taken at the battle of Gaza among the nomarchies of Egypt. They were probably settled as cleruchs; see F. Uebel, *Die Kleruchen Ägyptens unter den ersten sechs Ptolemäern*, AAB 1968, 3, 349.
4. Josephus, *Contra Apionem* I, 189.
5. Tcherikover and Fuks, CPJ I, 148.
6. Tcherikover and Fuks, CPJ I, 27f.; Launey, *Recherches* I, 541–56. Uebel, *Kleruchen*, see index p. 420 s.v. '*Ioudaios*'.
7. Josephus, *Contra Apionem* II, 44; E. Will, 'La Cyrénaïque et les partages successifs de l'empire d'Alexandre', *Antiquité Classique* 29, 1960, 369ff.; Hengel, *Judaism and Hellenism* I, 16; S. Applebaum, *Greeks and Jews in Ancient Cyrene*, Jerusalem 1969 (Hebrew).
8. Strabo according to Josephus, *Antt.* XIV, 115, see p. 59 above. For the *politeuma* of the Jews in Berenice see CIG III, 5361, 5362, supplemented by SEG XVI, 931.
9. CPJ I, 118ff. no. 1.
10. II Macc. 12,19,24,35; Hengel, *Judaism and Hellenism* I, 276.
11. Josephus, *Antt.* XII, 147–53, see pp. 39f. above and p. 104 below.
12. Launey, *Recherches* I, 89ff., 546ff.; Tcherikover, *Hellenistic Civilization*, 276f.; Fraser, *Ptolemaic Alexandria* I, 55ff., 83f., 689f.
13. Fraser, *Ptolemaic Alexandria* I, 74; Tcherikover, *Hellenistic Civilization*, 68f.; Hengel, *Judaism and Hellenism* I, 14ff., 48ff.
14. *SB* 8008, see p. 24 above.
15. *PCZ* 59092.

16. Rostovtzeff, *Social and Economic History* III, 1365 n. 28; 1393f. n. 119; Préaux, *L'économie*, 303ff.; Hengel, *Judaism and Hellenism* II, 32f. nn. 323, 324; Peremans, *Vreemdelingen*, 86f., 168.

17. Tcherikover and Fuks, CPJ I, 125ff., no. 4 = *SB* 6790.

18. Ps. Arist. 4.12ff., 22ff.; Josephus, *Antt.* XII, 7; cf. *Contra Apionem* I, 210.

19. Against E. L. Abel, 'The Myth of Jewish Slavery in Ptolemaic Egypt', *REJ* 127, 1968, 253–8.

20. IG II², 10678, cf. L. B. Urdahl, 'Jews in Attica', *Symbolae Osloenses* 43, 1968, 48.

21. M. Mitsos, *Archaiologike Ephemeris* 1952 (ed. 1955), 194–6.

22. J.-B. Frey, CIJ I, 512ff., no. 709/10.

23. Tcherikover and Fuks, CPJ I, 29; see also III, 173f.: Jewish prosopography in Egypt.

24. Tcherikover and Fuks, CPJ I, 131ff. nos. 9–15.

25. Braunert, *Binnenwanderung*, 40ff.

26. Tcherikover and Fuks, CPJ I, 158ff. no. 22; 171ff. no. 28; III, 206; Hengel, *Judaism and Hellenism* II, 11 n. 87; Uebel, *Kleruchen*, 188f.

27. CPJ I, 179ff., no. 33.

28. CPJ I, 164ff., no. 24 of 16.4.174 BC: two Jewish cavalrymen each possess eighty acres of land: cf. I, 13–16.

29. CPJ I, 175ff. nos. 30, 31, from the middle of the second century BC.

30. CPJ I, 13ff.; cf. Josephus, *Contra Apionem* II, 35ff.

31. CPJ I, 194ff., *sabbataios*: nos. 51–60; Simon: nos. 61–63, 90, 107; cf. I, 18f.

32. Josephus, *Contra Apionem* I, 189; Tcherikover, *Hellenistic Civilization*, 300.

33. Fraser, *Ptolemaic Alexandria* I, 54ff., 83f. For the Jewish *politeuma* see Ps. Arist. 310 = Josephus, *Antt.* XII, 108 and the *politeuma* in Bérenice, above n. 8; Hengel, 'Proseuche', 170 n. 57 (bibliography).

34. *CRAI* 1907, 234–43, 375–80; Frey, CIJ 1424–31; Fraser, *Ptolemaic Alexandria* I, 57; II, 141, n. 165.

35. Josephus, *Antt.* XII, 184, 200f.

36. *Antt.* XII, 187; cf. XIX, 276f.

37. Tcherikover, *Hellenistic Civilization*, 338ff.

38. *Contra Apionem* I, 60, cf. II, 294.

39. III Macc. 1.3; CPJ I, 230ff., no. 127; A. Fuks, 'Dositheos son of Drimylos, A prosopographical Note', *Journal of Juristic Papyrology* 7/8, 1953/54, 205–9.

40. CPJ I, 236ff., no. 128. Tcherikover stresses against F. Bozza, *Aegyptus* 14, 1934, 212ff., that this could also be a reference to a Jewess. The papyrus is badly damaged. Perhaps the 'Paeonian' Theodotos son

of Cassandros, CPJ I, 158ff., no. 22, was the son of a Gentile father and a Jewish mother. Tcherikover suggests that he was exclusively of Jewish origin.

41. Tcherikover, CPJ I, 32ff. For Philo see I. Heinemann, *Philons griechische und jüdische Bildung*, reprinted Darmstadt 1962, 541ff.

Chapter 10

1. See the inscriptions in the necropolis in Alexandria, above p. 162 n. 34; the early Ptolemaic Cowley papyrus 81, above p. 161 n. 2. An Aramaic papyrus fragment with a list of sales of oil to people bearing Greek names probably also comes from the same early period: E. Bresciani, 'Uno Papiro Aramaico di età tolemaica', *Atti della Accademia nationale dei Lincei 8. Ser. 17*, 1962, 258–64. There are further instances of Aramaic testimony from the Hellenistic period in Tcherikover, CPJ I, 30 n. 76. The inscription from Abydus may be expanded from M. Lidzbarski, *Ephemeris für Semitische Epigraphik* III, 1909–15, 103ff. The Nash papyrus, with the Hebrew text of the Decalogue and of Deut. 6.4ff., comes from a markedly later period and probably served the purpose of an amulet, see CPJ I, 107f.

2. CPJ I, 30ff.

3. CPJ I, 190ff., no. 46, 20f.: a Jewish potter and his son, who leased a pottery in the Fayum along with three Egyptians: I, 222 no. 107: the Jewish tax-farmer Simon son of Iazaros in Upper Egypt (see p. 90 above).

4. We have evidence only that individual Jews bore Egyptian names, and from time to time come up against Jewish influence in the demotic magical papyri.

5. See the prosopography of Jewish names in CPJ III, 167ff.; Hengel, *Judaism and Hellenism* I, 63ff.

6. Hengel, *Judaism and Hellenism* II, 46 n. 53. For Egypt, see CPJ I, 29; III, 191f.

7. Launey, *Recherches* II, 954ff., 959ff., 974ff., 1064ff.; see n. 10 below.

8. Cf. J. A. L. Lee, *JTS* 23, 1972, 430–7: 'In particular, the Israelite host in its journey from Egypt to Canaan is very like an army on the march, and is readily described in military language' (quot. 437). The same thing is already true of the 'expedition' of the patriarchs from the time of Abraham. B. H. Stricker, *De brief van Aristeas. De hellenistische codificaties der praehelleense godsdiensten*, Amsterdam 1956, overemphasizes and misinterprets the initiative of Ptolemy II as a drive towards Hellenization; see the criticism of R. Hanhart, 'Fragen um die Entstehung der LXX', *VT* 12, 1962, 156ff. Cf., however, Bickerman, 'Septuagint', 8ff.; and S. Jellicoe, *The Septuagint and Modern Study*, Oxford 1968, 55.

9. Taeger, *Charisma* I, 304 n. 137; N. Walter, *Der Thoraausleger*

Aristobulos, TU 86, Berlin 1964, 24f. n. 23; Fraser, *Ptolemaic Alexandria* II, 442 n. 770.

10. OGIS 737; Pap. Giss. 99 in F. Zucker, *Doppelinschrift spätptolemäischer Zeit aus der Garnison von Hermopolis Magna,* AAB 1937, 6, 13. Cf. U. Rapaport, 'Les Iduméens en Égypte', *Revue de Philologie* III, 43, 1969, 73–82; Fraser, *Ptolemaic Alexandria* I, 280f.; II, 438ff.

11. Hengel, *Judaism and Hellenism* I, 255ff.; Gager, *Moses,* passim.

12. Hengel, 'Proseuche', 162 n. 2.

13. Hengel, 'Proseuche', 161f.

14. CIJ 1440 = OGIS 726 from Schedia near Alexandria; CIJ 1532 A (reprinted in CPJ III, 164) = *SB* 8939 from Arsinoe–Krokodeilonpolis in the Fayum.

15. *Theos hypsistos:* CIJ 1433; 1443 (votive offering from the police officer Ptolemy and the Jews in Athribis); cf. also the inscriptions in Delos, CIJ 726–31, and the two prayers for vengeance from Rheneia, the island cemetery of Delos, CIJ 725. *Theos megas:* CIJ 1432 = OGIS 742; 1532: *theos megas megas hypsistos;* here Jewish derivation is uncertain. For the whole question see Hengel, *Judaism and Hellenism* I, 297ff.

16. Ganschinietz, 'Iao', in *PRECA* IX, 1914, 698–711.

17. Cf. S. Jellicoe, *The Septuagint and Modern Study,* 270ff. For the magical effect of the divine name see Artapanos, FGrHist 726 = Eusebius, *Praeparatio Evangelica* IX, 27, 24f.

18. Bickerman, *Septuagint*; but see H. S. Gehman, 'The Hebraic Character of LXX Greek', *VT* I, 1951, 81–90; 3, 1954, 141ff., and N. Turner, *Grammatical Insights into the New Testament,* Edinburgh 1965, 183ff., on the problem of Jewish Greek. See also S. Daniel, *Recherches sur le vocabulaire du culte dans la Septante,* Paris 1966, 364ff., 382ff.

19. J. Freudenthal, 'Are there Traces of Greek Philosophy in the LXX?', *JQR* 2, 1890, 205–22; R. Marcus, 'Jewish and Greek Elements in the LXX', in *Louis Ginzberg Jubilee Volume* II, New York 1945, 227–45.

20. Bickerman, 'Septuagint', 34f.; cf. J. Whittaker, 'Moses atticizing', *Phoenix* 21, 1967, 196–201.

21. W. Michaelis, *TDNT* III, 914f.

22. Cf. Gen. 18.25; Ex. 4.16; 15.3; 24.10f.; Num. 12.8; Deut. 14.23, etc., see C. T. Fritsch, *The Anti-anthropomorphisms of the Greek Pentateuch,* Philadelphia 1943; but cf. H. M. Orlinsky, *HUCA* 30, 1959, 153ff., especially on Job.

23. Cf. the *gigantes,* Gen. 6.4; 10.8f. etc., the *seirēnes* in the translations of the prophets, Isa. 13.21; 34.13, etc.; H. A. Redpath, 'Mythological Terms in the LXX', *American Journal of Theology* 9, 1905, 34f.; H. Kaupel, 'Sirenen in der LXX', *BZ* 23, 1935/36, 158–65.

24. H. A. Redpath, 'The Geography of the LXX', *American Journal of Theology* 7, 1903, 289–307.

25. Bickerman, 'Septuagint', 33f.

26. E. Bickerman, 'Two Legal Interpretations of the LXX', *Revue internationale des droits de l'antiquité* III, 3, 1956, 81–104, on the periphrastic translation of *mohar*, 'bride price', with *phernē*, 'dowry', and on the expansion of Ex. 22.4 to include damage done to the fields by cattle. The replacement of 'medical expenses' (*iatreia*) Ex. 21.19 with bodily injury and the omission of the distinction between the two Hebrew terms for pledge, *ḥᵃbol* and *ᶜᵃbōt*, in favour of the term *enechuron* is also in accord with Greek legal thinking, see M. David, 'Deux anciens termes bibliques pour le gage', *OTS* 2, 1943, 79–86.

27. Ps. Aristeas 121, cf. Hengel, *Judaism and Hellenism* I, 59ff.

28. Num. 25.3,5; Deut. 23.18; cf. I Kings 15.12; Ps. 105 (106). 28; Jer. 16.5; Hos. 4.14; Amos 7.9; Wisdom 12.3f.; 14.15, 22f.; Philo, *Spec. leg.* I, 319–23.

29. Philo, *Vit. Mos.* II, 205; *Spec. Leg.* I, 53; Josephus, *Antt.* IV, 207; *Contra Apionem* II, 237.

30. CPJ I, 24f., 63f., 96f.; Fraser, *Ptolemaic Alexandria* I, 88, 688f., 715f.

31. Cf. Isa. 9.12; Jer. 26 (46).16; 27 (50).16: *machaira hellēnikē* for *ḥerab hayyōnā*; Esther 9.24 and E (16), 10, 14; cf. CPJ I, 24 n. 61.

32. Fraser, *Ptolemaic Alexandria* I, 57.

33. Hengel, 'Anonymität', 234.

34. Text in A.-M. Denis, *Fragmenta Pseudepigraphorum quae supersunt Graeca*, Leiden 1970, 175ff. Cf. id., *Introduction aux pseudépigraphes grecs d'Ancien Testament*, Leiden 1970, 248ff.; Hengel, 'Anonymität', 235; Fraser, *Ptolemaic Alexandria* I, 690ff.; B. Z. Wacholder, 'Biblical Chronology in the Hellenistic World Chronicles', *HTR* 61, 1968, 451–84 (454ff.); E. Bickerman, in *Christianity* . . . (see p. 147 n. 48 above), 72–84.

35. Denis, *Fragmenta*, 186ff.; id., *Introduction*, 255ff.; Hengel, 'Anonymität', 239ff.; Fraser, *Ptolemaic Alexandria* I, 704ff.

36. Denis, *Fragmenta*, 207ff.; id., *Introduction*, 273ff.; B. Snell, 'Ezechiels Mosedrama', *Antike und Abendland* 13, 1967, 150–64; id., (ed.), *Tragicorum Graecorum Fragmenta* I, Göttingen 1971, 288–301, no. 128; Fraser, *Ptolemaic Alexandria* I, 707f.

37. CIG III 5361, and on that Hengel, 'Proseuche', 182, 178 n. 90.

38. Denis, *Fragmenta*, 204ff., 203f.; id., *Introduction*, 272f. 270f.; Fraser, *Ptolemaic Alexandria* I, 707.

39. Hengel, 'Anonymität', 286ff.; V. Nikiprowetzky, *La troisième Sibylle*, Paris 1970. J. J. Collins, *The Sibylline Oracles*, Missoula, Montana 1974.

40. He was writing after the battle of Cynoscephalae in 197 BC; see S. Josifović, *PRECA* Suppl. XI, 1968, 888–930 (925ff.).

41. K. Lowith, *Meaning in History*, Chicago 1949.

42. Denis, *Fragmenta*, 149ff., 199ff.; id., *Introduction*, 251ff., 262ff.; Hengel, 'Anonymität', 296ff., 301ff.

43. Denis, *Fragmenta*, 217ff.; id., *Introduction*, 277ff.; Walter, *Thoraausleger Aristobulos*; Hengel, *Judaism and Hellenism*; I, 163ff.; Fraser, *Ptolemaic Alexandria* I, 694ff. For his person see also II Macc. 1.10 and B. Z. Wacholder, *Eupolemus*, 239f.

44. Denis, *Fragmenta*, 163ff.; id., *Introduction*, 230ff.; Walter, *Thoraausleger Aristobulos*, 202ff.; Hengel, 'Anonymität', 293f.; this is extant in a number of versions. The oldest form has been preserved in Ps. Justin, *De monarchia*.

45. Walter, *Thoraausleger Aristobulos*, 41ff., 58ff., 141–9; W. Bousset, *Jüdisch-christlicher Schulbetrieb in Alexandria und Rom*, FRLANT NF 6, Göttingen 1915; M. J. Shroyer, *JBL* 55, 1936, 261ff.

46. A. Pelletier, *Lettre d'Aristée à Philocrate*, SC 89, Paris 1962; V. Tcherikover, 'The Ideology of the Letter of Aristeas', *HTR* 51, 1958, 59–85. For the dating see E. Van 't Dack, 'La date de la lettre d'Aristée', in *Antidotum W. Peremans*, Louvain 1968, 263–78; Fraser, *Ptolemaic Alexandria* I, 696ff.; bibliography in S. P. Brock, C. T. Fritsch and S. Jellicoe, *A Classified Bibliography to the Septuagint*, Leiden 1973, 44ff.

47. Walter, *Thoraausleger Aristobulos*, 166ff.; Heinemann, *Philons griechische und jüdische Bildung*, 498ff.; Hermippus according to Josephus, *Contra Apionem* I, 1964f.; for Ps. Ekphantos see W. Burkert in *Pseudepigrapha* I, Entretiens sur l'antiquité classique 18, Vandoeuvres-Genève 1972, 50–3; Numenius: H. C. Puech, 'Numenios d'Apamée et les théologes orientales', in *Mélanges J. Bidez*, Brussels 1934, 745–78; Dörrie, *Der Kleine Pauly* IV, 192ff.

48. Hengel, *Judaism and Hellenism* I, 163ff.; H. Cancik, *Mythische und historische Wahrheit*, SBS 48, Stuttgart 1970, 108–26. J. G. Bunge, *Untersuchungen zum zweiten Makkabäerbuch*, philosophical dissertation Bonn 1971.

49. H. J. Cadbury, 'The Grandson of Ben Sira', *HTR* 48, 1955, 219–25; P. Auvray, 'Notes sur le prologue de l'Ecclésiastique', in *Mélanges A. Robert*, Paris 1957, 281–7.

50. Gager, *Moses*; Hengel, 'Anonymität', 307f. Chronology makes it unthinkable that Callimachus knew the Septuagint of Isa. 14.12, etc., or that Theocritus knew Song of Songs 6.8–10, as is supposed by Fraser, *Ptolemaic Alexandria* I, 584, 714, 716; II, 1000, 1002 n. 255. It is even improbable that Agatharchides knew the LXX of Koh. 12.8 (II, 784 n. 204). The theme that the spirit returns to the giver or to the place of its origin can also be found in Greek literature: Hengel, *Judaism and Hellenism* II, 84 n. 134, on Koh. 3.28.

51. See the account, deriving from Hellenistic sources, in Pliny, *Historia naturalis* XXX, 11, and Apuleius, *Apol.* 90, where in each case Moses stands at the head of the 'Jewish' magicians.

52. Hengel, *Judaism and Hellenism* I, 234ff., 239ff.; Gager, *Moses*,

134ff.; W. and H. G. Gundel, *Astrologumena*, Sudhoffs Archiv, Beiheft 6, Wiesbaden 1966, 51–9. According to Vettius Valens II, 28f. (Kroll, p. 96), Hermippus (*c*. 220 BC), the pupil of Callimachus, who *inter alia* made Pythagoras an imitator of the Jews (see n. 47 above), is said to have known astrological books of the 'most remarkable Abraham' which gave horoscopes for journeys. Artapanus, the anonymous Samaritan and Eupolemus agree in making Abraham the transmitter or inventor of astrology.

53. Hengel, *Judaism and Hellenism* II, 48 n. 84.

54. CIJ II, nos. 1451–1530 (with supplements no. 1530 A–D in CPJ III, 162f.).

55. CPJ III 162 no. 1530A, cf. ibid., 151 nos. 1484, 1488; and on this L. Robert, *Hellenica* I, Paris 1940, 18–24.

56. Cf. H. Thyen, *Der Stil der Jüdisch-Hellenistischen Homilie*, FRLANT 65, Göttingen 1955; cf. pp. 98f. above.

57. Ps. Aristeas 16, cf. Josephus, *Antt.* XII, 22 and *Contra Apionem* II, 168; the euhemeristic etymology of the name of Zeus in Sib. III, 141 is very different. For the problem see Hengel, *Judaism and Hellenism* I, 264ff.

58. Eusebius, *Praeparatio evangelica* 13, 12, 7f. (GCS 43, 2, p. 195, ed. Mras).

59. Hengel, *Judaism and Hellenism* I, 261ff.

60. OGIS 73, 64 = CIJ II, 445 nos. 1537f.; cf. now A. Bernhard, *Le Paneion d'el kanais. Les inscriptions Grecques*, Leiden 1972, nos. 34, 42, pp. 95f., 105ff.; the Lazarus mentioned in nos. 24, 73, pp. 85f., 147, may also be of Jewish descent, see J. and L. Robert, *REG* 86, 1973, 202.

61. Lucan, *Pharsalia* II, 592f., cf. Livy in *Schol. Lucan* II, 531, and E. Bickerman, 'Anonymous Gods', *Journal of the Warburg Institute* 1, 1938, 187–96 (quot. 195).

62. Tacitus, *Histories* V, 5, 5 (translation from the Penguin Classics edition, Harmondsworth 1964, p. 274); further instances in Hengel, *Judaism and Hellenism* II, 175f. no. 47.

63. III Macc. 1.30; Hengel, *Judaism and Hellenism* I, 283f.; Fraser, *Ptolemaic Alexandria* I, 43ff., 202ff.; II, 344ff. See p. 37 above.

64. Bickerman, *Der Gott der Makkabäer*; Hengel, *Judaism and Hellenism* I, 283ff.

65. III Macc. 2.32.

66. Speculation on a form of gnosticism which is supposed to be chronologically pre-Christian shows no desire to come to an end. In this connection it should be pointed out that in his study which covers all the sources and spheres of life in pre-Roman Alexandria, Fraser, *Ptolemaic Alexandria*, does not include the term gnosis in an otherwise comprehensive index. Our sources do not give any indication that there was any form of gnostic speculation before Christianity in Alexandria, the place

where gnosis is supposed to have grown out of a popularized, syncretistic Platonism. One sometimes has the impression that some scholars researching into gnosticism have lost all sense of the realities of history in their all too intensive concern with their difficult material. A prime element in history is the chronology of sources. The gnostic may be forgiven if he does not know either the time or the hour, but not the historian.

Chapter 11

1. Josephus, *Antt.* XII, 147–53; see above, pp. 39f., 161 n. 11.
2. CIJ II, nos. 750–80, cf. L. Robert, *Hellenica*, XI/XII, Paris 1960, 380–439; A. T. Kraabel, *Judaism in Western Asia Minor*, Harvard Dissertation 1968.
3. CIJ II, no. 775.
4. CIJ II, no. 749; Schürer, *Geschichte des jüdischen Volkes* III, 16f.
5. Josephus, *Antt.* XII, 126.
6. *Contra Apionem* II, 258.
7. Josephus, *Antt.* XIV, 255.
8. B. V. Head, *Historia Numorum*, London [2]1911 (reprinted 1963), 666f.
9. I Macc. 15.15–24. Mention is made of Caria, Pamphylia, Lycia, Halicarnassus, Myndos, Cnidos, Phaselis, Side and the islands of Samos, Cos and Rhodes; cf. Tcherikover, *Hellenistic Civilization*, 288f.; A. Giovannini and H. Müller, 'Die Beziehungen zwischen Rom und den Juden im 2. Jh. v.Chr.', *MusHelv* 28, 1971, 156–71.
10. CIJ I, nos. 725–31; A. Plassart, in *Mélanges Holleaux*, Paris 1913, 201–15 = *RB* 11, 1914, 523–34; Hengel, 'Synagogeninschrift', 161 n. 53; 174 n. 97; P. Bruneau, *Recherches sur les cultes de Delos*, Bibliothèque des Écoles françaises d'Athènes et de Rome 217, Paris 1970, 480–93. The synagogue was erected on the site of a gymnasium which was given up after the plundering of Delos by Mithridates in 88.
11. CIJ I no. 725; cf. A. Deissmann, *Light from the Ancient East*, London 1927, 413–24: 'the whole style of the prayer . . . all adaptations to the Hellenic surroundings' (423); cf. the later, imperial inscription from Argos, CIJ I, no. 719.
12. II Macc. 5.9; see p. 116f. below.
13. L. B. Urdahl, 'Jews in Attica', *Symbolae Osloenses* 43, 1968, 39–56; cf. IG II[2] 12609: epitaph of a 'Simon Ananiu' (46) from the second century BC.
14. Josephus, *Contra Apionem* I, 180, from the writing *Peri Hypnou*, see F. Wehrli, *Die Schule des Aristoteles* III, Basle and Stuttgart [2]1969, 10f. fr. 6, and also the commentary, 48f.: 'Clearches' fiction serves to give the Greek doctrine of faith enhanced value through a representative of the much-admired East.' Cf. Hengel, *Judaism and Hellenism* I, 257f.

Text with commentary and bibliography also in Stern, *Greek and Latin Authors* I, 49ff.

15. W. Jaeger, *Diokles von Karystos*, Berlin 1938, 134ff.; id., 'Greeks and Jews', *JR* 18, 1938, 127–43 = *Scripta Minora* II, Rome 1960, 169–83; L. Robert, 'Inscriptions de la Bactriane', *CRAI* 1968, 443–54; cf. Stern, *Greek and Latin Authors* I, 8ff., 45ff.

16. Valerius Maximus I, 3,3. The report occurs in the *Epitome* of Julius Paris and the shorter version of Nepotianus, which mutually supplement each other, see Hengel, *Judaism and Hellenism* I, 262ff.; W. Fauth, 'Sabazius', in *Der Kleine Pauly* IV, Munich 1972, 1479f. It is utterly improbable that the whole thing is an invention of Valerius Maximus who wanted to please Tiberius in this way, as is argued by S. Alessandria, 'La presunta cacciata dei Giudei da Roma nel 139 a.Cr', *Studi classici e orientali* 17, 1968, 187–98. Cf. on the whole question Stern, *Greek and Latin Authors* I, 357ff.

17. L. Robert, 'Reliefs votifs et cultes d'Anatolie', *Anatolia* 3, 1958, 115f., 120ff.; cf. *Hellenica* XI/XII, 1960, 432ff. M. P. Nilsson, *Geschichte der Griechischen Religion* II, ²1961, 540 n. 7; 577 n. 1.

18. C. Roberts, T. Skeat and A. D. Nock, 'The Gild of Zeus Hypsistos', *HTR* 29, 1936, 39–88; Hengel, *Judaism and Hellenism* I, 297ff.; G. Bertram, *hypsistos*, *TDNT* 8, 614ff.; C. Colpe, 'Hypsistos', *Der Kleine Pauly* II, 1291f.; Kraabel, *Judaism in Western Asia Minor*.

19. E. Lohse, *sabbaton*, *TDNT* 7, 17f.

20. J. Keil and A. von Premerstein, *Bericht über eine zweite Reise in Lydien*, Denkschriften der kaiserlichen Akademie der Wissenschaften in Wien 54, 1911, 117f., no. 224; cf. also the inscription of Sabazius, 113 no. 218. Cf. the definition of the Jewish God in Hecataeus of Abdera, Diodore 40,3,4, see Stern, *Greek and Latin Authors* I, 26: *ton periechonta tēn gēn ouranon monon einai theon*, and Strabo XVI, 2, 35, see Stern, *Greek and Latin Authors* I, 294: *hen touto monon theos to periechon hēmas hapantas kai gēn kai thalattan*.

21. Schürer, *Geschichte des jüdischen Volkes* III, 562f. n. 136; OGIS 573. For what follows see V. Tcherikover, 'The Sambathions', CPJ III, 43–56.

22. CIJ 752.

23. *SB* 12, see Tcherikover, 'The Sambathions', CPJ III, 47.

24. E. Schürer, *Die Juden im bosporanischen Reiche und die Genossenschaften der sebomenoi theon hypsiston*, SAB 1897, 200–25; E. R. Goodenough, 'The Bosporus Inscriptions to the Most High God', *JQR* 47, 1956/7, 221–44; M. Hengel, 'Proseuche', 173ff.

25. Hengel, 'Proseuche', 179; B. Wyss, *Phyllobolia P. von der Mühll*, 1946, 174.

26. For the 'godfearers' and sympathizers among the non-Jews see

now F. Siegert, *JSJ* 4, 1973, 109–64, and H. Hommel in *Istanbuler Mitteilungen* 25, 1975, 167–95.

27. Josephus, *Antt.* XII, 119–24; *BJ* VII, 44; *Contra Apionem* II, 39; cf. Tcherikover, *Hellenistic Civilization*, 328f.

28. II Macc. 4.35.

29. Josephus, *BJ* VII, 44f.; Hengel, *Judaism and Hellenism* I, 274.

30. E. Bickerman, 'Les Maccabées de Malala', *Byzantion* 21, 1951, 63–83; R. Renehan, 'The Greek Philosophic Background of Fourth Maccabees', *RheinMus* 115, 1972, 223–38.

31. Cf. CIJ II, 870–75, 877–81, and the numerous Greek inscriptions of the Jewish tombs in Bet Šeʿarim, some of which come from Jews from the cities of Phoenicia and Syria. On this see M. Schwabe and B. Lifshitz, *Beth Shearim* II, Jerusalem 1967, nos. 96f., 147f., 164, 172, 199, etc.; J. N. Sevenster, *Do You Know Greek?*, SupplNovTest 19, Leiden 1968; B. Lifshitz, *Euphrosyne* 4, 1970, 113–33; M. Treu, 'Die Bedeutung des Griechischen für die Juden im römischen Reich', *Kairos* 15, 1973, 122ff.

Chapter 12

1. Cf. H. Gese, 'Anfang und Ende der Apokalyptik dargestellt am Sacharjabuch', *ZThK* 70, 1973, (20–49) 41ff.

2. Zech. 9.13; Dan. 7.7ff.; 8.5ff.; Ethiopian Enoch 90.1ff.; cf. also the allegory of the shepherds in Zech. 11.4ff.

3. II Chron. 26.9–15; see pp. 19f. above.

4. Alt, *Kleine Schriften* II, 396ff.

5. Hengel, *Judaism and Hellenism* I, 37f., 248; Smith, *Palestinian Parties*, 71.

6. M. Smith, in *Fischer Weltgeschichte* V (*Griechen und Perser*, ed. H. Bengtson), Frankfurt am Main 1965, 364ff.; id., *Palestinian Parties*, 158ff.; he wants to ascribe this literature to 'pious members of the assimilationist party' (159); Hengel, *Judaism and Hellenism* I, 113ff.

7. Hengel, *Judaism and Hellenism* I, 107ff., 247ff.

8. Smith, *Palestinian Parties*, 63ff. (quot. 64); Hengel, *Judaism and Hellenism* I, 14f.

9. Rostovtzeff, *Social and Economic History* I, 213ff.; Tcherikover, *Hellenistic Civilization*, 64ff., 132ff.

10. Tcherikover and Fuks, CPJ I, 115ff., nos. 1–5; B. Mazar, 'The Tobiads', *IEJ* 7, 1957, 137–45; 229–38; Smith, *Palestinian Parties*, 92, 132f., 258 n. 38; see also p. 27 above.

11. V. Tcherikover, 'Palestine under the Ptolemies', *Mizraim* 4/5, 1937, 37, 49f.; Hengel, *Judaism and Hellenism* I, 59f., 267ff.

12. Josephus, *Antt.* XII, 160ff.; see pp. 37f. above. Quot. XII, 222.

13. Josephus, *BJ* I, 31ff.; *Antt.* XII, 239f.; the sons of Tobias sup-

port the radical Menelaus. Cf. Schürer, Vermes and Millar, *History* I, 149f. no. 30.

14. Koh. 10.19; cf. Hengel, *Judaism and Hellenism* I, 47ff.

15. J. P. Peters and H. Thiersch, *Painted Tombs in the Necropolis of Marissa*, London 1905; F.-M. Abel, 'Tombeaux récemment découverts à Marisa', *RB* 34, 1925, 267–75; Hengel, *Judaism and Hellenism* I, 62ff.

16. G. E. Wright, *Shechem*, London and New York 1964, 183; Hengel, *Judaism and Hellenism* I, 62f.

17. E. R. Goodenough, *Jewish Symbols in the Greco-Roman Period* I, New York 1953, 74.

18. I Macc. 12.16; 14.22,24; 15.15; cf. Josephus, *Antt.* XIII, 169; XIV, 146. On this and what follows see Hengel, *Judaism and Hellenism* I, 64f.

19. II Macc. 4.7ff.; I Macc. 1.11ff.; cf. Hengel, *Judaism and Hellenism* I, 73ff., 277ff.

20. II Macc. 3.4; 4.23ff., 29, 39ff.; and Hengel, *Judaism and Hellenism* I, 279ff.

21. *T. Sukka* 4.28 (line 200): *j. Sukka* 55d, 40ff.; *b. Sukka* 56b. For mixed marriages see Smith, *Palestinian Parties*, 84ff., 154, 174, 195, though of course he exaggerates.

22. *Greek Anthology* 5, 160; cf. 172f.

23. II Macc. 12.19,24,35; see p. 86 above and Hengel, *Judaism and Hellenism* I, 276.

24. II Macc. 4.11; cf. I Macc. 8.17; see p. 172 n. 44 below.

25. Ps. Aristeas 47–50.

26. 121: *alla kai tēs tōn hellēnikōn ephrontisan ou parergōs kataskeuēs.*

27. Josephus, *Contra Apionem* I, 176–81; see above, pp. 168f. n. 14.

28. II Macc. 4.5f.; 14.4ff.; I Macc. 8; 12.1ff.; 14.16ff. etc.

29. A good example of this from Roman times is the Theodotus inscription CIJ II, 333 no. 1404, cf. Sevenster, *Do You Know Greek?*, 131ff.; Hengel, *ZThK* 72, 1975, 184f., cf. 156ff. on the significance of Greek in Jerusalem in the New Testament period.

30. Cf. II Macc. 2.15; cf. also the colophon to the Greek book of Esther, and E. Bickerman, 'The Colophon of the Greek Book of Esther', *JBL* 63, 1944, 339–62.

31. Daniel 3.5,7,10,15; Hengel, *Judaism and Hellenism* I, 60.

32. Hengel, *Judaism and Hellenism* II, 44 n. 24.

33. Hengel, *Judaism and Hellenism* I, 74ff.

34. I Macc. 12.6–23 (10.21); II Macc. 5.9; Josephus, *Antt.* XII, 226f.; XII, 167; earlier literature in R. Marcus, *Josephus* VII, Loeb Classical Library 1961, 769; Hengel, *Judaism and Hellenism* I, 72f.; B. Cardauns, 'Juden und Spartaner', *Hermes* 95, 1967, 317–24; S. Schüller, 'Some Problems connected with the Supposed Common Ancestry of Jews and Spartans . . .', *JSS* 1, 1956, 257–68; Schürer,

Vermes and Millar, *History* I, 184f. n. 33. Smith, *Palestinian Parties*, 177f., transfers the first contacts as far back as the Persian period.
    35. *PRECA* XIV, 1, 786, alluding to a saying by Heinrich Heine.
    36. Cf. also the tomb in Modein, I Macc. 13.25ff.; Josephus, *Antt.* XIII, 210ff.; C. Watzinger, *Denkmäler Palästinas* II, Leipzig 1935, 22f., and Jason's tomb, L. Y. Rahmani et al., *Atiqot* 4, 1964.
    37. P. Roussel, 'Épitaphe de Gaza commémorant deux officiers de la garnison ptolémaïque', *Aegyptus* 13, 1933, 145–51; W. Peek, *Griechische Grabgedichte*, Darmstadt 1960, 112 n. 162. Presumably an epidemic caused a number of deaths in the family. Cf. Hengel, *Judaism and Hellenism* II, 20 n. 79.
    38. E. Bickerman, 'Sur une inscription grecque de Sidon', *Mélanges R. Dussaud* I, Paris 1939, 91–9; Hengel, *Judaism and Hellenism* I, 71f.
    39. W. Cronert, 'Das Lied von Marisa', *RheinMus* 64, 1909, 433f., Hengel, *Judaism and Hellenism* II, 56 n. 192.
    40. Schürer, Vermes and Millar, *History* I, 191; cf. also the curse inscription, CIJ 1184.
    41. XVI, 2, 29 (759).
    42. Hengel, *Judaism and Hellenism* I, 83–8.
    43. II Macc. 4.18ff.; cf. 4.32,39.
    44. Eusebius, *Praeparatio Evangelica* IX, 34, 16 = Jacoby, FGrHist 723 F 2; Hengel, *Judaism and Hellenism* I, 94; cf. Dio in Josephus, *Contra Apionem* I, 112f.; Menander, *Contra Apionem* I, 118; Theophilus, Eusebius, *Praeparatio Evangelica* IX, 34, 19 = Jacoby, FGrHist 733. The theme already occurs in Herodotus II, 44, 1. See Hadas, *Hellenistic Culture*, 95f., who sees in this reference a sign of a 'considerable latitudinarism, or perhaps a tendency towards syncretism'.
    45. Clement of Alexandria, *Strom.* I, 114, 2, and Tatian, *ad Graecos* 37 = Jacoby, FGrHist 784 F la and b.
    46. Athenagoras IV, 157b, cf. Hadas, *Hellenistic Culture*, 83.
    47. *PCZ* 59004 = CPJ no. 2a/col. I, 3; *PCZ* 59005 = CPJ no. 2b; Hecataeus of Abdera according to Diodore 40 fr. 3.3 = Jacoby, FGrHist 264 F 5,3. Of course we do not know for certain whether Photius, who has preserved this fragment for us, or Diodore later 'Graecized' the names. Ps. Hecataeus (second century BC) also knows the Greek form of the name, see Josephus, *Contra Apionem* I, 197. On the other hand, Clearchus of Soli (first half of the third century BC) still has *Hierousalēmē*, *Contra Apionem* I, 179. This is probably a 'Graecism' from the Latin translator (*hierosolyma*). The Greek name was taken over by all the later non-Jewish writers from the third century BC on (Berossus, Ps.(?) Manetho, Agartharchides of Cnidus). See J. Jeremias, *ZNW* 65, 1974, 273ff. and Reinach, *Textes*, index s.v. 'Jerusalem', 370. In the LXX the new form appears in the later writings: I–IV Maccabees; I Esdras; Tobias.

48. Eusebius, *Praeparatio Evangelica* IX, 17 and 18,2 = Jacoby, FGrHist 724; cf. Hengel, *Judaism and Hellenism* I, 88f.; A.-M. Denis, *Introduction aux pseudépigraphes grecs d'Ancien Testament*, Leiden 1970, 261.

49. Hengel, *Judaism and Hellenism* I, 115–30; R. Braun, *Kohelet und die frühhellenistische Popularphilosophie*, passim; Smith, *Palestinian Parties*, 159ff. 'Though there is no reason to suppose that he knew Epicurus' work, the similarities of temper and attitude are unmistakable' (160). Cf. also Bickerman, *Four Strange Books of the Bible*, 139–67.

50. Braun, *Kohelet*, 44ff.

51. Hengel, *Judaism and Hellenism* I, 123ff.

52. See the surveys in Braun, *Kohelet*, 146ff., 158ff.

53. K. Galling, *Der Prediger*, HAT I, 18, Tübingen ²1969, 75ff.: 'The corrections made by QR² contradict the scope of the sentence in question' (76).

54. Sir. 50.27, see Hengel, *Judaism and Hellenism* I, 79.

55. Sir. 24.30f.; 33.16a, 25ff.; 38.34–39.8 (numeration following V. Hamp); Hengel, *Judaism and Hellenism* I, 134ff.

56. 1.1–20; 24.1–34; cf. Hengel, *Judaism and Hellenism* I, 157ff.; Marböck, *Weisheit*.

57. 41.8f.; 10.6–25; 16.4; Hengel, *Judaism and Hellenism* I, 150ff.

58. 39.24–34; Hengel, *Judaism and Hellenism* I, 141ff.; cf. Marböck, *Weisheit*, 134ff.; R. Pautrel, 'Ben Sira et le stoïcisme', *RechSR* 51, 1963, 535–49; J. L. Crenshaw, 'The Problem of Theodicy in Sirach . . .', *JBL* 94, 1975, 47–64.

59. 43.27, cf. Marböck, *Weisheit*, 150 n. 13; 170 n. 46.

60. 34 (G31).24–27; 13.2–5; 4.1ff., 8ff.; 21.5; Hengel, *Judaism and Hellenism* I, 136f.; Tcherikover, *Hellenistic Civilization*, 144ff.

61. 10.27; 13.24; 25.3, etc.; 31.12ff.; 32.3ff.; 34.9ff.; 38.1,12 (but cf. II Chron. 16.12, which is a little earlier); see Marböck, *Weisheit*, 160ff.

62. Middendorp, *Stellung*, 7–34, gives a large number of parallels.

63. 44.1–50.24; T. Maertens, *L'Éloge des Pères (Ecclésiastique XLIV–L)*, Bruges 1956; E. Bickerman, 'La chaîne de la tradition pharisienne', *RB* 59, 1952, 44ff.; Hengel, *Judaism and Hellenism* I, 136.

64. Sir. 50.23f.

65. Sir. 36.1–22; see pp. 47f. above.

66. Most recently, Middendorp, *Stellung*, has tried to describe Ben Sira as an out-and-out 'Hellenist'. But even he has to concede that Ben Sira stands on the side of the high priest Simon and is an opponent of the Tobiads, 167ff. Marböck, *Weisheit*, 168ff., is more restrained in his judgment. See my review of Middendorp's book in *JSJ* 5, 1974, 83–7.

67. See Smith, *Palestinian Parties*, 79ff., and his warning against false alternatives.

68. I Macc. 2.42; 7.13; and II Macc. 14.6; cf. Hengel, *Judaism and Hellenism* I, 175ff.; Schürer, Vermes and Millar, *History* I, 157.

69. Hengel, *Judaism and Hellenism* I, 244ff.; W. Tyloch, 'Les Thiases et la Communauté de Qumran', in *Fourth World Congress of Jewish Studies, Papers* I, Jerusalem 1967, 225–8.

70. Hengel, 'Qumran und der Hellenismus', in *Qumrân. Sa piété, sa théologie et son milieu*, ed. M. Delcor, Paris and Louvain 1978, 333–72.

71. Thus rather one-sidedly in the otherwise valuable book by O. Plöger, *Theokratie und Eschatologie*, WMANT 2, Neukirchen 1959. This is already clear from the significance of the Temple in the book of Daniel and the fight of Hasidim, Essenes and Pharisees for the purity of the Temple and its worship.

72. Thus above all the Persian loanword *raz* in Daniel 2.18f., 27–30, 47, and the Qumran writings and Ethiopian Enoch 16.3; 38.3; 103.2; 104.12. Cf. Hengel, *Judaism and Hellenism* I, 202f.

73. Hengel, *Judaism and Hellenism* I, 209–18.

74. Dan. 12.2f.; Ethiopian Enoch 104.2. T. F. Glasson, *Greek Influence in Jewish Eschatology*, London 1961; Hengel, *Judaism and Hellenism* I, 196–202; G. W. E. Nickelsburg, *Resurrection, Immortality and Eternal Life in Intertestamental Judaism*, Harvard Dissertation 1972; G. Stemberger, *Der Leib der Auferstehung*, Analecta Biblica 56, Rome 1972; E. M. Meyers, *Jewish Ossuaries, Reburial and Birth*, Biblica et Orientalia 24, Rome 1971.

75. Hengel, *Judaism and Hellenism* I, 181ff.; B. Gatz, *Weltzeitalter, goldene Zeit und sinnverwandte Vorstellungen*, Spudasmata 16, Hildesheim 1967.

76. H. C. Gottoff, 'On the Fourth Eclogue of Vergil', *Philologus* 111, 1967, 66–79; Gatz, *Weltzeitalter*, 87ff.

77. Hengel, *Judaism and Hellenism* I, 104ff., 311ff.; Smith, *Palestinian Parties*, 81: 'We shall do better to recognize "Hellenistic" as a cultural classification distinct both from "Greek" and from "oriental", and see the civil conflicts of the Seleucid and Ptolemaic empires as conflicts between various groups of a single cultural continuum – the Hellenistic.'

DISCARD
Mt. Angel Abbey Library

Mt. Angel Abbey Library
St. Benedict, Oregon 97373